# MICHAEL S. HARPER

*and*

# ANTHONY WALTON

*The Vintage Book of African American Poetry*

≡

Michael S. Harper is the author of nine books of poetry: *Songlines in Michaeltree; Honorable Amendments; Dear John, Dear Coltrane; History Is Your Own Heartbeat; Song: I Want a Witness; Debridement; Nightmare Begins Responsibility; Images of Kin;* and *Healing Songs for the Inner Ear.* He has twice been nominated for the National Book Award and has been cited or given awards by the National Institute of Arts and Letters, the National Endowment for the Arts, and the Guggenheim Foundation. He is University Professor, Brown University, and lives in Providence, Rhode Island.

Anthony Walton is the author of a memoir, *Mississippi: An American Journey.* His poems have appeared widely in magazines, including *The Kenyon Review* and *The Oxford American.* He is a graduate of the University of Notre Dame and Brown University, and the recipient of a 1998 Whiting Writers' Award. He teaches at Bowdoin College, and lives in Brunswick, Maine.

*The Vintage Book of*

# AFRICAN AMERICAN POETRY

≡

≡

≡

*The Vintage Book of*

# AFRICAN AMERICAN POETRY

≡

≡

≡

*Edited and with an Introduction*

*by Michael S. Harper and Anthony Walton*

VINTAGE BOOKS

*A Division of Random House, Inc.*

*New York*

A VINTAGE ORIGINAL, FEBRUARY 2000

Copyright © 2000 by Michael S. Harper and Anthony Walton

All rights reserved under International and Pan-American Copyright Conventions. Published in the United States by Vintage Books, a division of Random House, Inc., New York, and simultaneously in Canada by Random House of Canada Limited, Toronto.

Vintage and colophon are registered trademarks of Random House, Inc.

Library of Congress Cataloging-in-Publication Data
The Vintage book of African American poetry / edited by Michael S. Harper and Anthony Walton.
p.   cm.
"A Vintage original."
Includes bibliographical references.
ISBN 0-375-70300-4 (alk. paper)
1. American poetry—Afro-American authors. 2. Afro-Americans—Poetry.
I. Harper, Michael S., 1938–   . II. Walton, Anthony, 1960–
PS591.N4V56   2000
811.008'0896073—dc21      99-39428
CIP

Book design by Rebecca Aidlin

www.vintagebooks.com

Printed in the United States of America
10  9  8

For our parents—
Walter Warren Harper
Katherine Johnson Harper (1913–1988)
and
Claude Edward Walton
Dorothy Cannon Visor Walton
*who believed the burden of past, present, and future*
*is best handled with the grip of literacy*

# ACKNOWLEDGMENTS

The editors would like to acknowledge Deborah Murphy and Rowan Ricardo Phillips for their work on the headnotes and bibliography. They would also like to thank the editor, Robert Grover, for his diligence and good humor throughout the project, and their agent, Sloan Harris, for riding shotgun.

# CONTENTS

## COUNTEE CULLEN

## ROBERT HAYDEN

## JAY WRIGHT

## MICHAEL S. HARPER

## ISHMAEL REED

## AL YOUNG

# INTRODUCTION

It is highly likely that the story of the people known as African Americans—the chronicle of their journey from captivity to an ever-evolving and complicated status as full members of American society—will become one of the most inspiring narratives in the development of human aspiration from the Dark Ages to the Space Age. The poetry of this group, ranging from the plaintive classicism of slave-born Phillis Wheatley:

> *Filled with the praise of him who gives the light,*
> *And draws the sable curtains of the night,*
> *Let placid slumbers soothe each weary mind,*
> *At morn to wake, more heavenly, more refined.*
> ("An Hymn to the Evening")

to the jazzy irony of Elizabeth Alexander, born some two hundred years later, in her dramatic monologue of the global sports hero Muhammad Ali:

> *I said to Joe Frazier,*
> *. . . Always*
> *keep one good Cadillac.*
> *And watch how you dress*
> *with that cowboy hat,*
> *pink suits, white shoes—*
> *that's how pimps dress,*
> *or kids, and you a champ,*
> *or wish you were, 'cause*
> *I can whip you in the ring*
> *or whip you in the street*

has served as pulse and barometer of both the panoramic American scene and the lives, individual and collective, of the members of one of its most integral ethnic groups.

America was the first true experiment in democracy in human history; the treatment of African Americans has been both this country's greatest triumph and its greatest failing. "The Negro," Richard Wright wrote, "is America's metaphor"—a people uprooted from a traditional homeland and left to survive, endure, and create self and soul in a strange and hostile environment. The experience of American blacks offers not a marginal but an essential glimpse into this country—its darkest and brightest aspects, its promised equality and entrenched hierarchy, the violence upon which it was founded and the hope toward which it fitfully moves.

Our founding documents, despite their rhetoric—"we hold these truths to be self-evident, that all men are created equal"—were never intended by their authors, many of them slaveholders, to be inclusive. But through what Kenneth Burke calls "the power of the negative" (when we say that we *are* something, for example a democracy, this implies that we are *not* something else, a feudal state), we are constantly prodded toward their stated truths. African Americans have from the outset been at the heart of this push-and-pull. As Ralph Ellison wrote: "Materially, psychologically, and culturally, part of the nation's heritage is Negro American, and whatever it becomes will be shaped in part by the Negro's presence. Which is fortunate, for today it is the black American who puts pressure upon the nation to live up to its ideals."

There is another sense, beyond this reminder of the distance between our ideals and fact, in which African American culture and its artifacts are not just of marginal but of central importance to the nation. To be "American" is to be in constant search of one's identity. Richard Slotkin, in his brilliant trilogy *Regeneration Through Violence, The Fatal Environment,* and *Gunfighter Nation,* argues that our national identity has in large part been formed by insecurity, Europeans needing in this strange land to justify their leaving the "old country" by claiming as their own the virtues and native mores of the new land, while at the same time asserting cultural superiority over the new land's native inhabitants by claiming as their own the Old World's values.

Our national identity has thus been formed as a constant flux of appropriation and contrast from and with the margins of society. This pattern continues to the present day—witness popular slang and pop music, with its use of black "hip-hop" beats and attitude, as they play against the persistent racism of our social institutions in what Ellison termed the "antagonistic cooperation" that unifies the country. Understanding this paradox of the mainstream's relationship to minority groups is essential in assessing any aspect of black culture—for as much as it has been mocked and dismissed as "ethnic," this culture is and always has been a fundamental part of who we are, who we *all* are, shaping everything from dress and music to speech itself, in what Ellison called the stretching, modifying, and expanding of the "American tongue."

Insofar as their culture and work *can* be separated out, African American artists, in this instance African American poets, forced by the dominant culture, which constantly negates them, to question what it means to be human, American, and black, have kept closest in their writing to the definitive American quest for identity. Their work represents a unique blending of the public and private, as the lonely existential search for self-definition and transcendence becomes by necessity a public journey toward voice and freedom. This quest for identity and a belonging that will not compromise the self is the theme, if there can be said to be one theme, that animates the tradition from its beginning. To quote the spiritual, the endeavors of these authors are those of a "true believer far from home."

≡

The first black American poets, to follow the analysis of Robert Hayden, turned exclusively to British models of poetic practice, to Alexander Pope, Samuel Johnson, Jonathan Swift, and other contemporaries. Phillis Wheatley's neoclassical stylings lack the element of personal psychology that we today consider an essential part of the American literary tradition, but this is true of all American poetry until the mid-nineteenth century. Emerson's intellectual declaration of independence with its celebration of the self, it should be remembered, was not written until 1837.

African American poets writing before the Civil War—Jupitor Hammon, George Moses Horton, George Boyer Vashon, James M. Whitfield, and Frances E. W. Harper, among others—tended with few exceptions abstractly to explore the questions of slavery and freedom, drawing heavily on myth and allegory. While their poems are generally equal in quality to those written in the same period by Anglo Americans, they are of interest today largely for their sociohistorical relevance (George Boyer Vashon, James M. Whitfield, and Frances E. W. Harper published often in abolitionist periodicals) and for the feat of their having been written at all under conditions of slavery, social isolation, educational deprivation, and poverty.

The autobiographical element, the quest for self-discovery and voice characteristic of the American Renaissance launched by Emerson and exemplified in Frederick Douglass's *Narrative,* did not enter African American poetry until after the Civil War, in the work of Paul Laurence Dunbar, James Weldon Johnson, Anne Spencer, Georgia Douglas Johnson, and William Stanley Braithwaite. The more intricate and personal literary journeys of these authors mirrored in part the changed national aesthetic, and in part the more gnarled and complex social situation that developed as the straightforward hopes of Emancipation and Reconstruction collapsed into Jim Crow in both the North and the South. In his intensely lyric meditations of love, yearning, and lamentation, Dunbar questions his personal and public status quo, expressing desire for a life and experience beyond that prescribed for blacks:

> *I know why the caged bird sings, ah me,*
> *When his wing is bruised and his bosom sore,*
> *When he beats his bars and he would be free;*
> *It is not a carol of joy or glee,*
> *But a prayer that he sends from his heart's deep core.*

The fabled Harlem Renaissance of the 1920s and '30s represents a crucial turning point in the tradition, for at this point it could first be said to have become self-conscious, aware of itself *as* a tradition. In this period the first anthologies of African American poetry were compiled. Harlem Renaissance writers and critics encouraged an experimentation with form paralleling that of the modernists; works like Jean Toomer's *Cane* embody a new melding of genres, tenses, and viewpoints equal to the highest literary accomplishment of any American. The small details, triumphs, and disappointments of black daily life that had occasionally been explored by poets like Dunbar and Georgia Douglas Johnson were brought to the fore and celebrated as valid subject matter by this new generation, by Toomer, Langston Hughes, Gwendolyn Bennett, Claude McKay, Countee Cullen, and Sterling A. Brown (discussed in further detail below). And poets like Cullen developed a nuanced, critical awareness of the black poet's paradoxical relationship to the mainstream—

marginalized and dismissed for being black and choosing black subject matter, yet conscious of great literature as an attempt to encompass just such questionings of society and self: "Yet do I marvel at this curious thing:/To make a poet black, and bid him sing!"

Robert Hayden, born just after these masters of the Harlem Renaissance, is another of the tradition's luminaries. One of the most skilled practitioners in the English language, Hayden was dedicated in his work to an exploration of soul and race that has influenced all African American poets since as well as changed the way we see and read his literary ancestors. With poems such as "A Letter from Phillis Wheatley" and "Paul Laurence Dunbar," Hayden strove to foreground the often-overlooked personal suffering (much of it socially imposed) that informed the work of these poets, giving them, as he once said, an inner life. In "Middle Passage," "Runagate, Runagate," and "The Ballad of Sue Ellen Westerfield," Hayden explored collective and folk experience further to animate and foreground a painful, otherwise forgotten past. And in another vein, that of "The Night-Blooming Cereus" and "Ice Storm," he voiced his own private loss and longing:

> *The trees themselves, as in winters past,*
> *will survive their burdening,*
> *broken thrive. And am I less to You,*
> *my God, than they?*

Gwendolyn Brooks, born just four years later, is another master of the tradition—pushing the rural folk subjects and voicings skillfully treated by Sterling Brown into the modern, industrial North, creating a record of an entire people that goes beyond anything in the mainstream American tradition and must be compared in its scope and vision with the work of Chaucer, Dante, and Joyce. Brooks has so deeply influenced how we see the black South Side of Chicago, the inner lives of its inhabitants, that she can be said to have helped create it in the popular imagination. Her 1950 Pulitzer Prize was the first ever awarded a Negro writer (Margaret Walker had, in another signal moment, been awarded the Yale Younger Poets Prize earlier in the decade), and in many ways marked the arrival of black poets into the national elite. But Brooks's public, socially engaged career seems in the end to have won her no more of the wider culture's regard than did Hayden's quiet, almost monkish one gained him, reflecting again that problematic relationship of black writers to the mainstream: both poets have been underappreciated, underknown, and underpraised.

The African American poetic tradition from the post–World War II period to the present day has fragmented into several different, at times contradictory, strands, reflecting the complexities for both blacks and the nation at large of the movement into the modern and postmodern eras. Poets such as Jay Wright, Michael S. Harper, C. S. Giscombe, and Rita Dove have continued Hayden's quest to locate the self in relation to the past; those in the Black Arts Movement and cultural nationalists, Amiri Baraka, Sonia Sanchez, and Haki Madhubuti (Don L. Lee) among them, have sought a more engaged and politically "relevant" poetic practice, one that would fuel or guide the kinds of radical political transformations these practitioners believe still necessary to the full purchase on the American promise.

A younger generation, featuring such poets as Yusef Komunyakaa, Thylias Moss, and Reginald Shepherd, is benefiting from an unprecedented access to the institutional life of the poetic establishment. These poets enjoy as well the postmodern freedom of the practitioner to draw from the whole of their tradition and of the world tradition, to publish any kind of poem, from blazing political tract to private love lyric—often in the same book or magazine—in any style, from four-beat rap quatrains to Spenserian sonnets. These poets at their best have used this freedom as a tool in exploring the complexities of their private lives as well as the related complexities and contradictions inherent in a nation that has given unprecedented wealth and personal freedom to so many African Americans while leaving many more mired in the socially constructed nightmares of the inner cities and impoverished rural South.

≡

**B**ut no broad outline such as the preceding of the African American tradition could serve to convey its importance and its troubled relationship to the mainstream so much as understanding in some depth the career and body of work of perhaps its most accomplished practitioner, Sterling A. Brown.

A consummate literary critic, writing seminal texts on African American art and folklore and having studied the Irish Renaissance with an eye toward applying its lessons to the situation of black Americans, Brown was also an extraordinary poet, capable of fusing his critical awareness with narrative, rhythm, meter, and tone to create a singular reflection of a people's experience and consciousness.

From the "adopt" and "adapt" phases of African American poetry—its adoption of rhetoric and form from English poetry in Wheatley and others and its adaptation of these forms to distinctly black subjects in the Harlem Renaissance—this tradition could be said to have come into its own with Brown's "adept" creation of an entirely new prosody. Though often confused with the work of "dialect poets," poets who simply forced black speech into English forms in some of their poems (Dunbar and Hughes among them), Brown's poetic project was in fact quite different. His life's work was to foreground the "folk." He strove to show that rural southern blacks in particular, while generally dismissed by white Americans, even those who worked for social reform, as passive sufferers, had in fact developed a system of active strategies for encompassing the harsh economic and social situations in which they found themselves. Brown's poetry does not ennoble his subjects but serves to underscore their preexisting nobility.

Just as Yeats drew from folk myths to "create" a national identity, to voice the experiences and aspirations of a people written out of history, so did Brown turn to black folk myths, folk expressions, work songs, blues, and spirituals. His verse is not "dialect," for no one talks like his narrators talk: rather, Brown distilled the rhythms of black speech and song, merging them with English form and rhetoric to create a wholly invented language that, as such, takes us both through and beyond history into myth, beyond the apparent face of things into the commonality of human hopes and ambitions hidden by social forms.

In the refrain of "After Winter,"

> *Butter beans fo' Clara*
> *Sugar corn fo' Grace*
> *An' fo' de little feller*
> *Runnin' space*

Brown distills and prosodically sifts the words of a sharecropper to underscore his striving and deep humanity. The first line of this refrain consists of three trochées (stressed-unstressed), and the second line, also of three beats, continues this rhythm. In the third line Brown shifts the rhythm to iambic (unstressed-stressed) to create a tension strikingly resolved in the final line—where the shift back to trochaic rhythm comes as a slight surprise but at the same time (as it represents a return to the trochaic metric contract established at the refrain's beginning) feels "right," like a true resolution. The hard sound of the *Ru* in *Runnin'*, which contrasts with the soft vowels and consonants of the rest of the stanza, and the two beats of the final line, which oppose the three-beat lines throughout, give this line still further emphasis. With his creative patterning of vernacular speech, Brown thus makes his stanza act out the emotion of his speaker—his tenderness and delicacy in the first lines and, in the last, the sheer force of his hope and determination.

In "Southern Road," Brown abstracts the rhythms of a work song to make it slightly more regular and so to emphasize the grinding, repetitive nature of the chain gang. In the following stanza he brilliantly compresses the tragicomic awareness of their situation through which the chain gang's men, society's lowest of the low, endure and so transcend it:

> *White man tells me—hunh—*
> *Damn yo' soul;*
> *White man tells me—hunh—*
> *Damn yo' soul;*
> *Got no need, bebby,*
> *To be tole.*

Few poets in the African American tradition have approached Brown's level of vision and accomplishment, and no poet has been so overlooked. Brown received no awards for his poetry, though other, more immediately accessible black poets were feted in this time; and his third book, *No Hiding Place,* did not find a publisher until it was included in his *Collected Poems.*

This dismissal of Brown by the white publishing establishment, white critics, and even black critics, goes to the heart of the problem of the African American literary tradition and, beyond that, to the problem of the color line itself. In his book of essays *Goin' to the Territory,* Ralph Ellison described a situation of the kind that Brown attempted in his work to encompass. Ellison wrote of a group of speakers from the Mississippi Freedom Democratic Party in 1964:

> To the facile eye, one of the men who talked there might well have been mistaken for the Sambo stereotype. He was southern, rural; his speech was heavily idiomatic, his tempo slow. A number of his surface characteristics seemed to support the stereotype. But had you accepted him as an incarnation of Sambo, you would have missed a very courageous man—a man who understood only too well that his activities in aiding and protecting the young Northern students working in the Freedom Movement placed his life in constant contact with death, but continued to act. Now, I'm not going to reject that man because some misinformed person, some prejudiced person, sees him as the embodiment of Uncle Tom or Sambo.

Brown's life's work was to hold up the face of this man and make us look behind it. He aimed to take his reader through the looking glass in a sense—into that part of society that "society" has defined itself against. His work was dismissed because the face he held up *is* in fact a looking glass: to see that face accurately we would first have to see ourselves, to see those things about ourselves and the country we have made that we still, even at this late date, do not like to see. The problem of the Mississippi Freedom Democratic Party worker's identity is the problem of *our* identity; the centuries-long struggle for identity of African Americans in this country is not just a *part* of who we are, it *is* who we are. Ellison concluded his paragraph: "What's inside you, brother; what's your heart like? What are your real values? What human qualities are hidden beneath your idiom?"

≡

Language has an essential role in the life of the United States; more than a tool for communication, it is the very stuff out of which the nation is made. From the simultaneous promise and betrayal of the founding documents—"We hold these truths to be self-evident, that all men are created equal" on the one hand, to "three-fifths of all other persons" on the other—what Americans have dared to dream, and say, has had a way of coming true. African Americans have pulled America with them from the latter quotation toward the promise of the former in their long journey, in Ellison's stretching, modifying, and expanding of the American tongue beyond its first intentions.

As a nation we have regularly fallen asleep in the comfortable notion that we have reached the promised land, only like Jay Gatsby to be jarred awake by tragedy—John F. Kennedy and Martin Luther King, the *Challenger* and Columbine—to the reality that somewhere in our constant rush forward we have lost our bearings, things are not as we thought they were.

This existential void is the space in which African Americans have been forced to live; shut out of society, they have been forced to hear the invisible echoes, the tonalities above and below our rhetoric. And they have developed cultural strategies, most notably the blues with its tragicomic vision, to teach themselves and by extension all Americans to survive and endure. From the jazz age of the 1920s to the beat 1950s, the politically torn 1960s and '70s, and the turbulent youth culture of today, the American mainstream has turned to black cultural forms to voice its heartache and discontent as well as its hopes and ambitions. The African American poetic tradition has borne witness to that space just out of sight that is the web of personal, social, and biological realities that in the end circumscribes us all—lamenting and celebrating what the poet Cornelius Eady has termed "this/Rent party above the/Slaughter-house."

Torn from a past we have already forgotten and hurtling through the unknown world to an uncertain future, the heroes of American myth have all been "poor wayfaring strangers"—Hawkeye, Ishmael, Huckleberry Finn, the Invisible Man, and Shane. African American poets—Wheatley, Dunbar, Brown, Hayden, Brooks, Dove, and hundreds of others—have been on this same quest, the quest that is the true theme of American literature:

> *Sometimes I feel like a motherless child,*
> *Sometimes I feel like a motherless child,*
> *Long ways from home, long ways from home,*
> *True believer far from home.*

It is our hope that this book may help to carry that quest forward, doing honor to those who have gone on, encouraging those who read and those who write in the present day, and preserving one piece of our cultural heritage and promise for those Americans to come.

Michael S. Harper
Anthony Walton
May 1999
Providence, Rhode Island

*The Vintage Book of*

# AFRICAN AMERICAN
# POETRY

≡

≡

≡

# JUPITOR HAMMON *(1720?–1800?)*

Jupitor Hammon was born on the Long Island plantation of Henry Lloyd sometime between 1720 and 1730. He remained the property of the Lloyd family, accompanying them to Hartford, Connecticut, during the Revolutionary War. Hammon achieved fame as an opponent of slavery. Though not as forceful a critic as Richard Allen or Prince Hall, Hammon argued for reforms in the chattel system as it stood and for the immediate manumission of younger blacks.

In 1761, at about the age of forty-one, Hammon published "An Evening Thought: Salvation by Christ, with Penetential Cries." Seventeen years later he published a fairly long (twenty-one stanzas) poem entitled "An Address to Miss Phillis Wheatly, Ethiopian Poetess" (an early example of poetic discourse, one of the vestments of any poetic tradition). Hammon continued to publish his poetry and prose as the eighteenth century pushed toward completion, all the while remaining a slave. His poetry displays the strong flavor of William Cowper, an English contemporary, and of the hymnists Charles Wesley and John Newton, favorites of Hammon, a lifelong, devoted Methodist.

*An Address to Miss Phillis Wheatly [sic], Ethiopian Poetess, in Boston, who came from Africa at eight years of age, and soon became acquainted with the gospel of Jesus Christ.*

### 1.

O, come, you pious youth! adore
    The wisdom of thy God,
In bringing thee from distant shore,
    To learn His holy word.

### 2.

Thou mightst been left behind,
   Amidst a dark abode;
God's tender mercy still combined,
   Thou hast the holy word.

### 3.

Fair Wisdom's ways are paths of peace,
   And they that walk therein,
Shall reap the joys that never cease,
   And Christ shall be their King.

### 4.

God's tender mercy brought thee here;
   Tossed o'er the raging main;
In Christian faith thou hast a share,
   Worth all the gold of Spain.

### 5.

While thousands tossed by the sea,
   And others settled down,
God's tender mercy set thee free
   From dangers that come down.

### 6.

That thou a pattern still might be,
   To youth of Boston town,
The blessed Jesus set thee free
   From every sinful wound.

### 7.

The blessed Jesus, who came down,
   Unveiled his sacred face,

To cleanse the soul of every wound,
    And give repenting grace.


### 8.

That we poor sinners may obtain
    The pardon of our sin,
Dear blessed Jesus, now constrain,
    And bring us flocking in.


### 9.

Come, you, Phillis, now aspire,
    And seek the living God,
So step by step thou mayst go higher,
    Till perfect in the word.


### 10.

While thousands moved to distant shore,
    And others left behind,
The blessed Jesus still adore;
    Implant this in thy mind.


### 11.

Thou hast left the heathen shore;
    Through mercy of the Lord,
Among the heathen live no more;
    Come magnify thy God.


### 12.

I pray the living God may be,
    The shepherd of thy soul;
His tender mercies still are free,
    His mysteries to unfold.

### 13.

Thou, Phillis, when thou hunger hast,
      Or pantest for thy God,
Jesus Christ is thy relief,
      Thou hast the holy word.

### 14.

The bounteous mercies of the Lord
      Are hid beyond the sky,
And holy souls that have His word
      Shall taste them when they die.

### 15.

These bounteous mercies are from God,
      The merits of His Son;
The humble soul that loves His word
      He chooses for His own.

### 16.

Come, dear Phillis, be advised
      To drink Samaria's flood;
There nothing that shall suffice
      But Christ's redeeming blood.

### 17.

While thousands muse with earthly toys,
      And range about the street,
Dear Phillis, seek for heaven's joys,
      Where we do hope to meet.

### 18.

When God shall send His summons down,
      And number saints together,

Blessed angels chant (triumphant sound),
    Come live with me forever.


### 19.

The humble soul shall fly to God,
    And leave the things of time,
Start forth as 'twere at the first word,
    To taste things more divine.


### 20.

Behold! the soul shall waft away,
    Whene'er we come to die,
And leave its cottage made of clay,
    In twinkling of an eye.


### 21.

Now glory be to the Most High,
    United praises given,
By all on earth, incessantly,
    And all the host of heaven.


## An Evening Thought: Salvation by Christ, with Penetential Cries

Salvation comes by Christ alone,
    The only Son of God;
Redemption now to every one,
    That love his holy Word.

Dear Jesus, we would fly to Thee,
    And leave off every Sin,
Thy tender Mercy well agree;
    Salvation from our King.

Salvation comes now from the Lord,
    Our victorious King.
His holy Name be well ador'd,
    Salvation surely bring.

Dear Jesus, give thy Spirit now,
    Thy Grace to every Nation,
That han't the Lord to whom we bow,
    The Author of Salvation.

Dear Jesus, unto Thee we cry,
    Give us the Preparation;
Turn not away thy tender Eye;
    We seek thy true Salvation.

Salvation comes from God we know,
    The true and only One;
It's well agreed and certain true,
    He gave his only Son.

Lord, hear our penetential Cry:
    Salvation from above;
It is the Lord that doth supply,
    With his Redeeming Love.

Dear Jesus, by thy precious Blood,
    The World Redemption have:
Salvation now comes from the Lord,
    He being thy captive slave.

Dear Jesus, let the Nations cry,
    And all the People say,
Salvation comes from Christ on high,
    Haste on Tribunal Day.

We cry as Sinners to the Lord,
    Salvation to obtain;
It is firmly fixed, his holy Word,
    *Ye shall not cry in vain.*

Dear Jesus, unto Thee we cry,
    And make our Lamentation:
O let our Prayers ascend on high;
    We felt thy Salvation.

Lord, turn our dark benighted Souls;
    Give us a true Motion,
And let the Hearts of all the World,
    Make Christ their Salvation.

Ten Thousand Angels cry to Thee,
    Yea, louder than the Ocean.
Thou art the Lord, we plainly see;
    Thou art the true Salvation.

Now is the Day, excepted Time;
    The Day of Salvation;
Increase your Faith, do not repine:
    Awake ye, every Nation.

Lord, unto whom now shall we go,
    Or seek a safe abode?
Thou hast the Word Salvation Too,
    The only Son of God.

Ho! every one that hunger hath,
    Or pineth after me,
Salvation be thy leading Staff,
    To set the Sinner free.

Dear Jesus, unto Thee we fly;
    Depart, depart from Sin,
Salvation doth at length supply,
    The Glory of our King.

Come, ye Blessed of the Lord,
    Salvation greatly given;
O turn your Hearts, accept the Word,
    Your Souls are fit for Heaven.

Dear Jesus, we now turn to Thee,
    Salvation to obtain;
Our Hearts and Souls do meet again,
    To magnify thy Name.

Come, Holy Spirit, Heavenly Dove,
    The Object of our Care;
Salvation doth increase our Love;
    Our Hearts hath felt they fear.

Now Glory be to God on High,
    Salvation high and low;
And thus the Soul on Christ rely,
    To Heaven surely go.

Come, Blessed Jesus, Heavenly Dove,
    Accept Repentance here;
Salvation give, with tender Love;
    Let us with Angels share.     Finis.

# BENJAMIN BANNEKER *(1731–1806)*

Benjamin Banneker was born in Maryland in 1731. His father had been born in Africa; his mother, an indentured servant, purchased her husband's freedom after their marriage. Banneker's schooling at an integrated private school outside Baltimore left him with an extraordinary range of interests that included astronomy, engineering, and architecture. Through his close relationship with George Ellicott, a Quaker, Banneker gained access to a private library that enabled him further to pursue his studies, in particular in astronomy. *Mayer's Tables, Ferguson's Astronomy,* and *Leadbeater's Lunar Tables* supplemented Banneker's own research and culminated in the 1790 publication of his first *Almanac.*

Along with his scholarly accomplishments, Banneker was a vocal opponent of slavery. His 1791 letter to then Secretary of State Thomas Jefferson, with which Banneker enclosed a volume of his *Almanac,* is one of the brightest examples of rhetorical protest against systematized bigotry. Jefferson's expeditious and carefully worded response, as well as his forwarding of Banneker's *Almanac* to Monsieur de Condorcet, secretary of the Academy of Sciences in Paris, and to members of the Philanthropic Society, speaks for Banneker's dynamic voice and mind. Banneker later served on the commission responsible for constructing the street designs of the District of Columbia. He was not strictly a poet, but his "A Mathematical Problem in Verse" is yet another example of his talent and accomplishment. Banneker died in 1806.

## A Mathematical Problem in Verse

A Cooper and Vintner sat down for a talk,
Both being so groggy, that neither could walk,
Says Cooper to Vintner, "I'm the first of my trade,
There's no kind of vessel, but what I have made,
And of any shape, Sir,—just what you will,—
And of any size, Sir,—from a ton to a gill!"
"Then," says the Vintner, "you're the man for me,—

Make me a vessel, if we can agree.
The top and the bottom diameter define,
To bear that proportion as fifteen to nine,
Thirty-five inches are just what I crave,
No more and no less, in the depth, will I have;
Just thirty-nine gallons this vessel must hold,—
Then I will reward you with silver or gold,—
Give me your promise, my honest old friend?"
"I'll make it tomorrow, that you may depend!"
So the next day the Cooper his work to discharge,
Soon made the new vessel, but made it too large;—
He took out some staves, which made it too small,
And then cursed the vessel, the Vintner and all.
He beat on his breast, "By the Powers!"—he swore,
He never would work at his trade any more.
Now my worthy friend, find out, if you can,
The vessel's dimensions and comfort the man!*

*The greater diameter would be 24.7460 inches, the lesser 14.8476.

# PHILLIS WHEATLEY  *(1753?–1784)*

Phillis Wheatley holds a distinction that most poets suffer in reverse—her name is more widely known than her work. Those who have followed her in the African American tradition have tended to view her poetry with a mixture of gratitude and contempt, to be both attentive toward and dismissive of her influence. While citing her limitations as a poet, these critics nonetheless acknowledge her poetic efforts to be little short of miraculous given the high hour of slavery in America.

Wheatley's work could indeed suffer at times from the sentimentality, prolixity, and overuse of allusion characteristic of the neoclassical style, but her keen awareness of the English tradition, her ability to translate emotion into language, and her abiding Christian faith are worthy of note.

Wheatley was born in West Africa, presumably in 1753. Her kidnapping for sale brought her to Boston; in July 1761 she was sold to John Wheatley from the slave ship *Phillis*. Wheatley would spend most of her short life in Boston. Encouraged in her early interest in books by her owners, Wheatley received great acclaim as a poet at the age of seventeen with her "A Poem, by Phillis, A Negro Girl in Boston, on the Death of the Reverend George Whitfield."

Wheatley's verse brought her international attention; in 1773 she traveled to London, where she was received by the countess of Huntingdon and was the object of a great deal of courtly interest. But before she could fulfill her arranged meeting at the court of George III, Wheatley, herself quite frail, rushed back to the American colonies to aid her ailing mistress.

After enduring an unhappy and poverty-stricken marriage, the loss of her three children in early childhood, and a long unproductive period, toward the end of her life Wheatley published several new poems displaying a patriotic (though poetically diplomatic) verve, indications, after all she had endured, of the importance poetry held in her life. Wheatley died on December 5, 1784. With the posthumous appearance of *Poems on Various Subjects, Religious and Moral by Phillis Wheatley* in 1793, Wheatley became the first African American to publish a volume of literature.

## On Being Brought from Africa to America

'Twas mercy brought me from my *Pagan* land,
Taught my benighted soul to understand
That there's a God, that there's a *Saviour* too:
Once I redemption neither sought nor knew.
Some view our sable race with scornful eye,
"Their colour is a diabolic die."
Remember, *Christians*, *Negros*, black as *Cain*,
May be refin'd, and join th' angelic train.

## To S.M.,* A Young African Painter, on Seeing His Works

To show the lab'ring bosom's deep intent,
And thought in living characters to paint,
When first thy pencil did those beauties give,
And breathing figures learnt from thee to live,
How did those prospects give my soul delight,
A new creation rushing on my sight!
Still, wondrous youth! each noble path pursue;
On deathless glories fix thine ardent view:
Still may the painter's and the poet's fire,
To aid thy pencil and thy verse conspire!
And may the charms of each seraphic theme
Conduct thy footsteps to immortal fame!
High to the blissful wonders of the skies
Elate thy soul, and raise thy wishful eyes.
Thrice happy, when exalted to survey
That splendid city, crowned with endless day,
Whose twice six gates on radiant hinges ring:
Celestial Salem blooms in endless spring.
Calm and serene thy moments glide along,

*Scipio Moorhead.

And may the muse inspire each future song!
Still, with the sweets of contemplation blessed,
May peace with balmy wings your soul invest!
But when these shades of time are chased away,
And darkness ends in everlasting day,
On what seraphic pinions shall we move,
And view the landscapes in the realms above!
There shall thy tongue in heavenly murmurs flow,
And there my muse with heavenly transport glow;
No more to tell of Damon's tender sighs,
Or rising radiance of Aurora's eyes;
For nobler themes demand a nobler strain,
And purer language on the ethereal plain.
Cease, gentle Muse! the solemn gloom of night
Now seals the fair creation from my sight.

## On the Death of the Rev. Mr. George Whitefield

Hail, happy saint! on thine immortal throne,
Possest of glory, life, and bliss unknown:
We hear no more the music of thy tongue;
Thy wonted auditories cease to throng.
Thy sermons in unequalled accents flowed,
And ev'ry bosom with devotion glowed;
Thou didst, in strains of eloquence refined,
Inflame the heart, and captivate the mind.
Unhappy, we the setting sun deplore,
So glorious once, but ah! it shines no more.

Behold the prophet in his towering flight!
He leaves the earth for heaven's unmeasured height,
And worlds unknown receive him from our sight.
There Whitefield wings with rapid course his way,
And sails to Zion through vast seas of day.
Thy prayers, great saint, and thine incessant cries,
Have pierced the bosom of thy native skies.
Thou, moon, hast seen, and all the stars of light,

How he has wrestled with his God by night.
He prayed that grace in ev'ry heart might dwell;
He longed to see America excel;
He charged its youth that ev'ry grace divine
Should with full lustre in their conduct shine.
That Saviour, which his soul did first receive,
The greatest gift that ev'n a God can give,
He freely offered to the numerous throng,
That on his lips with list'ning pleasure hung.

   "Take him, ye wretched, for your only good,
"Take him ye starving sinners, for your food;
"Ye thirsty, come to this life-giving stream,
"Ye preachers, take him for your joyful theme;
"Take him my dear Americans," he said,
"Be your complaints on his kind bosom laid:
"Take him, ye Africans, he longs for you;
"Impartial Saviour is his title due:
"Washed in the fountain of redeeming blood,
"You shall be sons, and kings, and priests to God."

   Great Countess,* we Americans revere
Thy name, and mingle in thy grief sincere;
New England deeply feels, the orphans mourn,
Their more than father will no more return.
   But though arrested by the hand of death,
Whitefield no more exerts his lab'ring breath,
Yet let us view him in th' eternal skies,
Let ev'ry heart to this bright vision rise;
While the tomb, safe, retains its sacred trust,
Till life divine reanimates his dust.

---

*The countess of Huntingdon, to whom Mr. Whitefield was chaplain.

# A Farewell to America

## I

Adieu, New-England's smiling meads,
　　Adieu, th' flow'ry plain:
I leave thine op'ning charms, O spring,
　　And tempt the roaring main.

## II

In vain for me the flow'rets rise,
　　And boast their gaudy pride,
While here beneath the northern skies
　　I mourn for health deny'd.

## III

Celestial maid of rosy hue,
　　Oh let me feel thy reign!
I languish till thy face I view,
　　Thy vanish'd joys regain.

## IV

Susannah mourns, nor can I bear
　　To see the crystal shower
Or mark the tender falling tear
　　At sad departure's hour;

## V

Not regarding can I see
　　Her soul with grief opprest
But let no sighs, no groans for me
　　Steal from her pensive breast.

## VI

In vain the feather'd warblers sing
    In vain the garden blooms
And on the bosom of the spring
    Breathes out her sweet perfumes.

## VII

While for Britannia's distant shore
    We weep the liquid plain,
And with astonish'd eyes explore
    The wide-extended main.

## VIII

Lo! Health appears! celestial dame!
    Complacent and serene,
With Hebe's mantle o'er her frame,
    With soul-delighting mien.

## IX

To mark the vale where London lies
    With misty vapors crown'd
Which cloud Aurora's thousand dyes,
    And veil her charms around.

## X

Why, Phoebus, moves thy car so slow?
    So slow thy rising ray?
Give us the famous town to view,
    Thou glorious King of day!

## XI

For thee, Britannia, I resign
    New-England's smiling fields;

To view again her charms divine,
    What joy the prospect yields!

## XII

But thou! Temptation hence away,
    With all thy fatal train,
Nor once seduce my soul away,
    By thine enchanting strain.

## XIII

Thrice happy they, whose heavenly shield
    Secures their souls from harm,
And fell Temptation on the field
    Of all its pow'r disarms.

# An Hymn to the Morning

Attend my lays, ye ever honored Nine,
Assist my labors, and my strains refine;
In smoothest numbers pour the notes along,
For bright Aurora now demands my song.

Aurora hail! and all the thousand dies,
Which deck thy progress through the vaulted skies:
The morn awakes, and wide extends her rays,
On ev'ry leaf the gentle zephyr plays;
Harmonious lays the feathered race resume,
Dart the bright eye, and shake the painted plume.

Ye shady groves, your verdant bloom display,
To shield your poet from the burning day:
Calliope, awake the sacred lyre,
While thy fair sisters fan the pleasing fire.
The bowers, the gales, the variegated skies,
In all their pleasures in my bosom rise.

See in the east, th'illustrious king of day!
His rising radiance drives the shades away—
But oh! I feel his fervid beams too strong,
And scarce begun, concludes the abortive song.

## An Hymn to the Evening

Soon as the sun forsook the eastern main,
The pealing thunder shook the heavenly plain;
Majestic grandeur! From the zephyr's wing,
Exhales the incense of the blooming spring.
Soft purl the streams, the birds renew their notes,
And through the air their mingled music floats.

Through all the heavens what beauteous dyes are spread!
But the west glories in the deepest red:
So may our breasts with ev'ry virtue glow,
The living temples of our God below!

Filled with the praise of him who gives the light,
And draws the sable curtains of the night,
Let placid slumbers soothe each weary mind,
At morn to wake, more heavenly, more refined;
So shall the labours of the day begin
More pure, more guarded from the snares of sin.

Night's leaden sceptre seals my drowsy eyes;
Then cease, my song, till fair Aurora rise.

# GEORGE MOSES HORTON (*1797?–1883?*)

George Moses Horton, at his best, was a poet of daring intensity and vast ambition. Born about 1797 in Northampton County, North Carolina, he was a slave for most of his life, until Emancipation in 1865. Horton, who taught himself to read, found his way into the hearts of many unwitting belles of North Carolina through his selling of personalized love lyrics to students at nearby Chapel Hill. He furthered his education by borrowing what books he could from these students.

Many of Horton's best poems concern the topic of slavery. His "On Hearing of the Intention of a Gentleman to Purchase the Poet's Freedom," "On Liberty and Slavery," and "The Slave's Complaint" examine the slave's position in clean and learned verses. "George Moses Horton, Myself" captures in its paced, cool contemplativeness and terse lyrics some of the unresolved strivings of the poet.

Horton had hoped to purchase his freedom with the sales of his first book of poems, *The Hope of Liberty* (published in Raleigh in 1829), the first full volume of verse published by an African American since Phillis Wheatley's some thirty years before. But he fell short of this goal, living instead through three generations of Horton ownership.

*The Hope of Liberty* was reissued in 1837 in Philadelphia under the title *Poems by a Slave*. Horton's second volume, *Naked Genius*, came to print in 1865, the year in which he escaped to the Northern infantry then occupying Raleigh. Little was heard of Horton after this point, and it is generally presumed that he lived the remainder of his life in Philadelphia, where he died in about 1883.

## On Liberty and Slavery

Alas! and am I born for this,
    To wear this slavish chain?
Deprived of all created bliss,
    Through hardship, toil, and pain!

How long have I in bondage lain,
    And languished to be free!
Alas! and must I still complain—
    Deprived of liberty.

Oh, Heaven! and is there no relief
    This side the silent grave—
To soothe the pain—to quell the grief
    And anguish of a slave?

Come, Liberty, thou cheerful sound,
    Roll through my ravished ears!
Come, let my grief in joys be drowned,
    And drive away my fears.

Say unto foul oppression, Cease:
    Ye tyrants rage no more,
And let the joyful trump of peace,
    Now bid the vassal soar.

Soar on the pinions of that dove
    Which long has cooed for thee,
And breathed her notes from Afric's grove,
    The sound of Liberty.

Oh, Liberty! thou golden prize,
    So often sought by blood—
We crave thy sacred sun to rise,
    The gift of nature's God!

Bid Slavery hide her haggard face,
    And barbarism fly:
I scorn to see the sad disgrace
    In which enslaved I lie.

Dear Liberty! upon thy breast,
    I languish to respire;
And like the Swan unto her nest,
    I'd to thy smiles retire.

Oh, blest asylum—heavenly balm!
　　Unto thy boughs I flee—
And in thy shades the storm shall calm,
　　With songs of Liberty!

## On Hearing of the Intention of a Gentleman to Purchase the Poet's Freedom

When on life's ocean first I spread my sail,
I then implored a mild auspicious gale;
And from the slippery strand I took my flight,
And sought the peaceful haven of delight.

Tyrannic storms arose upon my soul,
And dreadful did their mad'ning thunders roll;
The pensive muse was shaken from her sphere,
And hope, it vanished in the clouds of fear.

At length a golden sun broke through the gloom,
And from his smiles arose a sweet perfume—
A calm ensued, and birds began to sing,
And lo! the sacred muse resumed her wing.

With frantic joy she chaunted as she flew,
And kiss'd the clement hand that bore her through;
Her envious foes did from her sight retreat,
Or prostrate fall beneath her burning feet.

'Twas like a proselyte, allied to Heaven—
Or rising spirits' boast of sins forgiven,
Whose shout dissolves the adamant away,
Whose melting voice the stubborn rocks obey.

'Twas like the salutation of the dove,
Borne on the zephyr through some lonesome grove,
When Spring returns, and Winter's chill is past,
And vegetation smiles above the blast.

'Twas like the evening of a nuptial pair,
When love pervades the hour of sad despair—
'Twas like fair Helen's sweet return to Troy,
When every Grecian bosom swell'd with joy.

The silent harp which on the osiers hung,
Was then attuned, and manumission sung;
Away by hope the clouds of fear were driven,
And music breathed my gratitude to Heaven.

Hard was the race to reach the distant goal,
The needle oft was shaken from the pole;
In such distress who could forbear to weep?
Toss'd by the headlong billows of the deep!

The tantalizing beams which shone so plain,
Which turned my former pleasures into pain—
Which falsely promised all the joys of fame,
Gave way, and to a more substantial flame.

Some philanthropic souls as from afar,
With pity strove to break the slavish bar;
To whom my floods of gratitude shall roll,
And yield with pleasure to their soft control.

And sure of Providence this work begun—
He shod my feet this rugged race to run;
And in despite of all the swelling tide,
Along the dismal path will prove my guide.

Thus on the dusky verge of deep despair,
Eternal Providence was with me there;
When pleasure seemed to fade on life's gay dawn,
And the last beam of hope was almost gone.

# Early Affection

I lov'd thee from the earliest dawn,
　　When first I saw thy beauty's ray,
And will, until life's eve comes on,
　　And beauty's blossom fades away;
And when all things go well with thee,
With smiles and tears remember me.

I'll love thee when thy morn is past,
　　And wheedling gallantry is o'er,
When youth is lost in age's blast,
　　And beauty can ascend no more,
And when life's journey ends with thee,
O, then look back and think of me.

I'll love thee with a smile or frown,
　　'Mid sorrow's gloom or pleasure's light,
And when the chain of life runs down,
　　Pursue thy last eternal flight,
When thou hast spread thy wing to flee,
Still, still, a moment wait for me.

I'll love thee for those sparkling eyes,
　　To which my fondness was betray'd,
Bearing the tincture of the skies,
　　To glow when other beauties fade,
And when they sink too low to see,
Reflect an azure beam on me.

# George Moses Horton, Myself

I feel myself in need
　　Of the inspiring strains of ancient lore,
My heart to lift, my empty mind to feed,
　　And all the world explore.

I know that I am old
    And never can recover what is past,
But for the future may some light unfold
    And soar from ages blast.

I feel resolved to try,
    My wish to prove, my calling to pursue,
Or mount up from the earth into the sky,
    To show what Heaven can do.

My genius from a boy,
    Has fluttered like a bird within my heart;
But could not thus confined her powers employ,
    Impatient to depart.

She like a restless bird,
    Would spread her wings, her power to be unfurl'd,
And let her songs be loudly heard,
    And dart from world to world.

## The Slave's Complaint

Am I sadly cast aside,
On misfortune's rugged tide?
Will the world my pains deride
        Forever?

Must I dwell in Slavery's night,
And all pleasure take its flight,
Far beyond my feeble sight,
        Forever?

Worst of all, must hope grow dim,
And withhold her cheering beam?
Rather let me sleep and dream
        Forever!

Something still my heart surveys,
Groping through this dreary maze;
Is it Hope?—they burn and blaze
          Forever!

Leave me not a wretch confined,
Altogether lame and blind—
Unto gross despair consigned,
          Forever!

Heaven! in whom can I confide?
Canst thou not for all provide?
Condescend to be my guide
          Forever:

And when this transient life shall end,
Oh, may some kind, eternal friend
Bid me from servitude ascend,
          Forever!

## To Eliza

Eliza, tell thy lover why
Or what induced thee to deceive me?
    Fare thee well—away I fly—
I shun the lass who thus will grieve me.

Eliza, still thou art my song,
Although by force I may forsake thee;
    Fare thee well, for I was wrong
To woo thee while another take thee.

Eliza, pause and think awhile—
Sweet lass! I shall forget thee never:
    Fare thee well! although I smile,
I grieve to give thee up for ever.

Eliza, I shall think of thee—
My heart shall ever twine about thee;
Fare thee well—but think of me,
Compell'd to live and die without thee.
"Fare thee well!—and if for ever,
Still for ever fare thee well!"

# GEORGE BOYER VASHON  *(1820–1878)*

George Boyer Vashon was born in Carlisle, Pennsylvania, in 1820 and graduated from Oberlin College in 1844. He received a master's degree in 1849 and became a professor at New York Central College, an abolitionist school. Later he was admitted as a lawyer to the New York City bar.

While teaching at College Faustin in Haiti, Vashon learned the story of Vincent Ogé, a mulatto, friend of Lafayette, and early martyr in the cause of Haitian independence. Vashon's *Autographs for Freedom,* published in 1854, contains a remembrance of Oge, which is one of the first narrative poems written by an African American. "Vincent Ogé" suffers in part from exaggerated Byronic tendencies, but the poem does achieve a sustained model for later poems that seek to use the heroic mode as a lens through which to view black history. The poem is also of interest in its prophetic warning of the racial conflict that would explode on the world stage in the next 150 years. He died in 1878.

## Vincent Ogé

There is, at times, an evening sky—
  The twilight's gift—of sombre hue,
All checkered wild and gorgeously
  With streaks of crimson, gold and blue;—
A sky that strikes the soul with awe,
  And, though not brilliant as the sheen,
Which in the east at morn we saw,
  Is far more glorious, I ween;—
So glorious that, when night hath come
And shrouded in its deepest gloom,
We turn aside with inward pain
And pray to see that sky again,
Such sight is like the struggle made
When freedom bids unbare the blade,

And calls from every mountain-glen—
    From every hill—from every plain,
Her chosen ones to stand like men,
    And cleanse their souls from every stain
Which wretches, steeped in crime and blood,
Have cast upon the form of God.
Though peace like morning's golden hue,
    With blooming groves and waving fields,
Is mildly pleasing to the view,
    And all the blessings that it yields
Are fondly welcomed by the breast
    Which finds delight in passion's rest,
That breast with joy foregoes them all,
While listening to Freedom's call.
Though red the carnage,—though the strife
Be filled with groans of parting life,—
Though battle's dark, ensanguined skies
Give echo but to agonies—
    To shrieks of wild despairing,—
We willingly suppress a sigh—
Nay, gaze with rapture in our eye,
Whilst "Freedom!" is the rally-cry
    That calls to deeds of daring.

The waves dash brightly on thy shore,
    Fair island of the southern seas!
As bright in joy as when of yore
    They gladly hailed the Genoese,—
That daring soul who gave to Spain
A world—last trophy of her reign!
Basking in beauty, thou dost seem
A vision in a poet's dream!
Thou look'st as though thou claim'st not birth
While sea and sky and other earth,
That smile around thee but to show
Thy beauty in a brighter glow,—
That are unto thee as the foil
    Artistic hands have neatly set
Around Golconda's radiant spoil,
    To grace some lofty coronet,—

A foil, which serves to make the gem
The glory of that diadem!

If Eden claimed a favored haunt,
    Most hallowed of that blessed ground,
Where tempting fiend with guileful taunt
    A resting-place would ne'er have found,—
As shadowing it well might seek
    The loveliest home in that fair isle,
Which in its radiance seemed to speak
    As to the charmed doth Beauty's smile,
That whispers of a thousand things
For which words find no picturings.
Like to the gifted Greek who strove
    To paint a crowning work of art,
And from his ideal Queen of Love,
    By choosing from each grace a part,
Blending them in one beauteous whole,
To charm the eye, transfix the soul,
And hold it in enraptured fires,
Such as a dream of heaven inspires,—
So seem the glad waves to have sought
'    From every place its richest treasure,
And borne it to that lovely spot,
    To found thereon a home of pleasure;—
A home where balmy airs might float
    Through spicy bower and orange grove;
Where bright-winged birds might turn the note
    Which tells of pure and constant love;
Where earthquake stays its demon force,
And hurricane its wrathful course;
Where nymph and fairy find a home,
And foot of spoiler never come.

And Ogé stands mid this array
    Of matchless beauty, but his brow
Is brightened not by pleasure's play;
    He stands unmoved—nay, saddened now,
As doth the lorn and mateless bird
That constant mourns, whilst all unheard,

The breezes freighted with the strains
Of other songsters sweep the plain,—
That ne'er breathes forth a joyous note,
Though odors on the zephyrs float—
The tribute of a thousand bowers,
Rich in their store of fragrant flowers.
Yet Oge's was a mind that joyed
    With nature in her every mood,
Whether in sunshine unalloyed
    With darkness, or in tempest rude
And, by the dashing waterfall,
    Or by the gently flowing river,
Or listening to the thunder's call,
    He'd joy away his life forever.
But ah! life is a changeful thing,
    And pleasures swiftly pass away,
And we may turn, with shuddering,
    From what we sighed for yesterday.
The guest, at banquet-table spread
With choicest viands, shakes with dread,
Nor heeds the goblet bright and fair,
Nor tastes the dainties rich and rare,
Nor bids his eye with pleasure trace
The wreathed flowers that deck the place,
If he but knows there is a draught
Among the cordials, that, if quaffed,
Will send swift poison through his veins.
    So Ogé seems; nor does his eye
With pleasure view the flowery plains,
    The bounding sea, the spangled sky,
As, in the short and soft twilight,
    The stars peep brightly forth in heaven,
And hasten to the realms of night,
    As handmaids of the Even.


        The loud shouts from the distant town,
            Joined in with nature's gladsome lay;
        The lights went glancing up and down,
            Riv'ling the stars—nay, seemed as they
        Could stoop to claim, in their high home,

A sympathy with things of earth,
    And had from their bright mansions come,
        To join them in their festal mirth.
For the land of the Gaul had arose in its might,
And swept by as the wind of a wild, wintry night;
And the dreamings of greatness—the phantoms of power,
Had passed in its breath like the things of an hour.
Like the violet vapors that brilliantly play
Round the glass of the chemist, then vanish away,
The visions of grandeur which dazzlingly shone,
Had gleamed for a time, and all suddenly gone.
And the fabric of ages—the glory of kings,
Accounted most sacred mid sanctified things,
Reared up by the hero, preserved by the sage,
And drawn out in rich hues on the chronicler's page,
Had sunk in the blast, and in ruins lay spread,
While the altar of freedom was reared in its stead.
And a spark from that shrine in the free-roving breeze,
Had crossed from fair France to that isle of the seas;
And a flame was there kindled which fitfully shone
Mid the shout of the free, and the dark captive's groan;
As, mid contrary breezes, a torch-light will play,
Now streaming up brightly—now dying away.

        The reptile slumbers in the stone,
            Nor dream we of his pent abode;
        The heart conceals the anguished groan,
            With all the poignant griefs that goad
                The brain to madness;
        Within the hushed volcano's breast,
            The molten fires of ruin lie;—
        Thus human passions seem at rest,
            And on the brow serene and high,
                Appears no sadness.
        But still the fires are raging there,
        Of vengeance, hatred, and despair;
        And when they burst, they wildly pour
            Their lava flood of woe and fear,
        And in one short—one little hour,
            Avenge the wrongs of many a year.

And Ogé standeth in his hall;
    But now he standeth not alone;—
A brother's there, and friends; and all
    Are kindred spirits with his own;
For mind will join with kindred mind,
As matter's with its like combined.
They speak of wrongs they had received—
Of freemen, of their rights bereaved;
And as they pondered o'er the thought
Which in their minds so madly wrought,
Their eyes gleamed as the lightning's flash,
Their words seemed as the torrent's dash
That falleth, with a low, deep sound,
Into some dark abyss profound,—
A sullen sound that threatens more
Than other torrent's louder roar.
Ah! they had borne well as they might,
    Such wrongs as freemen ill can bear;
And they had urged both day and night,
    In fitting words, a freeman's prayer;
And when the heart is filled with grief,
    For wrongs of all true souls accurst,
In action it must seek relief,
    Or else, o'ercharged, it can but burst.
Why blame we them, if they oft spake
Words that were fitted to awake
The soul's high hopes—its noblest parts—
The slumbering passions of brave hearts,
And send them as the simoon's breath,
Upon a work of woe and death?
And woman's voice is heard amid
    The accents of that warrior train;
And when has woman's voice e'er bid,
    And man could from its hest refrain?
Hers is the power o'er his soul
    That's never wielded by another,
And she doth claim this soft control
    As sister, mistress, wife, or mother.
So sweetly doth her soft voice float
    O'er hearts by guilt or anguish rifen,

It seemeth as a magic note
    Struck from earth's harps by hands of heaven.
And there's the mother of Ogé,
    Who with firm voice, and steady heart,
And look unaltered, well can play
    The Spartan mother's hardy part;
And send her sons to battle-fields,
    And bid them come in triumph home,
Or stretched upon their bloody shields,
    Rather than bear the bondman's doom.
"Go forth," she said, "to victory;
Or else, go bravely forth to die!
Go forth to fields where glory floats
In every trumpet's cheering notes!
Go forth to where a freeman's death
Glares in each cannon's fiery breath!
Go forth and triumph o'er the foe;
Or, failing that, with pleasure go
To molder on the battle-plain,
Freed ever from the tyrant's chain!
But if your hearts should craven prove,
Forgetful of your zeal—your love
For rights and franchises of men,
My heart will break; but even then,
Whilst bidding life and earth adieu,
This be the prayer I'll breathe for you:
'Passing from guilt to misery,
May this for aye your portion be,—
A life, dragged out beneath the rod—
An end, abhorred of man and God—
As monument, the chains you nurse—
As epitaph, your mother's curse!' "

A thousand hearts are breathing high,
And voices shouting "Victory!"
    Which soon will hush in death;
The trumpet clang of joy that speaks,
Will soon be drowned in the shrieks
    Of the wounded's stifling breath,
The tyrant's plume in dust lies low—

Th' oppressed has triumphed o'er his foe.
But ah! the lull in the furious blast
May whisper not of ruin past;
It may tell of the tempest hurrying on,
To complete the work the blast begun.
With the voice of a Syren, it may whisp'ringly tell
 As a moment of hope in the deluge of rain;
And the shout of the free heart may rapt'rously swell,
 While the tyrant is gath'ring his power again.
Though the balm of the leech may soften the smart,
 It never can turn the swift barb from its aim;
And thus the resolve of the true freeman's heart
 May not keep back his fall, though it free it from shame.
Though the hearts of those heroes all well could accord
With freedom's most noble and loftiest word;
Their virtuous strength availeth them nought
With the power and skill that the tyrant brought.
Gray veterans trained in many a field
Where the fate of nations with blood was sealed,
In Italia's vales—on the shores of the Rhine—
Where the plains of fair France give birth to the vine—
Where the Tagus, the Ebro, go dancing along,
Made glad in their course by the Muleteer's song—
All these were poured down in the pride of their might,
On the land of Oge in that terrible fight.
Ah! dire was the conflict, and many the slain,
Who slept the last sleep on that red battle-plain!
The flash of the cannon o'er valley and height
Danced like the swift fires of a northern night,
Or the quivering glare which leaps forth as a token
That the King of the Storm from his cloud-throne has spoken.
And oh! to those heroes how welcome the fate
Of Sparta's brave sons in Thermopylae's strait;
With what ardor of soul they then would have given,
Their last look at earth for a long glance at heaven!
Their lives to their country—their backs to the sod—
Their hearts' blood to the sword, and their souls to their God!
But alas! although many lie silent and slain,
More blest are they far than those clanking the chain,

In the hold of the tyrant, debarred from the day;—
And among these sad captives is Vincent Ogé!

Another day's bright sun has risen,
And shines upon the insurgent's prison;
Another night has slowly passed,
And Ogé smiles, for 'tis the last
He'll droop beneath the tyrant's power—
The galling chains! Another hour,
And answering to the jailor's call,
He stands within the Judgment Hall.
They've gathered there;—they who have pressed
Their fangs into the soul distressed,
To pain its passage to the tomb
With mock'ry of a legal doom.
They've gathered there;—they who have stood
Firmly and fast in hour of blood,—
Who've seen the lights of hope all die,
As stars fade from a morning sky,—
They've gathered there, in that dark hour—
The latest of the tyrant's power,—
An hour that speaketh of the day
Which never more shall pass away,—
The glorious day beyond the grave,
Which knows no master—owns no slave.
And there, too, are the rack—the wheel—
The torturing screw—the piercing steel,—
Grim powers of death all crusted o'er
With other victims' clotted gore.
Frowning they stand, and in their cold,
Silent solemnity, unfold
The strong one's triumph o'er the weak—
The awful groan—the anguished shriek—
The unconscious mutt'rings of despair—
The strained eyeball's idiot stare—
The hopeless clench—the quiv'ring frame—
The martyr's death—the despot's shame.
The rack—the tyrant—victim,—all
Are gathered in that Judgment Hall.

Draw we the veil, for 'tis a sight
But friends can gaze on with delight.
The sunbeams on the rack that play,
For sudden terror flit away
From this dread work of war and death,
As angels do with quickened breath,
From some dark deed of deepest sin,
Ere they have drunk its spirit in.

No mighty host with banners flying,
   Seems fiercer to a conquered foe,
Than did those gallant heroes dying,
   To those who gloated o'er their woe;—
Grim tigers, who have seized their prey,
They turn and shrink abashed away;
Quail 'neath the flashing of the eye,
Which tells that though the life has started,
The will to strike has not departed.

Sad was your fate, heroic band!
Yet mourn we not, for yours the stand
Which will secure to you a fame,
That never dieth, and a name
That will, in coming ages, be
A signal word for Liberty.
Upon the slave's o'erclouded sky,
   Your gallant actions traced the bow,
Which whispered of deliv'rance nigh—
   The meed of one decisive blow.
Thy coming fame, Ogé, is sure;
Thy name with that of L'Overture,
And all the noble souls that stood
With both of you, in times of blood,
Will live to be the tyrant's fear—
Will live, the sinking soul to cheer!

# JAMES MONROE WHITFIELD   *(1822–1871)*

James Monroe Whitfield was born in Exeter, New Hampshire, in 1822 but was to make a name for himself in Buffalo, New York, where he rose, with the help of Frederick Douglass, from barber to poet and African American spokesperson of national recognition. Whitfield's poems course with a taut, controlled energy that marks him as one of the more effective antislavery poets of his generation. His work was frequently published in the abolitionist periodicals *North Star* and *Frederick Douglass' Paper*.

On the heels of such profitable exposure Whitfield released, in 1853, the volume *America and Other Poems*. It is with "America" that Whitfield's reputation largely rests today. This poem introduced to African American poetics the irony and sarcasm already characteristic of the blues and folk idioms.

Using his newfound popularity as a springboard into politics, Whitfield joined Martin R. Delany in 1854 in organizing the National Emigration Convention, whose platform was that emigration to Central America would better suit disenfranchised blacks in North America. A break with Frederick Douglass, who publicly criticized Whitfield's stance, inevitably followed. Whitfield died in San Francisco in 1871 without having published another volume.

## America

America, it is to thee,
Thou boasted land of liberty,—
It is to thee I raise my song,
Thou land of blood, and crime, and wrong.
It is to thee, my native land,
From whence has issued many a band
To tear the black man from his soil,
And force him here to delve and toil;
Chained on your blood-bemoistened sod,
Cringing beneath a tyrant's rod,
Stripped of those rights which Nature's God

Bequeathed to all the human race,
Bound to a petty tyrant's nod,
    Because he wears a paler face.
Was it for this that freedom's fires
Were kindled by your patriot sires?
Was it for this they shed their blood,
On hill and plain, on field and flood?
Was it for this that wealth and life
Were staked upon that desperate strife,
Which drenched this land for seven long years
With blood of men, and women's tears?
When black and white fought side by side,
    Upon the well-contested field,—
Turned back the fierce opposing tide,
    And made the proud invader yield—
When, wounded, side by side they lay,
    And heard with joy the proud hurrah
From their victorious comrades say
    That they had waged successful war,
The thought ne'er entered in their brains
That they endured those toils and pains,
To forge fresh fetters, heavier chains
For their own children, in whose veins
Should flow that patriotic blood,
So freely shed on field and flood.
Oh, no; they fought, as they believed,
    For the inherent rights of man;
But mark, how they have been deceived
    By slavery's accursed plan.
They never thought, when thus they shed
    Their hearts' best blood, in freedom's cause,
That their own sons would live in dread,
    Under unjust, oppressive laws:
That those who quietly enjoyed
    The rights for which they fought and fell,
Could be the framers of a code,
    That would disgrace the fiends of hell!
Could they have looked, with prophet's ken,
    Down to the present evil time,
    Seen free-born men, uncharged with crime,

Consigned unto a slaver's pen,—
Or thrust into a prison cell,
With thieves and murderers to dwell—
While that same flag whose stripes and stars
Had been their guide through freedom's wars
As proudly waved above the pen
Of dealers in the souls of men!
Or could the shades of all the dead,
    Who fell beneath that starry flag,
Visit the scenes where they once bled,
    On hill and plain, on vale and crag,
By peaceful brook, or ocean's strand,
    By inland lake, or dark green wood,
Where'er the soil of this wide land
    Was moistened by their patriot blood,—
And then survey the country o'er,
    From north to south, from east to west,
And hear the agonizing cry
Ascending up to God on high,
From western wilds to ocean's shore,
    The fervent prayer of the oppressed;
The cry of helpless infancy
    Torn from the parent's fond caress
By some base tool of tyranny,
    And doomed to woe and wretchedness;
The indignant wail of fiery youth,
    Its noble aspirations crushed,
Its generous zeal, its love of truth,
    Trampled by tyrants in the dust;
The aerial piles which fancy reared,
    And hopes too bright to be enjoyed,
Have passed and left his young heart seared,
    And all its dreams of bliss destroyed.
The shriek of virgin purity,
Doomed to some libertine's embrace,
Should rouse the strongest sympathy
    Of each one of the human race;
And weak old age, oppressed with care,
    As he reviews the scene of strife,
Puts up to God a fervent prayer,

To close his dark and troubled life,
The cry of fathers, mothers, wives,
     Severed from all their hearts hold dear,
And doomed to spend their wretched lives
     In gloom, and doubt, and hate, and fear;
And manhood, too, with soul of fire,
And arm of strength, and smothered ire,
Stands pondering with brow of gloom,
Upon his dark unhappy doom,
Whether to plunge in battle's strife,
And buy his freedom with his life,
And with stout heart and weapon strong,
Pay back the tyrant wrong for wrong
Or wait the promised time of God,
     When his Almighty ire shall wake,
And smite the oppressor in his wrath,
And hurl red ruin in his path,
And with the terrors of his rod,
     Cause adamantine hearts to quake.
Here Christian writhes in bondage still,
     Beneath his brother Christian's rod,
And pastors trample down at will,
     The image of the living God.
While prayers go up in lofty strains,
     And pealing hymns ascend to heaven,
The captive, toiling in his chains,
     With tortured limbs and bosom riven,
Raises his fettered hand on high,
     And in the accents of despair,
To him who rules both earth and sky,
     Puts up a sad, a fervent prayer,
To free him from the awful blast
     Of slavery's bitter galling shame—
Although his portion should be cast
     With demons in the eternal flame!
Almighty God! 'tis this they call
     The land of liberty and law;
Part of its sons in baser thrall
     Than Babylon or Egypt saw—
Worse scenes of rapine, lust and shame,

Than Babylonian ever knew,
Are perpetrated in the name
    Of God, the holy, just, and true;
And darker doom than Egypt felt,
May yet repay this nation's guilt.
Almighty God! thy aid impart,
And fire anew each faltering heart,
And strengthen every patriot's hand,
Who aims to save our native land.
We do not come before thy throne,
    With carnal weapons drenched in gore,
Although our blood has freely flown,
    In adding to the tyrant's store.
Father! before thy throne we come,
    Not in the panoply of war,
With pealing trump, and rolling drum,
    And cannon booming loud and far;
Striving in blood to wash out blood,
    Through wrong to seek redress for wrong;
For while thou'rt holy, just and good,
    The battle is not to the strong;
But in the sacred name of peace,
    Of justice, virtue, love and truth,
We pray, and never mean to cease,
    Till weak old age and fiery youth
In freedom's cause their voices raise,
And burst the bonds of every slave;
Till, north and south, and east and west,
The wrongs we bear shall be redressed.

# Lines on the Death of John Quincy Adams

The great, the good, the just, the true,
    Has yielded up his latest breath;
The noblest man our country knew,
    Bows to the ghastly monster, Death;

The son of one whose deathless name
    Stands first on history's brightest page;
The highest on the list of fame
    As statesman, patriot, and sage.

In early youth he learned to prize
    The freedom which his father won;
The mantle of the patriot sire
    Descended on his mightier son.
Science her deepest hidden lore
    Beneath his potent touch revealed;
Philosophy's abundant store,
    Alike his mighty mind could wield.

The brilliant page of poetry
    Received additions from his pen,
Of holy truth and purity,
    And thoughts which rouse the souls of men,
Eloquence did his heart inspire,
    And from his lips in glory blazed,
Till nations caught the glowing fire,
    And senates trembled as they praised.

While all the recreant of the land
    To slavery's idol bowed the knee—
A fawning, sycophantic band,
    Fit tools of petty tyranny—
He stood amid the recreant throng,
    The chosen champion of the free,
And battled fearlessly and long
    For justice, right, and liberty.

What though grim Death has sealed his doom
    Who faithful proved to God and us;
And slavery, o'er the patriot's tomb
    Exulting pours its deadliest curse?
Among the virtuous and free
    His memory will ever live;
Champion of right and liberty,
    The blessings, truth and virtue give.

# FRANCES E. W. HARPER (1825–1911)

Frances Ellen Watkins Harper was born free in Baltimore in 1825. By the time of her death in 1911, she had become almost an institution in both literary and political circles. Harper used what seems to have been a tireless energy to publish countless poems, articles, essays, and novels examining both racial and gender division among Americans. Often thought of as the inaugural "protest poet," she presented her themes in graceful rhetoric, skillful metaphor, allusion, and allegory, embracing the demands of her craft along with the exigencies of the social moment.

Harper worked ably and extensively in her lifetime with the Underground Railroad, the Maine Anti-Slavery Society, the Woman's Christian Temperance movement, the African Methodist Episcopal Church, the American Equal Rights Association, the Universal Peace Union, the National Council of Women, and the National Association of Colored Women. Her *Poems on Miscellaneous Subjects* was published in 1854, with a preface by William Lloyd Garrison. This volume proved so popular that it went through over twenty reprints in the author's lifetime.

Harper was also the author of *Moses: A Story of the Nile,* published in 1869, *Poems* in 1871, and *Sketches of Southern Life* in 1873. *Iola Leroy,* one of the more widely read novels written by an African American of the nineteenth century, was published in 1893.

## The Slave Mother

> Heard you that shriek? It rose
>    So wildly on the air,
> It seemed as if a burden'd heart
>    Was breaking in despair.
>
> Saw you those hands so sadly clasped—
>    The bowed and feeble head—
> The shuddering of that fragile form—
>    That look of grief and dread?

Saw you the sad, imploring eye?
   Its every glance was pain,
As if a storm of agony
   Were sweeping through the brain.

She is a mother pale with fear,
   Her boy clings to her side,
And in her kirtle vainly tries
   His trembling form to hide.

He is not hers, although she bore
   For him a mother's pains;
He is not hers, although her blood
   Is coursing through his veins!

He is not hers, for cruel hands
   May rudely tear apart
The only wreath of household love
   That binds her breaking heart.

His love has been a joyous light
   That o'er her pathway smiled,
A fountain gushing ever new,
   Amid life's desert wild.

His lightest word has been a tone
   Of music round her heart,
Their lives a streamlet blent in one—
   Oh, Father! must they part?

They tear him from her circling arms,
   Her last and fond embrace.
Oh! never more may her sad eyes
   Gaze on his mournful face.

No marvel, then, these bitter shrieks
   Disturb the listening air:
She is a mother, and her heart
   Is breaking in despair.

# Let the Light Enter

*The Dying Words of Goethe*

"Light! more light! the shadows deepen,
　　And my life is ebbing low,
Throw the windows widely open:
　　Light! more light! before I go.

"Softly let the balmy sunshine
　　Play around my dying bed,
E'er the dimly lighted valley
　　I with lonely feet must tread.

"Light! more light! for Death is weaving
　　Shadows 'round my waning sight,
And I fain would gaze upon him
　　Through a stream of earthly light."

Not for greater gifts of genius;
　　Not for thoughts more grandly bright,
All the dying poet whispers
　　Is a prayer for light, more light.

Heeds he not the gathered laurels,
　　Fading slowly from his sight;
All the poet's aspirations
　　Centre in that prayer for light.

Gracious Saviour, when life's day-dreams
　　Melt and vanish from the sight,
May our dim and longing vision
　　Then be blessed with light, more light.

## The Slave Auction

The sale began—young girls were there,
　　Defenceless in their wretchedness,
Whose stifled sobs of deep despair
　　Revealed their anguish and distress.

And mothers stood with streaming eyes,
　　And saw their dearest children sold;
Unheeded rose their bitter cries,
　　While tyrants bartered them for gold.

And woman, with her love and truth—
　　For these in sable forms may dwell—
Gaz'd on the husband of her youth,
　　With anguish none may paint or tell.

And men, whose sole crime was their hue,
　　The impress of their Maker's hand,
And frail and shrinking children, too,
　　Were gathered in that mournful band.

Ye who have laid your love to rest,
　　And wept above their lifeless clay,
Know not the anguish of that breast,
　　Whose lov'd are rudely torn away.

Ye may not know how desolate
　　Are bosoms rudely forced to part,
And how a dull and heavy weight
　　Will press the life-drops from the heart.


## Songs for the People

Let me make the songs for the people,
　　Songs for the old and young;

Songs to stir like a battle-cry
   Wherever they are sung.

Not for the clashing of sabres,
   For carnage nor for strife;
But songs to thrill the hearts of men
   With more abundant life.

Let me make the songs for the weary,
   Amid life's fever and fret,
Till hearts shall relax their tension,
   And careworn brows forget.

Let me sing for little children,
   Before their footsteps stray,
Sweet anthems of love and duty,
   To float o'er life's highway.

I would sing for the poor and aged,
   When shadows dim their sight;
Of the bright and restful mansions,
   Where there shall be no night.

Our world, so worn and weary,
   Needs music, pure and strong,
To hush the jangle and discords
   Of sorrow, pain, and wrong.

Music to soothe all its sorrow,
   Till war and crime shall cease;
And the hearts of men grown tender
   Girdle the world with peace.

# President Lincoln's Proclamation of Freedom

It shall flash through coming ages;
   It shall light the distant years;

And eyes now dim with sorrow
    Shall be clearer through their tears.

It shall flush the mountain ranges;
    And the valleys shall grow bright;
It shall bathe the hills in radiance,
    And crown their brows with light.

It shall flood with golden splendor
    All the huts of Caroline,
And the sun-kissed brow of labor
    With lustre new shall shine.

It shall gild the gloomy prison,
    Darken'd by the nation's crime,
Where the dumb and patient millions
    Wait the better coming time.

By the light that gilds their prison,
    They shall seize its mould'ring key,
And the bolts and bars shall vibrate
    With the triumphs of the free.

Like the dim and ancient chaos,
    Shrinking from the dawn of light,
Oppression, grim and hoary,
    Shall cower at the sight.

And her spawn of lies and malice
    Shall grovel in the dust,
While joy shall thrill the bosoms
    Of the merciful and just.

Though the morning seemed to linger
    O'er the hill-tops far away,
Now the shadows bear the promise
    Of the quickly coming day.

Soon the mists and murky shadows
    Shall be fringed with crimson light,

And the glorious dawn of freedom
Break refulgent on the sight.

## A Double Standard

Do you blame me that I loved him?
    If when standing all alone
I cried for bread a careless world
    Pressed to my lips a stone.

Do you blame me that I loved him,
    That my heart beat glad and free,
When he told me in the sweetest tones
    He loved but only me?

Can you blame me that I did not see
    Beneath his burning kiss
The serpent's wiles, nor even hear
    The deadly adder hiss?

Can you blame me that my heart grew cold
    That the tempted, tempter turned;
When he was feted and caressed
    And I was coldly spurned?

Would you blame him, when you draw from me
    Your dainty robes aside,
If he with gilded baits should claim
    Your fairest as his bride?

Would you blame the world if it should press
    On him a civic crown;
And see me struggling in the depth
    Then harshly press me down?

Crime has no sex and yet to-day
    I wear the brand of shame;

Whilst he amid the gay and proud
   Still bears an honored name.

Can you blame me if I've learned to think
   Your hate of vice a sham,
When you so coldly crushed me down
   And then excused the man?

Would you blame me if to-morrow
   The coroner should say,
A wretched girl, outcast, forlorn,
   Has thrown her life away?

Yes, blame me for my downward course,
   But oh! remember well,
Within your homes you press the hand
   That led me down to hell.

I'm glad God's ways are not our ways,
   He does not see as man;
Within His love I know there's room
   For those whom others ban.

I think before His great white throne,
   His throne of spotless light,
That whited sepulchres shall wear
   The hue of endless night.

That I who fell, and he who sinned,
   Shall reap as we have sown;
That each the burden of his loss
   Must bear and bear alone.

No golden weights can turn the scale
   Of justice in His sight;
And what is wrong in woman's life
   In man's cannot be right.

## Bible Defence of Slavery

Take sackcloth of the darkest dye,
  And shroud the pulpits round!
Servants of Him that cannot lie,
  Sit mourning on the ground.

Let holy horror blanch each cheek,
  Pale every brow with fears;
And rocks and stones, if ye could speak,
  Ye well might melt to tears!

Let sorrow breathe in every tone,
  In every strain ye raise;
Insult not God's majestic throne
  With th' mockery of praise.

A "reverend" man, whose light should be
  The guide of age and youth,
Brings to the shrine of Slavery
  The sacrifice of truth!

For the direst wrong by man imposed,
  Since Sodom's fearful cry,
The word of life has been unclos'd,
  To give your God the lie.

Oh! when ye pray for heathen lands,
  And plead for their dark shores,
Remember Slavery's cruel hands
  Make heathens at your doors!


## Bury Me in a Free Land

Make me a grave where'er you will,
In a lowly plain, or a lofty hill;

Make it among earth's humblest graves,
But not in a land where men are slaves.

I could not rest if around my grave
I heard the steps of a trembling slave;
His shadow above my silent tomb
Would make it a place of fearful gloom.

I could not rest if I heard the tread
Of a coffle gang to the shambles led,
And the mother's shriek of wild despair
Rise like a curse on the trembling air.

I could not sleep if I saw the lash
Drinking her blood at each fearful gash,
And I saw her babes torn from her breast,
Like trembling doves from their parent nest.

I'd shudder and start if I heard the bay
Of bloodhounds seizing their human prey,
And I heard the captive plead in vain
As they bound afresh his galling chain.

If I saw young girls from their mother's arms
Bartered and sold for their youthful charms,
My eye would flash with a mournful flame,
My death-paled cheek grow red with shame.

I would sleep, dear friends, where bloated might
Can rob no man of his dearest right;
My rest shall be calm in any grave
Where none can call his brother a slave.

I ask no monument, proud and high,
To arrest the gaze of the passers-by;
All that my yearning spirit craves,
Is bury me not in a land of slaves.

## Learning to Read

Very soon the Yankee teachers
　　Came down and set up school;
But, oh! how the Rebs did hate it,—
　　It was agin' their rule.

Our masters always tried to hide
　　Book learning from our eyes;
Knowledge didn't agree with slavery—
　　'Twould make us all too wise.

But some of us would try to steal
　　A little from the book,
And put the words together,
　　And learn by hook or crook.

I remember Uncle Caldwell,
　　Who took pot-liquor fat
And greased the pages of his book,
　　And hid it in his hat.

And had his master ever seen
　　The leaves upon his head,
He'd have thought them greasy papers,
　　But nothing to be read.

And there was Mr. Turner's Ben,
　　Who heard the children spell,
And picked the words right up by heart,
　　And learned to read 'em well.

Well, the Northern folks kept sending
　　The Yankee teachers down;
And they stood right up and helped us,
　　Though Rebs did sneer and frown.

And, I longed to read my Bible,
　　For precious words it said;

But when I begun to learn it,
   Folks just shook their heads,

And said there is no use trying,
   Oh! Chloe, you're too late;
But as I was rising sixty,
   I had no time to wait.

So I got a pair of glasses,
   And straight to work I went,
And never stopped till I could read
   The hymns and Testament.

Then I got a little cabin—
   A place to call my own—
And I felt as independent
   As the queen upon her throne.

# JOSEPH SEAMAN COTTER, SR. *(1861–1949)*

Joseph Seaman Cotter, Sr., was born in Bardstown, Kentucky, in 1861. He did not begin his formal schooling until 1883, in his early twenties, but this late start did not deter him from astonishing accomplishments as a writer, teacher, and activist. Working as a laborer from early childhood, Cotter was educated in night school, becoming a legend as a teacher in the Louisville public school system and African American community.

His first collection of poetry, *A Rhyming,* was published in 1895. This work is markedly similar in its sound texture to Paul Laurence Dunbar's dialect poetry, but Cotter's verse is arguably more contentious toward the racial circumstances of the American South. He was hard on blacks but also celebratory of them, and he utilized a tremendous range of meters, forms, and technical structures to convey this variegated content. Cotter died in 1949.

## Dr. Booker T. Washington to the National Negro Business League

'Tis strange indeed to hear us plead
    For selling and for buying
When yesterday we said: "Away
    With all good things but dying."

The world's ago, and we're agog
    To have our first brief inning;
So let's away through surge and fog
    However slight the winning.

What deeds have sprung from plow and pick!
    What bank-rolls from tomatoes!
No dainty crop of rhetoric
    Can match one of potatoes.

Ye orators of point and pith,
   Who force the world to heed you,
What skeletons you'll journey with
   Ere it is forced to feed you.

A little gold won't mar our grace,
   A little ease our glory.
This world's a better biding place
   When money clinks its story.

## Frederick Douglass

O eloquent and caustic sage
Thy long and rugged pilgrimage
   To glory's shrine has ended;
And thou has passed the inner door,
And proved thy fitness o'er and o'er,
   And to the dome ascended.

In speaking of thy noble life
One needs must think upon the strife
   That long and sternly faced it;
But since those times have flitted by,
Just let the useless relic die
   With passions that embraced it.

There is no evil known to man
But what, if wise enough, he can
   Grow stronger in the bearing;
And so the ills we often scorn
May be of heavenly wisdom born
   To aid our onward faring.

Howe'er this be, just fame has set
Her jewels in thy coronet
   So firmly that the ages
To come will ever honor thee

And place thy name in company
  With patriots and sages.

Now thou art gone; the little men
Of fluent tongue and trashy pen
  Will strive to imitate thee;
And when they find they haven't sense
Enough to make a fair pretense,
  They'll turn and underrate thee.

## Ned's Psalm of Life for the Negro

Dis is Ned dat am er-speakin',
  Wid no wuds dat's cute an' fine.
Dis is Ned dat am er-seekin'
  Light fur dis heah race o' mine.

I don't know as I'se er prophit—
  Ef I is, I prophersy—
Smart folks, don' you dar ter scoff it:
  Dis race feelin's gwine ter die.

'Tain't er thing dat has er color—
  I'se gwine lib ter see it ain't.
Hit goes 'long wid black an' yeller,
  Kase you's not er wukin' saint.

When you wuks so dat de folks is
  Boun' ter lib by whut you does,
All dey feelin's an' dey jokes is
  Fur de man dat once you wuz.

Folks will 'cept you when you takes 'em
  By supplyin' all dey needs;
Dey will paint you when you makes 'em
  Jes' de color o' yo' deeds.

Atter while dey will be treatin'
    You de bery bes' dey can,
An' you'll nebber 'gret de meetin'
    Wid yo' brudder feller man.

Yes, dey's feelin' 'twixt de races,
    An' hit's gwine ter las' until
We jes' wuks ourselves ter places
    Udder folks has got ter fill.

Dis is Ned dat am er-speakin'—
    Smart folks, don' you dar ter scorn—
I'se er-prayin' an' er-seekin'
    Ways ter let dis race be born.

I'se got faith 'nuff in de Marster
    Fur ter know He'll do His part;
Ef we stomps out dire disarster
    Wid er wukin' brain an' heart.

## The Don't-Care Negro

Neber min' what's in your cran'um
    So your collar's high an' true.
Neber min' what's in your pocket
    So de blackin's on your shoe.

Neber min' who keeps you comp'ny
    So he halfs up what he's tuk.
Neber min' what way you's gwine
    So you's gwine away from wuk.

Neber min' de race's troubles
    So you profits by dem all.
Neber min' your leaders' stumblin'
    So you he'ps to mak' dem fall.

Neber min' what's true tomorrow
    So you libes a dream today.
Neber min' what tax is levied
    So it's not on craps or play.

Neber min' how hard you labors
    So you does it to de en'
Dat de judge is boun' to sen' you
    An' your record to de "pen."

Neber min' your manhood's risin'
    So you habe a way to stay it.
Neber min' folks' good opinion
    So you habe a way to slay it.

Neber min' man's why an' wharfo'
    So de world is big an' roun'.
Neber min' whar next you's gwine to
    So you's six foot under groun'.

## William Lloyd Garrison

His country seared its conscience through its gain,
    And had not wisdom to behold the loss.
It held God partner in the hellish stain,
    And saw Christ dying on a racial cross.

What unto it the shackled fellowman,
    Whose plea was mockery, and whose groans were mirth?
Its boasted creed was: "He should rule who can
    Make prey of highest heaven and dupe of earth."

From out this mass of century-tutored wrong
    A man stood God-like and his voice rang true.
His soul was sentry to the dallying throng,
    His thought was watchword to the gallant few.

He saw not as his fellow beings saw;
    He would not misname greed expediency.
He found no color in the nation's law,
    And scorned to meet it in its liberty.

He saw his duty in his neighbor's cause,
    And died that he might rise up strong and free—
A creature subject to the highest laws
    And master of a God-like destiny.

The thunder of a million armed feet,
    Reverberating 'till the land was stirred,
Was but the tension of his great heart-beat,
    The distant echo of his spoken word.

He speaks again: "Such as would miss the rod
    That ever chastens insufficiency,
Must purge their lives and make them fit for God,
    Must train their liberty and make it free."

# JAMES WELDON JOHNSON  *(1871–1938)*

James Weldon Johnson was born in Jacksonville, Florida, in 1871. He grew up in a middle-class household, his mother a schoolteacher, his father headwaiter at a luxury hotel. A graduate of Atlanta University, Johnson began his distinguished and wide-ranging professional life simply enough, as a Jacksonville school-teacher. Simultaneously pursuing studies in the law, Johnson embarked on a law career after passing the Florida bar, then moved to New York City to write for Broadway. He held a number of notable positions in the public sector, among them United States consul to Venezuela and Nicaragua, and general secretary of the NAACP.

Johnson is best known today for his 1901 poem "Lift Every Voice and Sing," as set to music by J. Rosamond Johnson, often referred to as the "black national anthem," though his true maturity as a poet was reached with *Fifty Years and Other Poems,* published in 1917. His novel *The Autobiography of an Ex-Colored Man,* published first in 1912 and again in 1927, is one of the more widely regarded—and controversial—literary moments from the Harlem Renaissance, portraying the distortions of a soul willing to pursue assimilation into a corrupt society at any cost. Johnson is also the author of *God's Trombones* (1927) and *Saint Peter Relates an Incident of the Resurrection Day* (1930). His 1922 anthology, *A Book of American Negro Poetry,* set the bar for all African American poetry anthologies to follow.

Johnson's professional and artistic development coincided with one of the more volatile periods of race relations in the United States, the collapse of Reconstruction and the implementation of Jim Crow. From within this vortex Johnson's poetry seeks to explore the complexities of human life, of human beings as both social and existential beings, the difficulty of self-knowledge, and our often flawed relationships with loved ones, strangers, geography, and God. In his vast explorations he drew on a remarkable range of voices and mixed idioms—rural southern, urban, folk, and high poetic. Johnson died in 1938.

# O Black and Unknown Bards

O black and unknown bards of long ago,
How came your lips to touch the sacred fire?
How, in your darkness, did you come to know
The power and beauty of the minstrels' lyre?
Who first from midst his bonds lifted his eyes?
Who first from out the still watch, lone and long,
Feeling the ancient faith of prophets rise
Within his dark-kept soul, burst into song?

Heart of what slave poured out such melody
As "Steal away to Jesus"? On its strains
His spirit must have nightly floated free,
Though still about his hands he felt his chains.
Who heard great "Jordan roll"? Whose starward eye
Saw chariot "swing low"? And who was he
That breathed that comforting, melodic sigh,
"Nobody knows de trouble I see"?

What merely living clod, what captive thing,
Could up toward God through all its darkness grope,
And find within its deadened heart to sing
These songs of sorrow, love and faith, and hope?
How did it catch that subtle undertone,
That note in music heard not with the ears?
How sound the elusive reed so seldom blown,
Which stirs the soul or melts the heart to tears.

Not that great German master in his dream
Of harmonies that thundered amongst the stars
At the creation, ever heard a theme
Nobler than "Go down, Moses." Mark its bars
How like a mighty trumpet-call they stir
The blood. Such are the notes that men have sung
Going to valorous deeds; such tones there were
That helped make history when Time was young.

There is a wide, wide wonder in it all,
That from degraded rest and servile toil
The fiery spirit of the seer should call
These simple children of the sun and soil.
O black slave singers, gone, forgot, unfamed,
You—you alone, of all the long, long line
Of those who've sung untaught, unknown, unnamed,
Have stretched out upward, seeking the divine.

You sang not deeds of heroes or of kings;
No chant of bloody war, no exulting paean
No arms-won triumphs; but your humble strings
You touched in chord with music empyrean.
You sang far better than you knew; the songs
That for your listeners' hungry hearts sufficed
Still live,—but more than this to you belongs:
You sang a race from wood and stone to Christ.


## Go Down Death

*A Funeral Sermon*


Weep not, weep not,
She is not dead;
She's resting in the bosom of Jesus.
Heart-broken husband—weep no more;
Grief-stricken son—weep no more;
She's only just gone home.

Day before yesterday morning,
God was looking down from his great, high heaven,
Looking down on all his children,
And his eye fell on Sister Caroline,
Tossing on her bed of pain.
And God's big heart was touched with pity,
With the everlasting pity.

And God sat back on his throne,
And he commanded that tall, bright angel standing at his
   right hand:
Call me Death!
And that tall, bright angel cried in a voice
That broke like a clap of thunder:
Call Death!—Call Death!
And the echo sounded down the streets of heaven
Till it reached away back to that shadowy place,
Where Death waits with his pale, white horses.

And Death heard the summons,
And he leaped on his fastest horse,
Pale as a sheet in the moonlight.
Up the golden street Death galloped,
And the hoof of his horse struck fire from the gold,
But they didn't make no sound.
Up Death rode to the Great White Throne,
And waited for God's command.

And God said: Go down, Death, go down,
Go down to Savannah, Georgia,
Down in Yamacraw,
And find Sister Caroline.
She's borne the burden and heat of the day,
She's labored long in my vineyard,
And she's tired—
She's weary—
Go down, Death, and bring her to me.

And Death didn't say a word,
But he loosed the reins on his pale, white horse,
And he clamped the spurs to his bloodless sides,
And out and down he rode,
Through heaven's pearly gates,
Past suns and moons and stars;
On Death rode,
And the foam from his horse was like a comet in the sky;
On Death rode,

Leaving the lightning's flash behind;
Straight on down he came.

While we were watching round her bed,
She turned her eyes and looked away,
She saw what we couldn't see;
She saw Old Death. She saw Old Death.
Coming like a falling star.
But Death didn't frighten Sister Caroline;
He looked to her like a welcome friend.
And she whispered to us: I'm going home,
And she smiled and closed her eyes.

And Death took her up like a baby,
And she lay in his icy arms,
But she didn't feel no chill.
And Death began to ride again—
Up beyond the evening star,
Out beyond the morning star,
Into the glittering light of glory,
On to the Great White Throne.
And there he laid Sister Caroline
On the loving breast of Jesus.

And Jesus took his own hand and wiped away her tears,
And he smoothed the furrows from her face,
And the angels sang a little song,
And Jesus rocked her in his arms,
And kept-a-saying: Take your rest,
Take your rest, take your rest.

Weep not—weep not,
She is not dead;
She's resting in the bosom of Jesus.

## Sence You Went Away

Seems lak to me de stars don't shine so bright,
Seems lak to me de sun done loss his light,
Seems lak to me der's nothin' goin' right,
    Sence you went away.

Seems lak to me de sky ain't half so blue,
Seems lak to me dat ev'ything wants you,
Seems lak to me I don't know what to do,
    Sence you went away.

Seems lak to me dat ev'ything is wrong,
Seems lak to me de day's jes twice as long,
Seems lak to me de bird's forgot his song,
    Sence you went away.

Seems lak to me I jes can't he'p but sigh,
Seems lak to me ma th'oat keeps gittin' dry,
Seems lak to me a tear stays in my eye,
    Sence you went away.

## The Creation

And God stepped out on space,
And he looked around and said:
I'm lonely—
I'll make me a world.

And far as the eye of God could see
Darkness covered everything,
Blacker than a hundred midnights
Down in a cypress swamp.

Then God smiled,
And the light broke,

And the darkness rolled up on one side,
And the light stood shining on the other,
And God said: That's good!

Then God reached out and took the light in his hands,
And God rolled the light around in his hands
Until he made the sun;
And he set that sun a-blazing in the heavens.
And the light that was left from making the sun
God gathered it up in a shining ball
And flung it against the darkness,
Spangling the night with the moon and stars.
Then down between
The darkness and the light
He hurled the world;
And God said: That's good!

Then God himself stepped down—
And the sun was on his right hand,
And the moon was on his left;
The stars were clustered about his head,
And the earth was under his feet.
And God walked, and where he trod
His footsteps hollowed the valleys out
And bulged the mountains up.

Then he stopped and looked and saw
That the earth was hot and barren.
So God stepped over to the edge of the world
And he spat out the seven seas—
He batted his eyes, and the lightnings flashed—
He clapped his hands, and the thunders rolled—
And the waters above the earth came down,
The cooling waters came down.

Then the green grass sprouted,
And the little red flowers blossomed,
The pine tree pointed his fingers to the sky,
And the oak spread out his arms,
The lakes cuddled down in the hollows of the ground,

And the rivers ran down to the sea;
And God smiled again,
And the rainbow appeared,
And curled itself around his shoulder.

Then God raised his arm and he waved his hand
Over the sea and over the land,
And he said: Bring forth! Bring forth!
And quicker than God could drop his hand,
Fishes and fowls
And beasts and birds
Swam the rivers and the seas,
Roamed the forests and the woods,
And split the air with their wings.
And God said: That's good!

Then God walked around,
And God looked around
On all that he had made.
He looked at his sun,
And he looked at his moon,
And he looked at his little stars;
He looked on his world
With all its living things,
And God said: I'm lonely still.

Then God sat down—
On the side of a hill where he could think;
By a deep, wide river he sat down;
With his head in his hands,
God thought and thought,
Till he thought: I'll make me a man!

Up from the bed of the river
God scooped the clay;
And by the bank of the river
He kneeled him down;
And there the great God Almighty
Who lit the sun and fixed it in the sky,
Who flung the stars to the most far corner of the night,

Who rounded the earth in the middle of his hand;
This Great God,
Like a mammy bending over her baby,
Kneeled down in the dust
Toiling over a lump of clay
Till he shaped it in his own image;

Then into it he blew the breath of life,
And man became a living soul.
Amen. Amen.

## The Glory of the Day Was in Her Face

The glory of the day was in her face,
The beauty of the night was in her eyes.
And over all her loveliness, the grace
Of Morning blushing in the early skies.

And in her voice, the calling of the dove;
Like music of a sweet, melodious part.
And in her smile, the breaking light of love;
And all the gentle virtues in her heart.

And now the glorious day, the beauteous night,
The birds that signal to their mates at dawn,
To my dull ears, to my tear-blinded sight
Are one with all the dead, since she is gone.

# PAUL LAURENCE DUNBAR (1872–1906)

Paul Laurence Dunbar is one of the two or three greatest poets in the African American tradition, and one of the greatest American poets. Born and educated in Dayton, Ohio, Dunbar wrote extensively in both black dialect and standard English. With the 1896 publication of *Lyrics of Lowly Life* and its introduction by William Dean Howells, Dunbar rose to a qualified fame among both whites and blacks though he never made enough money from his writing to quit the job as an elevator operator that he held until his death.

Nor did he attain the kind of reputation he deserved. Dunbar suffered from the literary establishment's deep prejudice against dialect, black dialect in particular, a prejudice that would plague later poets like Sterling A. Brown as well. Poems like "A Negro Love Song" and "When Malindy Sings," while enjoyed by the black audience, were never widely appreciated (except as a kind of minstrel show), though they are among his finest, masterpieces of compression, irony, emotional truth, and expressive use of rhythm. And the white literary audience never seemed able to reconcile the different voicings that informed Dunbar's craft: associating him with his dialect verse, critics never bothered seriously to examine his standard English verse, though poems such as "We Wear the Mask," "Ere Sleep Comes Down to Soothe the Weary Eyes," and "Sympathy" would stand in any tradition.

Dunbar published extensively: *Oak and Ivy,* in 1893; *Majors and Minors* in 1895; *Lyrics of the Hearthside* in 1899; *Lyrics of Love and Laughter* in 1903; *Lyrics of Sunshine and Shadow* in 1905, as well as novels. But Dunbar, an admirer of Keats, keenly felt the lack of serious literary consideration he was given and at times himself seemed ashamed of his dialect poems. His death in 1906 at the age of thirty-five followed years of declining health, including alcohol abuse and tuberculosis.

Without Paul Laurence Dunbar it is difficult to imagine Sterling A. Brown, Gwendolyn Brooks, or Michael S. Harper. Dunbar's ambition to merge the folk with the English tradition (the title of his first volume was a direct reference to Wordsworth's groundbreaking *Lyrical Ballads*) and perfect ear made him the first both to encompass and to transcend his political and historic context, to reach to the universally human. His work is perhaps the first in the African American tradition that can be appreciated outside its context—though, still absent from most American poetry anthologies, it has yet to receive this recognition.

## When Malindy Sings

G'way an' quit dat noise, Miss Lucy—
  Put dat music book away;
What's de use to keep on tryin'?
  Ef you practise twell you're gray,
You cain't sta't no notes a-flyin'
  Lak de ones dat rants and rings
F'om de kitchen to de big woods
  When Malindy sings.

You ain't got de nachel o'gans
  Fu' to make de soun' come right,
You ain't got de tu'ns an' twistin's
  Fu' to make it sweet an' light.
Tell you one thing now, Miss Lucy,
  An' I'm tellin' you fu' true,
When hit comes to raal right singin',
  'T ain't no easy thing to do.

Easy 'nough fu' folks to hollah,
  Lookin' at de lines an' dots,
When dey ain't no one kin sence it,
  An' de chune comes in, in spots;
But fu' real melojous music,
  Dat jes' strikes yo' hea't and clings,
Jes' you stan' an' listen wif me
  When Malindy sings.

Ain't you nevah hyeahd Malindy?
  Blessed soul, tek up de cross!
Look hyeah, ain't you jokin', honey?
  Well, you don't know whut you los'.
Y' ought to hyeah dat gal a-wa'blin',

Robins, la'ks, an' all dem things,
Heish dey moufs an' hides dey faces
    When Malindy sings.

Fiddlin' man jes' stop his fiddlin',
    Lay his fiddle on de she'f;
Mockin'-bird quit tryin' to whistle,
    'Cause he jes' so shamed hisse'f.
Folks a-playin' on de banjo
    Draps dey fingahs on de strings—
Bless yo' soul—fu'gits to move 'em,
    When Malindy sings.

She jes' spreads huh mouf and hollahs,
    "Come to Jesus," twell you hyeah
Sinnahs' tremblin' steps and voices
    Timid-lak a-drawin' neah;
Den she tu'ns to "Rock of Ages,"
    Simply to de cross she clings,
An' you fin' yo' teahs a-drappin'
    When Malindy sings.

Who dat says dat humble praises
    Wif de Master nevah counts?
Heish yo' mouf, I hyeah dat music,
    Ez hit rises up an' mounts—
Floatin' by de hills an' valleys,
    Way above dis buryin' sod,
Ez hit makes its way in glory
    To de very gates of God!

Oh, hit's sweetah dan de music
    Of an edicated band;
An hit's dearah dan de battle's
    Song o' triumph in de lan'.
It seems holier dan evenin'
    When de solemn chu'ch bell rings,
Ez I sit an' ca'mly listen
    While Malindy sings.

Towsah, stop dat ba'kin', hyeah me!
    Mandy, mek dat chile keep still;
Don't you hyeah de echoes callin'
    F'om de valley to de hill?
Let me listen, I can hyeah it,
    Th'oo de bresh of angels' wings,
Sof' an' sweet, "Swing Lo, Sweet Chariot,"
    Ez Malindy sings.

## A Negro Love Song

Seen my lady home las' night,
    Jump back, honey, jump back.
Hel' huh han' an' sque'z it tight,
    Jump back, honey, jump back.
Hyeahd huh sigh a little sigh,
Seen a light gleam f'om huh eye,
An' a smile go flittin' by—
    Jump back, honey, jump back.

Hyeahd de win' blow thoo de pine,
    Jump back, honey, jump back.
Mockin'-bird was singin' fine,
    Jump back, honey, jump back.
An' my hea't was beatin' so,
When I reached my lady's do',
Dat I could n't ba' to go—
    Jump back, honey, jump back.

Put my ahm aroun' huh wais',
    Jump back, honey, jump back.
Raised huh lips an' took a tase,
    Jump back, honey, jump back.
Love me, honey, love me true?
Love me well ez I love you?
An' she answe'd, "'Cose I do"—
    Jump back, honey, jump back.

## We Wear the Mask

We wear the mask that grins and lies,
It hides our cheeks and shades our eyes,—
This debt we pay to human guile;
With torn and bleeding hearts we smile,
And mouth with myriad subtleties.

Why should the world be over-wise,
In counting all our tears and sighs?
Nay, let them only see us, while
   We wear the mask.

We smile, but, O great Christ, our cries
To thee from tortured souls arise.
We sing, but oh the clay is vile
Beneath our feet, and long the mile;
But let the world dream other-wise,
   We wear the mask!

## Sympathy

I know what the caged bird feels, alas!
When the sun is bright on the upland slopes;
When the wind stirs soft through the springing grass,
And the river flows like a stream of glass;
When the first bird sings and the first bud opes,
And the faint perfume from its chalice steals—
I know what the caged bird feels!

I know why the caged bird beats his wing
Till its blood is red on the cruel bars;
For he must fly back to his perch and cling
When he fain would be on the bough a-swing;
And a pain still throbs in the old, old scars

And they pulse again with a keener sting—
I know why he beats his wing!

I know why the caged bird sings, ah me,
When his wing is bruised and his bosom sore,
When he beats his bars and would be free;
It is not a carol of joy or glee,
But a prayer that he sends from his heart's deep core,
But a plea, that upward to Heaven he flings—
I know why the caged bird sings!

## Dawn

An angel, robed in spotless white,
Bent down and kissed the sleeping Night.
Night woke to blush; the sprite was gone.
Men saw the blush and called it Dawn.

## Robert Gould Shaw

Why was it that the thunder voice of Fate
    Should call thee, studious, from the classic groves,
    Where calm-eyed Pallas with still footstep roves,
And charge thee seek the turmoil of the state?
What bade thee hear the voice and rise elate,
    Leave home and kindred and thy spicy loaves,
    To lead th' unlettered and despised droves
To manhood's home and thunder at the gate?

Far better the slow blaze of Learning's light,
    The cool and quiet of her dearer fane,
Than this hot terror of a hopeless fight,
    This cold endurance of the final pain,—
Since thou and those who with thee died for right
    Have died, the Present teaches, but in vain!

# Jealous

Hyeah come Caesar Higgins,
Don't he think he's fine?
Look at dem new riggin's
Ain't he tryin' to shine?
Got a standin' collar
An' a stove-pipe hat,
I'll jes' bet a dollar
Some one gin him dat.

Don't one o' you mention,
Nothin' 'bout his cloes,
Don't pay no attention,
Er let on you knows.
Dat he's got 'em on him,
Why, 't 'll mek him sick,
Jes go on an' sco'n him,
My, ain't dis a trick!

Look hyeah, whut's he doin'
Lookin' t' othah way?
Dat ere move 's a new one,
Some one call him, "Say!"
Can't you see no pusson—
Puttin' on you' airs,
Sakes alive, you 's wuss'n
Dese hyeah millionaires.

Need n't git so flighty,
Case you got dat suit.
Dem cloes ain't so mighty,—
Second hand to boot,
I's a-tryin' to spite you!
Full of jealousy!
Look hyeah, man, I'll fight you,
Don't you fool wid me!

## Frederick Douglass

A hush is over all the teeming lists,
    And there is pause, a breath-space in the strife;
A spirit brave has passed beyond the mists
    And vapors that obscure the sun of life.
And Ethiopia, with bosom torn,
Laments the passing of her noblest born.

She weeps for him a mother's burning tears—
    She loved him with a mother's deepest love.
He was her champion thro' direful years,
    And held her weal all other ends above.
When Bondage held her bleeding in the dust,
He raised her up and whispered, "Hope and Trust."

For her his voice, a fearless clarion, rung
    That broke in warning on the ears of men;
For her the strong bow of his power he strung,
    And sent his arrows to the very den
Where grim Oppression held his bloody place
And gloated o'er the mis'ries of a race.

And he was no soft-tongued apologist;
    He spoke straightforward, fearlessly uncowed;
The sunlight of his truth dispelled the mist,
    And set in bold relief each dark hued cloud;
To sin and crime he gave their proper hue,
And hurled at evil what was evil's due.

Through good and ill report he cleaved his way
    Right onward, with his face set toward the heights,
Nor feared to face the foeman's dread array,—
    The lash of corn, the sting of petty spites.
He dared the lightning in the lightning's track,
And answered thunder with his thunder back.

When men maligned him, and their torrent wrath
    In furious imprecations o'er him broke,

He kept his counsel as he kept his path;
   'T was for his race, not for himself he spoke.
He knew the import of his Master's call,
And felt himself too mighty to be small.

No miser in the good he held was he,—
   His kindness followed his horizon's rim.
His heart, his talents, and his hands were free
   To all who truly needed aught of him.
Where poverty and ignorance were rife,
He gave his bounty as he gave his life.

The place and cause that first aroused his might
   Still proved its power until his latest day.
In Freedom's lists and for the aid of Right
   Still in the foremost rank he waged the fray;
Wrong lived; his occupation was not gone.
He died in action with his armor on!

We weep for him, but we have touched his hand,
   And felt the magic of his presence nigh,
The current that he sent throughout the land,
   The kindling spirit of his battle-cry.
O'er all that holds us we shall triumph yet,
And place our banner where his hopes were set!

Oh, Douglass, thou hast passed beyond the shore,
   But still thy voice is ringing o'er the gale!
Thou 'st taught thy race how high her hopes may soar,
   And bade her seek the heights, nor faint, nor fail.
She will not fail, she heeds thy stirring cry,
She knows thy guardian spirit will be nigh,
And, rising from beneath the chast'ning rod,
She stretches out her bleeding hands to God!

## An Ante-Bellum Sermon

We is gathahed hyeah, my brothahs,
   In dis howlin' wildaness,
Fu' to speak some words of comfo't
   To each othah in distress.
An' we chooses fu' ouah subjic'
   Dis—we'll 'splain it by an' by;
   "An' de Lawd said, 'Moses, Moses,'
   An' de man said, 'Hyeah am I.'"

Now ole Pher'oh, down in Egypt,
   Was de wuss man evah bo'n,
An' he had de Hebrew chillun
   Down dah wukin' in his co'n;
'T well de Lawd got tiahed o' his foolin',
   An' sez he: "I'll let him know—
Look hyeah, Moses, go tell Pher'oh
   Fu' to let dem chillun go."

"An' ef he refuse to do it,
   I will make him rue de houah,
Fu' I'll empty down on Egypt
   All de vials of my powah."
Yes, he did—an' Pher'oh's ahmy
   Was n't wuth a ha'f a dime;
Fu' de Lawd will he'p his chillun,
   You kin trust him evah time.

An' yo' enemies may 'sail you
   In de back an' in de front;
But de Lawd is all aroun' you,
   Fu' to ba' de battle's brunt.
Dey kin fo'ge yo' chains an' shackles
   F'om de mountains to de sea;
But de Lawd will sen' some Moses
   Fu' to set his chillun free.

An' de lan' shall hyeah his thundah,
   Lak a blas' f'om Gab'el's ho'n,

Fu' de Lawd of hosts is mighty
  When he girds his ahmor on.
But fu' feah some one mistakes me,
  I will pause right hyeah to say,
Dat I'm still a-preachin' ancient,
  I ain't talkin' 'bout to-day.

But I tell you, fellah christuns,
  Things'll happen mighty strange;
Now, de Lawd done dis fu' Isrul,
  An' his ways don't nevah change,
An' de love he showed to Isrul
  Was n't all on Isrul spent;
Now don't run an' tell yo' mastahs
  Dat I's preachin' discontent.

'Cause I isn't; I'se a-judgin'
  Bible people by deir ac's;
I'se a-givin' you duh Scriptuah,
  I'se a-handin' you de fac's.
Cose ole Pher'oh b'lieved in slav'ry,
  But de Lawd he let him see,
Dat de people he put bref in,—
  Evah mothah's son was free.

An' dahs othahs thinks lak Pher'oh,
  But dey calls de Scriptuah liar,
Fu' de Bible says "a servant
  Is a-worthy of his hire."
An' you cain't git roun' nor thoo dat,
  An' you cain't git ovah it,
Fu' whatevah place you git in,
  Dis hyeah Bible too 'll fit.

So you see de Lawd's intention,
  Evah sence de worl' began,
Was dat his almighty freedom
  Should belong to evah man,
But I think it would be bettah,
  Ef I'd pause agin to say,

Dat I'm talkin' 'bout ouah freedom
    In a Bibleistic way.

But de Moses is a-comin',
    An' he's comin', suah and fas'
We kin hyeah his feet a-trompin',
    We kin hyeah his trumpit blas'.
But I want to wa'n you people,
    Don't you git too brigity;
An' don't you git to braggin'
    'Bout dese things, you wait an' see.

But when Moses wif his powah
    Comes an' sets us chillun free,
We will praise de gracious Mastah
    Dat has gin us liberty;
An' we'll shout ouah halleluyahs,
    On dat mighty reck'nin' day,
When we'se reco'nised ez citiz'—
    Huh uh! Chillun, let us pray!

## Accountability

Folks ain't got no right to censuah othah folks about dey habits;
Him dat giv' de squir'ls de bushtails made de bobtails fu' de
    rabbits.
Him dat built de great big mountains hollered out de little valleys,
Him dat made de streets an' driveways wasn't shamed to make de
    alleys.

We is all constructed diff'ent, d'ain't no two of us de same;
We cain't he'p ouah likes an' dislikes, ef we'se bad we ain't to
    blame.
Ef we'se good, we need n't show off, case you bet it ain't ouah
    doin'
We gits into su'tain channels dat we jes' cain't he'p pu'suin'.

But we all fits into places dat no othah ones could fill,
An' we does the things we has to, big er little, good er ill.
John cain't tek de place o' Henry, Su an' Sally ain't alike;
Bass ain't nuthin' like a suckah, chub ain't nuthin like a pike.

When you come to think about it, how it's all plannned out it's
    splendid.
Nuthin's done er evah happens, 'dout hit's somefin' dat's intended;
Don't keer whut you does, you has to, an' hit sholy beats de
    dickens,—
Viney, go put on de kittle, I got one o' mastah's chickens.


## A Plea

        Treat me nice, Miss Mandy Jane,
           Treat me nice.
        Dough my love has tu'ned my brain,
           Treat me nice.
        I ain't done a t'ing to shame,
        Lovahs all ac's jes' de same:
        Don't you know we ain't to blame?
           Treat me nice!

        Cose I know I's talkin' wild;
           Treat me nice;
        I cain't talk no bettah, child,
           Treat me nice;
        Whut a pusson gwine to do,
        W'en he come a-cout'in' you
        All a-trimblin' thoo and thoo?
           Please be nice.

        Reckon I mus' go de paf
           Othahs do:
        Lovahs lingah, ladies laff;
           Mebbe you

Do' mean all the things you say,
An' pu'haps some latah day
W'en I baig you ha'd, you may
    Treat me nice!

## Douglass

Ah, Douglass, we have fall'n on evil days,
    Such days as thou, not even thou didst know,
    When thee, the eyes of that harsh long ago
Saw, salient, at the cross of devious ways,
And all the country heard thee with amaze.
    Not ended then, the passionate ebb and flow,
    The awful tide that battled to and fro;
We ride amid a tempest of dispraise.

Now, when the waves of swift dissension swarm,
    And Honor, the strong pilot, lieth stark,
Oh, for thy voice high-sounding o'er the storm,
    For thy strong arm to guide the shivering bark,
The blast-defying power of thy form,
    To give us comfort through the lonely dark.

## Ere Sleep Comes Down to Soothe the Weary Eyes

Ere sleep comes down to soothe the weary eyes,
    Which all the day with ceaseless care have sought
The magic gold which from the seeker flies;
    Ere dreams put on the gown and cap of thought,
And make the waking world a world of lies,—
    Of lies most palpable, uncouth, forlorn,
That say life's full of aches and tears and sighs,—
    Oh, how with more than dreams the soul is torn,
Ere sleep comes down to soothe the weary eyes.

Ere sleep comes down to soothe the weary eyes,
    How all the griefs and heartaches we have known
Come up like pois'nous vapors that arise
    From some base witch's caldron, when the crone,
To work some potent spell, her magic plies.
    The past which held its share of bitter pain,
Whose ghost we prayed that Time might exorcise,
    Comes up, is lived and suffered o'er again,
Ere sleep comes down to soothe the weary eyes.

Ere sleep comes down to soothe the weary eyes,
    What phantoms fill the dimly lighted room;
What ghostly shades in awe-creating guise
    Are bodied forth within the teeming gloom.
What echoes faint of sad and soul-sick cries,
    And pangs of vague inexplicable pain
That pay the spirit's ceaseles enterprise,
    Come thronging through the chambers of the brain,
Ere sleep comes down to soothe the weary eyes.

Ere sleep comes down to soothe the weary eyes,
    Where ranges forth the spirit far and free?
Through what strange realms and unfamiliar skies
    Tends her far course to lands of mystery?
To lands unspeakable—beyond surmise,
    Where shapes unknowable to being spring,
Till, faint of wing, the Fancy fails and dies
    Much wearied with the spirit's journeying,
Ere sleep comes down to soothe the weary eyes.

Ere sleep comes down to soothe the weary eyes,
    How questioneth the soul that other soul,—
The inner sense which neither cheats nor lies,
    But self exposes unto self, a scroll
Full writ with all life's acts unwise or wise,
    In characters indelible and known;
So, trembling with the shock of sad surprise,
    The soul doth view its awful self alone,
Ere sleep comes down to soothe the weary eyes.

Ere sleep comes down to soothe the weary eyes,
    The last dear sleep whose soft embrace is balm,
And whom sad sorrow teaches us to prize
    For kissing all our passions into calm,
Ah, then, no more we heed the sad world's cries,
    Or seek to probe th' eternal mystery,
Or fret our souls at long-withheld replies,
    At glooms through which our visions cannot see,
When sleep comes down to seal the weary eyes.

# WILLIAM STANLEY BRAITHWAITE *(1878–1962)*

**W**illiam Stanley Braithwaite was an unabashed lover of poetry, channeling his energy into reviews, anthologies, and teaching as well as his own verse. Born in Boston, the son of West Indian parents, in 1878, Braithwaite was largely self-taught, studying on his own the British poets of the eighteenth and nineteenth centuries. His poetry reflects his love of formal stanzaic deployment and the "universal" themes of loneliness and passion. Though his personal poetics tended toward the conservative, Braithwaite spoke and wrote in encouragement of the experimentalists emerging with modernism and the Harlem Renaissance.

Braithwaite served on the editorial staff of the *Boston Transcript* and between 1913 and 1929 published an annual *Anthology of Magazines in Verse*. Also to his editorial credit are *The Book of Elizabethan Verse* (1906), *The Book of Georgian Verse* (1908), and *The Book of Restoration Verse* (1909). His own *Lyrics of Life* was first published in 1904, *The House of Falling Leaves* in 1908. A professor of literature at Atlanta University, Braithwaite died in 1962.

## The House of Falling Leaves

### I

Off our New England coast the sea to-night
Is moaning the full sorrow of its heart:
There is no will to comfort it apart
Since moon and stars are hidden from its sight.
And out beyond the furthest harbor-light
There runs a tide that marks not any chart
Wherewith man knows the ending and the start
Of that long voyage in the infinite.

If change and fate and hapless circumstance
May baffle and perplex the moaning sea,

And day and night in alternate advance
Still hold the primal Reasoning in fee,
Cannot my Grief be strong enough to chance
My voice across the tide I cannot see?


## II

We go from house to house, from town to town,
And fill the distance full of smiles and words;
We take all pleasure that our strength affords
And care not if the sun be up or down.
The way of it no man has ever known—
But suddenly there is a snap of chords
Within the heart that sounds like hollow boards,—
We question every shadow that is thrown.

O to be near when the last word is said!
And see the last reflection in the eye—
For when the word is brought our friend is dead,
How bitter is the tear that will not dry,
Because so far away our steps are led
When Love should draw us close to say Good-bye!


## III

Four seasons are there to the circling year:
Four horses where the dreams of men abide—
The stark and naked Winter without pride,
The Spring like a young maiden soft and fair;
The Summer like a bride about to bear
The issue of the love she deified;
And lastly, Autumn, on the turning tide
That ebbs the voice of nature to its bier.

Four houses with two spacious chambers each,
Named Birth and Death, wherein Time joys and grieves.
Is there no Fate so wise enough to teach
Into which door Life enters and retrieves?

What matter since his voice is out of reach,
And Sorrow fills My House of Falling Leaves!

### IV

The House of Falling Leaves we entered in—
He and I—we entered in and found it fair;
At midnight some one called him up the stair,
And closed him in the Room I could not win.
Now must I go alone out in the din
Of hurrying days: for forth he cannot fare;
I must go on with Time, and leave him there
In Autumn's house where dreams will soon grow thin.

When Time shall close the door unto the house
And opens that of Winter's soon to be,
And dreams go moving through the ruined boughs—
He who went in comes out a Memory.
From his deep sleep no sound may e'er arouse,—
The moaning rain, nor wind-embattled sea.

## The Watchers

Two women on the lone wet strand,
   *(The wind's out with a will to roam)*
The waves wage war on rocks and sand,
   *(And a ship is long due home.)*

The sea sprays in the women's eyes—
   *(Hearts can writhe like the sea's wild foam)*
Lower descend the tempestuous skies,
   *(For the wind's out with a will to roam.)*

"O daughter, thine eyes be better than mine,"
   *(The waves ascend high as yonder dome)*
"North or south is there never a sign?"
   *(And a ship is long due home.)*

They watched there all the long night through—
  *(The wind's out with a will to roam)*
Wind and rain and sorrow for two,—
  *(And heaven on the long reach home.)*

# ANNE SPENCER (1882–1975)

Upon graduating from Virginia Seminary, Anne Spencer made Lynchburg, Virginia, her permanent home. She cultivated there a renowned, lushly cultivated garden (memorialized by Sterling A. Brown in his poem "To a Certain Lady"), which also served as the most alluring feature of a warm, open house that functioned as an unofficial home away from home and conference center for many other black poets of the era.

Although the self-effacingly generous Spencer would not publish a volume of poetry during her lifetime, her presence as a significant poet of the period is evidenced in anthologies both past and present, as well as in respected literary journals of the 1920s, such as *Opportunity* and *Crisis*. Spencer's most rigorous poems engage the reader through piercing images and chiseled, precise language. Internal and meditative, these poems encompass personal and existential, rather than social concerns; race is rarely her explicit subject.

Born in 1882 in Bramwell, West Virginia, Spencer worked for many years as the librarian of Dunbar High School in Lynchburg, before her death in 1975.

## Letter to My Sister

It is dangerous for a woman to defy the gods;
To taunt them with the tongue's thin tip,
Or strut in the weakness of mere humanity,
Or draw a line daring them to cross;
The gods own the searing lightning,
The drowning waters, tormenting fears,
And anger of red sins.

Oh, but worse still if you mince timidly—
Dodge this way or that, or kneel or pray,
Be kind, or sweat agony drops
Or lay your quick body over your feeble young;

If you have beauty or plainness, if celibate
Or vowed—the gods are Juggernaut,
Passing over . . . over . . .

This you may do:
Lock your heart, then, quietly,
And lest they peer within,
Light no lamp when dark comes down
Raise no shade for sun;
Breathless must your breath come through
If you'd die and dare deny
The gods their god-like fun.

## White Things

Most things are colorful things—the sky, earth, and sea.
    Black men are most men; but the white are free!
White things are rare things; so rare, so rare
They stole from out a silvered world—somewhere.
Finding earth-plains fair plains, save greenly grassed,
They strewed white feathers of cowardice, as they passed;
    The golden stars with lances fine
    The hills all red and darkened pine,
They blanced with their wand of power;
And turned the blood in a ruby rose
To a poor white poppy-flower.

## Lines to a Nasturtium

*(A Lover Muses)*

Flame-flower, Day-torch, Mauna Loa,
I saw a daring bee, today, pause and soar,
    Into your flaming heart;

Then did I hear crisp, crinkled laughter
As the furies after tore him apart?
    A bird, next, small and humming,
Looked into your startled depths and fled . . .
Surely, some dread sight, and dafter
    Than human eyes as mine can see,
Set the stricken air waves drumming
    In his flight.

Day-torch, Flame-flower, cool-hot Beauty,
I cannot see, I cannot hear your flutey
Voice lure your loving swain,
But I know one other to whom you are in beauty
Born in vain:
Hair like the setting sun,
Her eyes a rising star,
Motions gracious as reeds by Babylon, bar
All your competing;
Hands like, how like, brown lilies sweet,
Cloth of gold were fair enough to touch her feet . . .
Ah, how the sense floods at my repeating,
*As once in her fire-lit heart I felt the furies*
Beating, beating.

## Dunbar

        Ah, how poets sing and die!
        Make one song and Heaven takes it;
        Have one heart and Beauty breaks it;
        Chatterton, Shelley, Keats and I—
        Ah, how poets sing and die!

# Neighbors

Ah, you are cruel;
You ask too much;
Offered a hand, a finger-tip,
You must have a soul to clutch.

# GEORGIA DOUGLAS JOHNSON *(1886–1966)*

Georgia Douglas Johnson published four volumes of poetry: *The Heart of a Woman and Other Poems* (1918), *Bronze: A Book of Poems* (1922), *An Autumn Love Cycle* (1928), and *Share My World* (1962), as well as numerous short stories, plays, and newspaper articles. Her poems speak frequently to affairs of the heart, often in rhymed lyrics, which at their best have a sharpness of observation, a rare, delicate pathos, and measured wit. Johnson's work and her sustained patronage of a group of young African American writers that included Langston Hughes garnered her the most respect and acclaim a black woman poet had received since Frances E. W. Harper and a preeminent position within the Harlem Renaissance.

Johnson was born in 1886 in Atlanta, Georgia. A graduate of Atlanta University and the Oberlin Conservatory, she settled in Washington, DC, with her husband, a prominent black Republican, and was herself rewarded by Calvin Coolidge with a position in his administration. Johnson was the recipient of an honorary doctorate from Atlanta University in 1965. She died in 1966.

## The Heart of a Woman

The heart of a woman goes forth with the dawn,
As a lone bird, soft winging, so restlessly on,
Afar o'er life's turrets and vales does it roam
In the wake of those echoes the heart calls home.

The heart of a woman falls back with the night,
And enters some alien cage in its plight,
And tries to forget it has dreamed of the stars
While it breaks, breaks, breaks on the sheltering bars.

# I Want to Die While You Love Me

I want to die while you love me,
  While yet you hold me fair,
While laughter lies upon my lips
  And lights are in my hair.

I want to die while you love me,
  And bear to that still bed,
Your kisses—turbulent, unspent,
  To warm me when I'm dead.

I want to die while you love me,
  Oh, who would care to live
'Till love has nothing more to ask
  And nothing more to give?

I want to die while you love me,
  And never, never see
The glory of this perfect day
  Grow dim or cease to be!

# Little Son

The very acme of my woe,
  The pivot of my pride,
My consolation, and my hope
  Deferred, but not denied.
The substance of my every dream,
  The riddle of my plight,
The very world epitomized
  In turmoil and delight.

## Old Black Men

They have dreamed as young men dream
Of glory, love and power;
They have hoped as youth will hope
Of life's sun-minted hour.

They have seen as others saw
Their bubbles burst in air,
They have learned to live it down
As though they did not care.

# CLAUDE MCKAY  *(1889–1948)*

The verse of Claude McKay sits at the center of the Harlem Renaissance. Negotiated carefully between form and content and conveyed in the forceful economy of his lines, McKay's poems speak with unambiguous clarity against the manifestations of racism in the early-twentieth-century metropolis. Particularly of note is his use of the sonnet as a vehicle for social argument, exemplified by McKay's composition, in the aftermath of the tragic race riots of 1919, of "If We Must Die." (Winston Churchill would read this poem in the House of Commons during World War II; many British soldiers carried copies of it.)

Born in Clarendon, Jamaica, in 1889, McKay was taught as a youth by his brother, Clarendon's schoolmaster. In 1912 McKay published his first book of verse, *Songs of Jamaica,* and soon after left to study in the United States. After brief stints at Tuskegee University and Kansas State, McKay made his way to New York, finding friends and supportive colleagues in Max Eastman and Greenwich Village's literati.

The year 1919 brought McKay to England, where he published *Spring in New Hampshire and Other Poems* (1920). Upon returning to the United States, McKay published his best-known volume, *Harlem Shadows* (1922), generally regarded as the inaugural literary event of the Harlem Renaissance. McKay's politics and restless spirit took him in the following years to various sites in Europe and North Africa, during which time he established himself as a writer of prose fiction with *Home to Harlem* (1928), the first of his three well-received novels. He died in 1948.

## If We Must Die

If we must die, let it not be like hogs
Hunted and penned in an inglorious spot,
While round us bark the mad and hungry dogs,
Making their mock at our accursèd lot.
If we must die, O let us nobly die,

So that our precious blood may not be shed
In vain; then even the monsters we defy
Shall be constrained to honor us though dead!
O kinsmen! we must meet the common foe!
Though far outnumbered let us show us brave,
And for their thousand blows deal one deathblow!
What though before us lies the open grave?
Like men we'll face the murderous, cowardly pack,
Pressed to the wall, dying, but fighting back!

## The White House

Your door is shut against my tightened face,
And I am sharp as steel with discontent;
But I possess the courage and the grace
To bear my anger proudly and unbent.
The pavement slabs burn loose beneath my feet,
A chafing savage, down the decent street;
And passion rends my vitals as I pass,
Where boldly shines your shuttered door of glass.
Oh, I must search for wisdom every hour,
Deep in my wrathful bosom sore and raw,
And find in it the superhuman power
To hold me to the letter of your law!
Oh, I must keep my heart inviolate
Against the potent poison of your hate.

## The Harlem Dancer

Applauding youths laughed with young prostitutes
And watched her perfect, half-clothed body sway;
Her voice was like the sound of blended flutes
Blown by black players upon a picnic day.
She sang and danced on gracefully and calm,

The light gauze hanging loose about her form;
To me she seemed a proudly-swaying palm
Grown lovelier for passing through a storm.
Upon her swarthy neck black shiny curls
Luxuriant fell; and tossing coins in praise,
The wine-flushed, bold-eyed boys, and even the girls,
Devoured her shape with eager, passionate gaze;
But looking at her falsely-smiling face,
I knew her self was not in that strange place.

## The Tropics in New York

Bananas ripe and green, and ginger-root,
　　Cocoa in pods and alligator pears,
And tangerines and mangoes and grape fruit,
　　Fit for the highest prize at parish fairs,

Set in the window, bringing memories
　　Of fruit-trees laden by low-singing rills,
And dewy dawns, and mystical blue skies
　　In benediction over nun-like hills.

My eyes grew dim, and I could no more gaze;
　　A wave of longing through my body swept,
And, hungry for the old, familiar ways,
　　I turned aside and bowed my head and wept.

# JEAN TOOMER  (1894–1967)

Jean Toomer's rise to the national literary stage was matched in its meteoric intensity only by his subsequent disappearance. With the 1923 publication of *Cane*, Toomer emerged as the author of one of the twentieth century's most original and challenging works. Full of lush prose and penetrating lyric poetry marked by imagistic density and metaphoric brilliance, *Cane* concerns the dialectic of change—racial, demographic, and psychic—that is the subject of all great literature.

Toomer's childhood of uncertainty and change laid the groundwork for this high modernist masterpiece. Born in Washington, DC, in 1894, he was the maternal grandson of a Reconstruction congressman who moved from Louisiana to the District of Columbia after Reconstruction's end. Toomer's grandparents originally settled in a predominantly white neighborhood; their subsequent decision to move, as racial tensions escalated, to a predominantly black neighborhood brought issues of race and genealogy (he was light-skinned) to Toomer's doorstep quite literally. Toomer maintained throughout his life that he was the sum of his parts, a living "melting pot" of New World complexity. This stance would cause him much personal and psychic pain.

Attending five universities in a four-year span, Toomer never received a degree. Though *Cane* situated him as one of the brightest young writers of his time, Toomer was never again able to capture the intensity of focus and aesthetic drive that fueled the fire of his major triumph. He died in 1967, having virtually removed himself from black literary society.

## Cotton Song

> Come, brother, come. Let's lift it;
> Come now, hewit! roll away!
> Shackles fall upon the Judgment Day
> But let's not wait for it.

God's body's got a soul,
Bodies like to roll the soul,
Cant blame God if we dont roll,
Come, brother, roll, roll!

Cotton bales are the fleecy way
Weary sinner's bare feet trod,
Softly, softly to the throne of God,
"We aint agwine t wait until th Judgment Day!

Nassur; nassur,
Hump.
Eoho, eoho, roll away!
We aint agwine t wait until th Judgment Day!"

God's body's got a soul,
Bodies like to roll the soul,
Cant blame God if we don't roll,
Come, brother, roll, roll!

## Evening Song

Full moon rising on the waters of my heart,
Lakes and moon and fires,
Cloine tires,
Holding her lips apart.

Promises of slumber leaving shore to charm the moon,
Miracle made vesper-keeps,
Cloine sleeps,
And I'll be sleeping soon.

Cloine, curled like the sleepy waters where the moon-waves start,
Radiant, resplendently she gleams,
Cloine dreams,
Lips pressed against my heart.

## Georgia Dusk

The sky, lazily disdaining to pursue
    The setting sun, too indolent to hold
    A lengthened tournament for flashing gold,
Passively darkens for night's barbecue,

A feast of moon and men and barking hounds,
    An orgy for some genius of the South
    With blood-hot eyes and cane-lipped scented mouth,
Surprised in making folk-songs from soul-sounds.

The sawmill blows its whistle, buzz-saws stop,
    And silence breaks the bud of knoll and hill,
    Soft settling pollen where plowed lands fulfill
Their early promise of a bumper crop.

Smoke from the pyramidal sawdust pile
    Curls up, blue ghosts of trees, tarrying low
    Where only chips and stumps are left to show
The solid proof of former domicile.

Meanwhile, the men, with vestiges of pomp,
    Race memories of king and caravan,
    High-priests, an ostrich, and a juju-man,
Go singing through the footpaths of the swamp.

Their voices rise . . . the pine trees are guitars,
    Strumming, pine-needles fall like sheets of rain . . .
    Their voices rise . . . the chorus of the cane
Is caroling a vesper to the stars . . .

O singers, resinous and soft your songs
    Above the sacred whisper of the pines,
    Give virgin lips to cornfield concubines,
Bring dreams of Christ to dusky cane-lipped throngs.

# Harvest Song

I am a reaper whose muscles set at sundown. All my oats are
    cradled.
But I am too chilled, and too fatigued to bind them. And I
    hunger.

I crack a grain between my teeth. I do not taste it.
I have been in the fields all day. My throat is dry. I hunger.

My eyes are caked with dust of oatfields at harvest-time.
I am a blind man who stares across the hills, seeking stack'd
    fields of other harvesters.

It would be good to see them . . . crook'd, split, and iron-
    ring'd handles of the scythes. It would be good to see
    them, dust-caked and blind. I hunger.

(Dusk is a strange fear'd sheath their blades are dull'd in.)
My throat is dry. And should I call, a cracked grain like the
    oats . . . eoho—

I fear to call. What should they hear me, and offer me their
    grain, oats, or wheat, or corn? I have been in the fields all
    day. I fear I could not taste it. I fear knowledge of my
    hunger.

My ears are caked with dust of oatfields at harvest-time.
I am a deaf man who strains to hear the calls of other har-
    vesters whose throats are also dry.

It would be good to hear their songs . . . reapers of the
    sweet-stalk'd cane, cutters of the corn . . . even though
    their throats cracked and the strangeness of their voices
    deafened me.

I hunger. My throat is dry. Now that the sun has set and I
   am chilled, I fear to call. (Eoho, my brothers!)

I am a reaper, (Eoho!) All my oats are cradled. But I am too
   fatigued to bind them. And I hunger. I crack a grain. It
   has no taste to it. My throat is dry . . .

O my brothers, I beat my palms, still soft, against the stubble
   of my harvesting. (You beat your soft palms, too.) My
   pain is sweet. Sweeter than the oats or wheat or corn. It
   will not bring me knowledge of my hunger.


## November Cotton Flower

Boll-weevil's coming, and the winter's cold,
Made cotton-stalks look rusty, seasons old,
And cotton, scarce as any southern snow,
Was vanishing; the branch, so pinched and slow,
Failed in its function as the autumn rake;
Drouth fighting soil had caused the soil to take
All water from the streams; dead birds were found
In wells a hundred feet below the ground—
Such was the season when the flower bloomed.
Old folks were startled, and it soon assumed
Significance. Superstition saw
Something it had never seen before:
Brown eyes that loved without a trace of fear,
Beauty so sudden for that time of year.


## Reapers

Black reapers with the sound of steel on stones
Are sharpening scythes. I see them place the hones
In their hip-pockets as a thing that's done,

And start their silent swinging, one by one.
Black horses drive a mower through the weeds,
And there, a field rat, startled, squealing bleeds.
His belly close to ground. I see the blade,
Blood-stained, continue cutting weeds and shade.

# MELVIN B. TOLSON  *(1900?–1966)*

**M**elvin B. Tolson's ornate rhetoric and interweaving of diverse materials into a distinct poetic code marked him as an accomplished artist in the high modernist tradition of T. S. Eliot and Ezra Pound. Allen Tate compared his achievement with that of Hart Crane.

Tolson was born in Moberly, Missouri, around 1900. Originally matriculating at Fisk, he transferred and earned his bachelor's degree from Lincoln University in Lincoln, Pennsylvania. (He would be awarded an honorary doctorate by his alma mater in 1965.)

Tolson taught at Wiley College in Marshall, Texas, before taking an M.A. in comparative literature at Columbia University, where he wrote on the Harlem Renaissance. By the mid-1930s Tolson, whose commitment to poetry had been strong since childhood, was submitting poems to various journals and earning a reputation for his personality as well as his work. A Tolson reading was indeed part poem, part performance.

In 1939 his masterwork "Dark Symphony" won the national poetry contest sponsored by the American Negro Exposition in Chicago. After moving to Oklahoma's Langston University in 1947, Tolson served as mayor of Langston for four successive terms. In 1953 he was commissioned to write a poem commemorating the Liberian Centennial and International Exposition, which became his *Libretto for the Republic of Liberia.* Tolson was the author of two other volumes of poetry, *Rendezvous with America* (1944) and *Harlem Gallery* (1965), and was serving as the writer in residence and chair of humanities at Tuskegee Institute when he succumbed to cancer in 1966.

# Dark Symphony

## I

### *Allegro Moderato*

Black Crispus Attucks taught
       Us how to die
Before white Patrick Henry's bugle breath
Uttered the vertical
       Transmitting cry:
"Yea, give me liberty, or give me death."

And from that day to this
       Men black and strong
For Justice and Democracy have stood,
Steeled in the faith that Right
       Will conquer Wrong
And Time will usher in one brotherhood.

No Banquo's ghost can rise
       Against us now
And say we crushed men with a tyrant's boot,
Or pressed the crown of thorns
       On Labor's brow,
Or ravaged lands and carted off the loot.

## II

### *Lento Grave*

The centuries-old pathos in our voices
Saddens the great white world,
And the wizardry of our dusky rhythms
Conjures up shadow-shapes of ante-bellum years:

Black slaves singing *One More River to Cross*
In the torture tombs of slave-ships,
Black slaves singing *Steal Away to Jesus*
In jungle swamps,
Black slaves singing *The Crucifixion*
In slave-pens at midnight,
Black slaves singing *Swing Low, Sweet Chariot*
In cabins of death,
Black slaves singing *Go Down, Moses*
In the canebrakes of the Southern Pharaohs.

### III

*Andante Sostenuto*

They tell us to forget
The Golgotha we tread . . .
We who are scourged with hate,
A price upon our head.
They who have shackled us
Require of us a song,
They who have wasted us
Bid us o'erlook the wrong.

They tell us to forget
Democracy is spurned.
They tell us to forget
The Bill of Rights is burned.
Three hundred years we slaved,
We slave and suffer yet:
Though flesh and bone rebel,
They tell us to forget!

Oh, how can we forget
Our human rights denied?
Oh, how can we forget
Our manhood crucified?
When Justice is profaned
And plea with curse is met,

When Freedom's gates are barred,
Oh, how can we forget?


## IV

### *Tempo Primo*

The New Negro strides upon the continent
In seven league boots . . .
The New Negro
Who sprang from the vigor-stout loins
Of Nat Turner, gallows-martyr for Freedom,
Of Joseph Cinquez, Black Moses of the Amistad Mutiny,
Of Frederick Douglass, oracle of the Catholic Man,
Of Sojourner Truth, eye and ear of Lincoln's legions,
Of Harriet Tubman, St. Bernard of the Underground Railroad.


## V

### *Larghetto*

None in the Land can say
To us black men Today:
You send the tractors on their bloody path,
And create Oakies for *The Grapes of Wrath*.
You breed the slum that breeds a *Native Son*
To damn the good earth Pilgrim Fathers won.

None in the Land can say
To us black men Today:
You dupe the poor with rags-to-riches tales,
And leave the workers empty dinner pails.
You stuff the ballot-box, and honest men
Are muzzled by your demagogic din.

None in the Land can say
To us black men Today:
You smash stock markets with your coined blitzkriegs,

And make a hundred million guinea pigs.
You counterfeit our Christianity,
And bring contempt upon Democracy.

None in the Land can say
To us black men Today:
You prowl when citizens are fast asleep,
And hatch Fifth Column plots to blast the deep
Foundations of the State and leave the Land
A vast Sahara with a Fascist brand.

None in the Land can say
To us black men Today:
You send flame-gutting tanks, like swarms of flies,
And plump a hell from dynamiting skies.
You fill machine-gunned towns with rotting dead—
A No Man's Land where children cry for bread.

## VI

### *Tempo di Marcia*

Out of abysses of Illiteracy,
Through labyrinths of Lies,
Across wastelands of Disease . . .
We advance!

Out of dead-ends of Poverty,
Through wildernesses of Superstition,
Across barricades of Jim Crowism . . .
We advance!

With the Peoples of the World . . .
We advance!

# STERLING A. BROWN  *(1901–1989)*

**B**orn in Washington, DC, in 1901, Sterling Allen Brown was raised on and around the Howard University campus. He attended Dunbar High School, where he counted among his teachers Jessie Redmond Fauset, Carter G. Woodson, and Angelina Grimké. After graduating Phi Beta Kappa from Williams College, Brown earned a master's degree from Harvard.

The time between the end of Brown's formal education and the beginning of his professional career marks a significant period of both productivity and development. Brown earned an award from *Opportunity* magazine in 1925 and spent the following three years in Lynchburg, Virginia, as a teacher at the Virginia Seminary and College. It was within this intimate, rural niche of African American culture that his talents as a teacher and a folksayer without peer blossomed. He was fond of saying, "I learned the arts and sciences at Williams, I learned the humanities in Lynchburg, Virginia."

Brown melded his vision of African American experience with his classical training in literature, creating a breathtaking foundation for the poems that make up his first volume, *Southern Road*. Published in 1932 with an introduction by James Weldon Johnson, *Southern Road* was the definitive answer to dialect verse's possibilities as a vehicle for the consciousness of a race. Brown's ear exceeded even Dunbar's. In the "common, racy, living speech" of most of Brown's poems, one may also find echoes of the poet's greatest influences, particularly A. E. Housman and Thomas Hardy, English regionalists who invoked the ballad form and lyric as mediums for social discourse, as well as his awareness of the use of folk modes of expression as reflections of national consciousness in W. B. Yeats's Irish Renaissance. Brown's poetic goals were communal; his hope was to create a community of voices and readers in antiphony. His poems were primarily rural in setting, though not pastoral, and his use of irony and the echoes of classical myth mark his work as modernist.

Brown taught at Fisk, Lincoln, and Atlanta Universities before in 1929 joining the faculty of Howard University, where he remained until 1969. During this time he published and taught with extreme rigor, though his publications after *Southern Road* were largely academic. His second book of poetry, *The Last Ride of Wild Bill,* failed to find a publisher until late in his lifetime.

Brown's scholarship, including his 1931 *Outline for the Study of the Poetry of American Negroes, The Negro in American Fiction* (1937), and *Negro Poetry and Drama* (1937), marks a pioneering moment in African American literary criticism. And his contributions to *The Reader's Companion to World Literature* (1956), including entries for Heine, Housman, Dickinson, Baudelaire, Arnold, and Frost, indicate his vast knowledge and mastery of world poetry. In 1941 he coedited *The Negro Caravan,* an anthology of Afro-American literature and folk material that became the seminal text of its kind.

Brown also served as editor of Negro affairs for the Federal Writers' Project and contributed to the Carnegie-Myrdal Study of the Negro. He gave tireless attention to his students, regarding teaching as a vocation. Forty-three years after *Southern Road,* his second book of poems, *The Last Ride of Wild Bill,* was published. In 1980 *The Collected Poems of Sterling A. Brown* was edited by Michael S. Harper and published in the National Poetry Series, revealing for the first time the complete scope of a body of poetry that is one of the greatest in national vision, prosodic innovation, and poetic elegance produced by an American of this century. He died in 1989.

## After Winter

He snuggles his fingers
In the blacker loam
The lean months are done with,
The fat to come.

His eyes are set
On a brushwood-fire
But his heart is soaring
Higher and higher.

Though he stands ragged
An old scarecrow,

This is the way
His swift thoughts go,

> "Butter beans fo' Clara
> Sugar corn fo' Grace
> An' fo' de little feller
> Runnin' space.

"Radishes and lettuce
Eggplants and beets
Turnips fo' de winter
An' candied sweets

> "Homespun tobacco
> Apples in de bin
> Fo' smokin' an' fo' cider
> When de folks draps in."

He thinks with the winter
His troubles are gone;
Ten acres unplanted
To raise dreams on.

> The lean months are done with,
> The fat to come.
> His hopes, winter wanderers,
> Hasten home.

"Butterbeans fo' Clara
Sugar corn fo' Grace
An' fo' de little feller
Runnin' space. . . ."

## Frankie and Johnny

> *Oh Frankie and Johnny were lovers*
> *Oh Lordy how they did love!*

Old Ballad


Frankie was a halfwit, Johnny was a nigger,
    Frankie liked to pain poor creatures as a little 'un,
Kept a crazy love of torment when she got bigger,
    Johnny had to slave it and never had much fun.

Frankie liked to pull wings off of living butterflies,
    Frankie liked to cut long angleworms in half,
Frankie liked to whip curs and listen to their drawn out cries,
    Frankie liked to shy stones at the brindle calf.

Frankie took her pappy's lunch week-days to the sawmill,
    Her pappy, red-faced cracker, with a cracker's thirst,
Beat her skinny body and reviled the hateful imbecile,
    She screamed at every blow he struck, but tittered when he
        curst.

Frankie had to cut through Johnny's field of sugar corn
    Used to wave at Johnny, who didn't *'pay no min'*—
*Had had to work like fifty from the day that he was born,*
    *And wan't no cracker hussy gonna put his work behind*—.

But everyday Frankie swung along the cornfield lane,
    And one day Johnny helped her partly through the wood,
Once he had dropped his plow lines, he dropped them many times
        again—
    Though his mother didn't know it, else she'd have whipped him
        good.

Frankie and Johnny were lovers; oh Lordy how they did love!
    But one day Frankie's pappy by a big log laid him low,
To find out what his crazy Frankie had been speaking of;
    He found that what his gal had muttered was exactly so.

Frankie, she was spindly limbed with corn silk on her crazy head,
    Johnny was a nigger, who never had much fun—
They swung up Johnny on a tree, and filled his swinging hide with
        lead,
    And Frankie yowled hilariously when the thing was done.


## Idyll

I found me a cranny of perpetual dusk.
There for the grateful sense was pungent musk
Of rotting leaves, and moss, mingled with scents
Of heavy clusters freighting foxgrape vines.
The sun was barred except at close of day
When he could weakly etch in changing lines
A filigree upon the silver trunks
Of maple and of poplar. There were oaks
Their black bark fungus-spotted, and there lay
An old wormeaten segment of gray fence
Tumbling in consonant long forgot decay.
Motionless the place save when a little wind
Rippled the leaves, and soundless too it was
Save for a stream nearly inaudible,
That made a short stay in closewoven grass
Then in elusive whispers bade farewell;
Save for the noise of birds, whistling security.

One afternoon I lay there drowsily
Steeped in the crannies' love benevolence;
Peaceful the far dreams I was dreaming of. . . .
Sharply a stranger whistle screeched above
Once then again. Nearly as suddenly
A hawk dove, swooping past the sagging fence
Past a short shrub, and like a heavy rock
˙Striking the ground. I started up, the hawk
Flew off unhurriedly with fine insolence,
On vigorous wings, and settled on the limb

Of a dead chestnut. His sentinel mate
Screeched down another cry, almost too late.

On the matting of the leaves, a small bird lay
Spattering blood and on the little stream
A fluff of blue feathers floated away.
The hawk awhile gazed at me, I at him—
Splendid the corsair's breast and head of white
And dauntless, daring poise. Then with a cry
Frustrate, vindictive, he wheeled in graceful flight.
The wind stirred faintly, there was nothing more
Of sound, except a snatch of woodland song
As earlier. The stream purred listlessly along,
And all grew quite as peaceful as before.


## Long Track Blues

Went down to the yards
To see the signal lights come on;
Looked down the track
Where my lovin' babe done gone.

Red light in my block,
Green light down the line;
Lawdy, let yo' green light
Shine down on that babe o' mine.

Heard a train callin'
Blowin' long ways down the track;
Ain't no train due here,
Baby, what can bring you back?

Brakeman tell me
Got a powerful ways to go;
He don't know my feelin's
Baby, when he's talkin' so.

Lanterns a-swingin',
An' a long freight leaves the yard;
Leaves me here, baby,
But my heart it rides de rod.

Sparks a flyin',
Wheels rumblin' wid a mighty roar;
Then the red tail light,
And the place gets dark once more.

Dog in the freight room
Howlin' like he los' his mind;
Might howl myself,
If I was the howlin' kind.

Norfolk and Western,
Baby, and the C. & O.;
How come they treat
A hardluck feller so?

Red light in my block,
Green light down the line;
Lawdy, let yo' green light
Shine down on that babe o' mine.

## Ma Rainey

### I

When Ma Rainey
Comes to town,
Folks from anyplace
Miles aroun',
From Cape Girardeau,
Poplar Bluff,
Flocks in to hear
Ma do her stuff;

Comes flivverin' in,
Or ridin' mules,
Or packed in trains,
Picknickin' fools. . . .
That's what it's like,
Fo' miles on down,
To New Orleans delta
An' Mobile town,
When Ma hits
Anywheres aroun'.

## II

Dey comes to hear Ma Rainey from de little river settlements,
From blackbottom cornrows and from lumber camps;
Dey stumble in de hall, jes a-laughin' an' a-cacklin',
Cheerin' lak roarin' water, lak wind in river swamps.

An' some jokers keeps deir laughs a-goin' in de crowded aisles,
An' some folks sits dere waitin' wid deir aches an' miseries,
Till Ma comes out before dem, a-smilin' gold-toofed smiles
An' Long Boy ripples minors on de black an' yellow keys.

## III

O Ma Rainey,
Sing yo' song;
Now you's back
Whah you belong,
Git way inside us,
Keep us strong. . . .
O Ma Rainey,
Li'l an' low;
Sing us 'bout de hard luck
Roun' our do';
Sing us 'bout de lonesome road
We mus' go. . . .

## IV

I talked to a fellow, an' the fellow say,
"She jes' catch hold of us, somekindaway.
She sang Backwater Blues one day:
    *'It rained fo' days an' de skies was dark as night,*
    *Trouble taken place in de lowlands at night.*

    *'Thundered an' lightened an' the storm begin to roll*
    *Thousan's of people ain't got no place to go.*

    *'Den I went an' stood upon some high ol' lonesome hill,*
    *An' looked down on the place where I used to live.'*

An' den de folks, dey natchally bowed dey heads an' cried,
Bowed dey heavy heads, shet dey moufs up tight an' cried,
An' Ma lef' de stage, an' followed some de folks outside."

Dere wasn't much more de fellow say:
She jes' gets hold of us dataway.


## Odyssey of Big Boy

        Lemme be wid Casey Jones,
            Lemme be wid Stagolee,
        Lemme be wid such like men
            When Death takes hol' on me,
                When Death takes hol' on me. . . .

        Done skinned as a boy in Kentucky hills,
            Druv steel dere as a man,
        Done stripped tobacco in Virginia fiel's
            Alongst de River Dan,
                Alongst de River Dan;

        Done mined de coal in West Virginia,
            Liked dat job jes' fine,

Till a load o' slate curved roun' my head,
   Won't work in no mo' mine,
      Won't work in no mo' mine;

Done shocked de corn in Marylan',
   In Georgia done cut cane,
Done planted rice in South Caline,
   But won't do dat again,
      Do dat no mo' again.

Been roustabout in Memphis,
   Dockhand in Baltimore,
Done smashed up freight on Norfolk wharves,
   A fust class stevedore,
      A fust class stevedore. . . .

Done slung hash yonder in de North
   On de ole Fall River Line,
Done busted suds in li'l New York,
   Which ain't no work o' mine—
      Lawd, ain't no work o' mine.

Done worked and loafed on such like jobs,
   Seen what dey is to see,
Done had my time wid a pint on my hip
   An' a sweet gal on my knee,
      Sweet mommer on my knee:

Had stovepipe blond in Macon,
   Yaller gal in Marylan',
In Richmond had a choklit brown,
   Called me huh monkey man—
      Huh big fool monkey man.

Had two fair browns in Arkansaw
   And three in Tennessee,
Had Creole gal in New Orleans,
   Sho Gawd did two time me—
      Lawd two time, fo' time me—

But best gal what I evah had
   Done put it over dem,
A gal in Southwest Washington
   At Four'n half and M—
     Four'n half and M. . . .

Done took my livin' as it came,
   Done grabbed my joy, done risked my life;
Train done caught me on de trestle,
   Man done caught me wid his wife,
     His doggone purty wife. . . .

I done had my women,
   I done had my fun;
Cain't do much complainin'
   When my jag is done,
     Lawd, Lawd, my jag is done.

An' all dat Big Boy axes
   When time comes fo' to go,
Lemme be wid John Henry, steel drivin' man,
   Lemme be wid old Jazzbo,
     Lemme be wid ole Jazzbo. . . .


## Old Lem

     I talked to old Lem
     and old Lem said:
       "They weigh the cotton
       They store the corn
         We only good enough
         To work the rows;
       They run the commissary
       They keep the books
         We gotta be grateful
         For being cheated;

Whippersnapper clerks
Call us out of our name
   We got to say mister
   To spindling boys
They make our figgers
Turn somersets
We buck in the middle
   Say, 'Thankyuh, sah.'
    They don't come by ones
    They don't come by twos
    But they come by tens.

"They got the judges
They got the lawyers
They got the jury-rolls
They got the law
   They don't come by ones
They got the sheriffs
They got the deputies
    They don't come by twos
They got the shotguns
They got the rope
   We git the justice
   In the end
    And they come by tens.

"Their fists stay closed
Their eyes look straight
   Our hands stay open
   Our eyes must fall
    They don't come by ones
They got the manhood
They got the courage
    They don't come by twos
   We got to slink around
   Hangtailed hounds.
They burn us when we dogs
They burn us when we men
    They come by tens . . .

"I had a buddy
Six foot of man
Muscled up perfect
Game to the heart
    They don't come by ones
Outworked and outfought
Any man or two men
    They don't come by twos
He spoke out of turn
At the commissary
They gave him a day
To git out the county
He didn't take it.
He said 'Come and get me.'
They came and got him
    And they came by tens.
He stayed in the county—
He lays there dead.

    They don't come by ones
      They don't come by twos
    But they come by tens."


## Rain


Outside the cold, cold night; the dripping rain. . . .
The water gurgles loosely in the eaves,
The savage lashes stripe the rattling pane
And beat a tattoo on November leaves.
The lamp wick gutters, and the last log steams
Upon the ash-filled hearth. Chill grows the room.
The ancient clock ticks creakily and seems
A fitting portent of the gathering gloom.

This is a night we planned. This place is where
One day, we would be happy; where the light

Should tint your shoulders and your wild flung hair.—
Whence we would—oh, we planned a merry morrow—
Recklessly part ways with the old hag, Sorrow. . . .

Outside the dripping rain; the cold, cold night.


## Seeking Religion

Lulu walked forlornly in late April twilight,
Lulu sought religion, long urged by Parson Jones,
Lulu sought the pinewoods, sought the dusky graveyard,
Fought her fears and sat among the ghostlike stones.

Waiting for her visions, but not so very eager,
Lulu sat still with a crescent moon above,
Lulu dreamt dreams a creaky-jointed parson
Hadn't so much as warned her of.

Jim found Lulu sitting in the shadow,
Lulu was sobbing, her head upon her knees;
Jim spoke to Lulu, and realized her visions,
And scared off the strange things lurking in the trees.

Jim sought Lulu when harrowing was over,
The slim moon up; and with a convert's joy
Lulu sought religion in thick deep-shadowed pinewoods,
Lulu found religion in a chubby baby boy.


## Slim Greer

Listen to the tale
Of Ole Slim Greer,
Waitines' devil
Waitin' here;

Talkinges' guy
An' biggest liar,
With always a new lie
On the fire.

Tells a tale
Of Arkansaw
That keeps the kitchen
In a roar;

Tells in a long-drawled
Careless tone,
As solemn as a Baptist
Parson's moan.

How he in Arkansaw
Passed for white,
An' he no lighter
Than a dark midnight.

Found a nice white woman
At a dance,
Thought he was from Spain
Or else from France;

Nobody suspicioned
Ole Slim Greer's race
But a Hill Billy, always
Roun' the place,

Who called one day
On the trustful dame
An' found Slim comfy
When he came.

The whites lef' the parlor
All to Slim
Which didn't cut
No ice with him,

An' he started a-tinklin'
Some mo'nful blues,
An' a-pattin' the time
With No. Fourteen shoes.

The cracker listened
An' then he spat
An' said, "No white man
Could play like that. . . ."

The white jane ordered
The tattler out;
Then, female-like,
Began to doubt,

Crept into the parlor
Soft as you please,
Where Slim was agitatin'
The ivories.

Heard Slim's music—
An' then, hot damn!
Shouted sharp—"Nigger!"
An' Slim said, "Ma'am?"

She screamed and the crackers
Swarmed up soon,
But found only echoes
Of his tune;

'Cause Slim had sold out
With lightnin' speed;
"Hope I may die, sir—
Yes, indeed. . . ."

## Slim in Atlanta

Down in Atlanta,
   De whitefolks got laws
For to keep all de niggers
   From laughin' outdoors.

     Hope to Gawd I may die
        If I ain't speakin' truth
     Make de niggers do deir laughin
        In a telefoam booth.

Slim Greer hit de town
   An' de rebs got him told,—
"Dontcha laugh on de street,
   If you want to die old."

     Den dey showed him de booth,
        An' a hundred shines
     In front of it, waitin'
        In double lines.

Slim thought his sides
   Would bust in two,
Yelled, "Lookout, everybody,
   I'm coming through!"

     Pulled de other man out,
        An' bust in de box,
     An' laughed four hours
        By de Georgia clocks.

Den he peeked through de door,
   An' what did he see?
*Three* hundred niggers there
   In misery.—

     Some holdin' deir sides,
        Some holdin' deir jaws,

>       To keep from breakin'
>           De Georgia laws.
>
>   An' Slim gave a holler,
>       An' started again;
>   An' from three hundred throats
>       Come a moan of pain.
>
>       An' everytime Slim
>           Saw what was outside,
>       Got to whoopin' again
>           Till he nearly died.
>
>   An' while de poor critters
>       Was waitin' deir chance,
>   Slim laughed till dey sent
>       Fo' de ambulance.
>
>       De state paid de railroad
>           To take him away;
>       Den, things was as usual
>           In Atlanta, Gee A.

## Slim in Hell

### I

>   Slim Greer went to heaven;
>       St. Peter said, "Slim,
>   You been a right good boy."
>       An' he winked at him.
>
>       "You been a travelin' rascal
>           In yo' day.
>       You kin roam once mo';
>           Den you comes to stay.

"Put dese wings on yo' shoulders,
      An' save yo' feet."
Slim grin, and he speak up
      "Thankye, Pete."

            Den Peter say, "Go
                  To Hell an' see,
            All dat is doing, and
                  Report to me.

"Be sure to remember
      How everything go."
Slim say, "I be seein' yuh
      On de late watch, bo."

            Slim got to cavortin',
                  Swell as you choose,
            Like Lindy in de "Spirit
                  Of St. Louis Blues!"

He flew an' he flew,
      Till at last he hit
A hangar wid de sign readin'
      DIS IS IT.

            Den he parked his wings,
                  An' strolled aroun'
            Gettin' used to his feet
                  On de solid ground.

## II

Big bloodhound came aroarin'
      Like Niagry Falls,
Sicked on by white devils
      In overhalls.

Now Slim warn't scared,
      Cross my heart, it's a fac',

An' de dog went on a bayin'
   Some po' devil's track.

     Den Slim saw a mansion
       An' walked right in;
     De Devil looked up
       Wid a sickly grin.

"Suttinly didn't look
   Fo' you, Mr. Greer,
How it happen you comes
   To visit here?"

     Slim say—"Oh, jes' thought
       I'd drap by a spell."
     "Feel at home, seh, an' here's
       De keys to Hell."

Den he took Slim around
   An' showed him people
Raisin' hell as high as
   De First Church Steeple.

     Lots of folks fightin'
       At de roulette wheel,
     Like old Rampart Street,
       Or leastwise Beale.

Showed him bawdy houses
   An' cabarets,
Slim thought of New Orleans
   An' Memphis days.

     Each devil was busy
       Wid a devilish broad,
     An' Slim cried, "Lawdy,
       Lawd, Lawd, Lawd."

Took him in a room
   Where Slim see

De preacher wid a brownskin
  On each knee.

    Showed him giant stills,
      Going everywhere
    Wid a passel of devils,
      Stretched dead drunk there.

Den he took him to de furnace
  Dat some devils was firing,
Hot as hell, an' Slim start
  A mean presspirin';

    White devils wid pitchforks
      Threw black devils on,
    Slim thought he'd better
      Be gittin' along.

An' he say—"Dis makes
  Me think of home—
Vicksburg, Little Rock, Jackson,
  Waco, and Rome."

    Den de devil give Slim
      De big Ha-ha;
    An' turned into a cracker,
      Wid a sheriff's star.

Slim ran fo' his wings,
  Lit out from de groun'
Hauled it back to St. Peter,
  Safety boun'.

### III

    St. Peter said, "Well,
      You got back quick.
    How's de devil? An' what's
      His latest trick?"

An' Slim say, "Peter,
  I really cain't tell,
De place was Dixie
  Dat I took for Hell."

Then Peter say, "You must
  Be crazy, I vow,
Where'n hell dja think Hell *was*,
  Anyhow?

"Git on back to de yearth,
  Cause I got de fear,
You'se a leetle too dumb,
  Fo' to stay up here . . ."

## Southern Road

Swing dat hammer—hunh—
  Steady, bo';
Swing dat hammer—hunh—
  Steady, bo';
Ain't no rush, bebby,
  Long ways to go.

Burner tore his—hunh—
  Black heart away;
Burner tore his—hunh—
  Black heart away;
Got me life, bebby,
  An' a day.

Gal's on Fifth Street—hunh—
  Son done gone;
Gal's on Fifth Street—hunh—
  Son done gone;
Wife's in de ward, bebby,
  Babe's not bo'n.

My ole man died—hunh—
Cussin' me;
My ole man died—hunh—
Cussin' me;
Ole lady rocks, bebby,
Huh misery.

Doubleshackled—hunh—
Guard behin';
Doubleshackled—hunh—
Guard behin';
Ball and chain, bebby,
On my min'.

White man tells me—hunh—
Damn yo' soul;
White man tells me—hunh—
Damn yo' soul;
Got no need, bebby,
To be tole.

Chain gang nevah—hunh—
Let me go;
Chain gang nevah—hunh—
Let me go;
Po' los' boy, bebby,
Evahmo'. . . .


## Strong Men

*The young men keep coming on*
*The strong men keep coming on.*
　　　　　　　—Sandburg


*They dragged you from homeland,*
*They chained you in coffles,*

They huddled you spoon-fashion in filthy hatches,
They sold you to give a few gentlemen ease.

They broke you like oxen,
They scourged you,
They branded you,
They made your women breeders,
They swelled your numbers with bastards. . . .
They taught you the religion they disgraced.

You sang:
   Keep a-inchin' along
   Lak a po' inch worm. . . .

You sang:
   Bye and bye
   I'm gonna lay down dis heaby load. . . .

You sang:
   Walk togedder, chillen,
   Dontcha git weary. . . .
The strong men keep a-comin' on
The strong men git stronger.

They point with pride to the roads you built for them,
They ride in comfort over the rails you laid for them.
They put hammers in your hands
And said—Drive so much before sundown.

You sang:
   Ain't no hammah
   In dis lan',
   Strikes lak mine, bebby,
   Strikes lak mine.

They cooped you in their kitchens,
They penned you in their factories,
They gave you the jobs that they were too good for,
They tried to guarantee happiness to themselves
By shunting dirt and misery to you.

*You sang:*
  *Me an' muh baby gonna shine, shine*
  *Me an' muh baby gonna shine.*
  The strong men keep a-comin' on
  The strong men git stronger. . . .

*They bought off some of your leaders*
*You stumbled, as blind men will . . .*
*They coaxed you, unwontedly soft-voiced. . . .*
*You followed a way.*
*Then laughed as usual.*

*They heard the laugh and wondered;*
*Uncomfortable,*
*Unadmitting a deeper terror. . . .*
  The strong men keep a-comin' on
  Gittin' stronger. . . .

*What, from the slums*
*Where they have hemmed you,*
*What, from the tiny huts*
*They could not keep from you—*
*What reaches them*
*Making them ill at ease, fearful?*
*Today they shout prohibition at you*
*"Thou shalt not this"*
*"Thou shalt not that"*
*"Reserved for whites only"*
*You laugh.*

*One thing they cannot prohibit—*
  The strong men . . . coming on
  The strong men gittin' stronger.
  Strong men. . . .
  Stronger. . . .

## To a Certain Lady, in Her Garden

*For Anne Spencer*

Lady, my lady, come from out the garden,
Clay-fingered, dirty-smocked, and in my time
I too shall learn the quietness of Arden
Knowledge so long a stranger to my rhyme.

What were more fitting than your springtime task?
Here, close-engirdled by your vines and flowers
Surely there is no other grace to ask,
No better cloister from the bickering hours.

A step beyond, the dingy streets begin
With all their farce, and silly tragedy—
But here, unmindful of the futile din
. You grow your flowers, far wiser certainly.

You and your garden sum the same to me,
A sense of strange and momentary pleasure,
And beauty snatched—oh, fragmentarily
Perhaps, yet who can boast of other seizure?

Oh, you have somehow robbed, I know not how,
The secret of the loveliness of these
Whom you have served so long. Oh, shameless, now
You flaunt the winnings of your thieveries.

Thus, I exclaim against you, profiteer. . . .
For purpled evenings spent in pleasing toil,
Should you have gained so easily the dear
Capricious largesse of the miser soil?

Colorful living in a world grown dull,
Quiet sufficiency in weakling days,
Delicate happiness, more beautiful
For lighting up belittered, grimy ways—

Surely I think I shall remember this,
You in your old, rough dress, bedaubed with clay,
Your smudgy face parading happiness,
Life's puzzle solved. Perhaps, in turn, you may

One time, while clipping bushes, tending vines,
(Making your brave, sly mock at dastard days),
Laugh gently at these trivial, truthful lines—
And that will be sufficient for my praise.

# GWENDOLYN BENNETT  *(1902–1981)*

Gwendolyn Bennett was born in Giddings, Texas, in 1902. She studied fine arts at Columbia University and the Pratt Institute, and taught art for several years at Howard University. Her association with the Harlem Renaissance is well documented through her work for the movement's primary literary magazines, *Opportunity* and *Crisis*.

Bennett's verse articulations of black life are concrete in their detailing yet exemplary of the lyrical style for which the Harlem Renaissance is best known. Equally capable of trenchant if not mordant observation and naked, plangent declarations of romantic love, Bennett was one of the most skilled, delicate, and careful crafters of the period. Her literary career was cut short by financial difficulties attending the death of her husband and the Great Depression; forced to abandon art to make a living, Bennett never regained her early productivity. She died in Kutztown, Pennsylvania, in 1981.

## To a Dark Girl

I love you for your brownness
And the rounded darkness of your breast.
I love you for the breaking sadness in your voice
And shadows where your wayward eye-lids rest.

Something of old forgotten queens
Lurks in the lithe abandon of your walk,
And something of the shackled slave
Sobs in the rhythm of your talk.

Oh, little brown girl, born for sorrow's mate,
Keep all you have of queenliness,
Forgetting that you once were slave,
And let your full lips laugh at Fate!

## Sonnets

### I

He came in silvern armour, trimmed with black—
A lover come from legends long ago—
With silver spurs and silken plumes a-blow,
And flashing sword caught fast and buckled back
In a carven sheath of Tamarack.
He came with footsteps beautifully slow,
And spoke in voice meticulously low.
He came and Romance followed in his track. . . .

I did not ask his name—I thought him Love;
I did not care to see his hidden face.
All life seemed born in my intaken breath;
All thought seemed flown like some forgotten dove.
He bent to kiss and raised his visor's lace . . .
All eager-lipped I kissed the mouth of Death.

### II

Some things are very dear to me—
Such things as flowers bathed by rain
Or patterns traced upon the sea
Or crocuses where snow has lain . . .
The iridescence of a gem,
The moon's cool opalescent light,
Azaleas and the scent of them,
And honeysuckles in the night.
And many sounds are also dear—
Like winds that sing among the trees
Or crickets calling from the weir
Or Negroes humming melodies.
But dearer far than all surmise
Are sudden tear-drops in your eyes.

# LANGSTON HUGHES  *(1902–1967)*

**B**orn in Joplin, Missouri, in 1902, Langston Hughes was raised in
Kansas, Illinois, and Ohio. He attended Columbia University before
embarking as a sailor on a freighter, making stops in the Canary
Islands, the Azores, and West Africa. Hughes jumped ship in
Europe and settled in Paris, where he earned a piecemeal living as a
doorman and cook in a nightclub. During this period he was writ-
ing poetry already strongly laced with jazz and the blues.

By the time he returned to the United States, he had been pub-
lished in *Crisis*. His encounter with the poet Vachel Lindsay while
working as a busboy in a Washington, DC, hotel would prove a
springboard for his career. Lindsay, excited by Hughes's blues-
tinged meters and sharp yet loving depictions of urban life, champi-
oned his poetics as the new wave. By 1925 Hughes was deeply
associated with the Harlem Renaissance; in 1926 his first book of
verse, *The Weary Blues*, was published to great acclaim.

Hughes continued his formal education and received his B.A.
from Lincoln University in 1929—winning the Witter Bynner
poetry prize and completing his memoir *Not Without Laughter*
before graduating. These accomplishments marked only the begin-
ning for Hughes, who was to publish dozens of books: poetry,
drama, essays, children's stories, screenplays, anthologies, and
autobiography. His *Not Without Laughter* won the Harmon Award
in 1930, and in 1935 he was awarded a Guggenheim Fellowship.

Hughes became involved with the socialist movement in the
early 1930s. Though he did not turn away from the themes that
had made him the Harlem Renaissance's most visible black writer,
he did become more bitterly critical of social and racial inequalities.
His encounter with politics also increased the range of his concerns:
as a journalist Hughes voiced his strong support for the Republican
opposition in the Spanish Civil War and for the American Commu-
nist movement. Despite the distractions of a strident conservative
political opposition, he continued to write creatively and success-
fully.

Hughes was coeditor with Arna Bontemps of *The Poetry of the
Negro* (1950) and in 1964 edited another anthology, *New Negro
Poets: U.S.A.* In 1960 Hughes won the Spingarn Medal and in the
following year was elected to the American Academy of Arts and
Letters.

Hughes saw in both the structure and content of the blues poetic expression of a high order. The blues's succinct deployment of a story and ability to transcend weariness through humor—to contemplate and reconfigure anguish—characterize his best work. Along with *The Weary Blues,* Hughes's volumes of poetry include *Fine Clothes to the Jew* (1927), *Shakespeare in Harlem* (1942), and *Ask Your Mama: Twelve Moods for Jazz* (1961). He died in 1967.

## Cross

My old man's a white old man
And my old mother's black.
If ever I cursed my white old man
I take my curses back.

If ever I cursed my black old mother
And wished she were in hell,
I'm sorry for that evil wish
And now I wish her well.

My old man died in a fine big house.
My ma died in a shack.
I wonder where I'm gonna die,
Being neither white nor black?

## Christ in Alabama

Christ is a nigger,
Beaten and black:
Oh, bare your back!

Mary is His mother:
Mammy of the South,
Silence your mouth.

God is His father:
White Master above
Grant Him your love.

Most holy bastard
Of the bleeding mouth,
    Nigger Christ
    On the cross
    Of the South.


## Dream Variations


To fling my arms wide
In some place of the sun,
To whirl and to dance
Till the white day is done.
Then rest at cool evening
Beneath a tall tree
While night comes on gently,
    Dark like me—
That is my dream!

To fling my arms wide
In the face of the sun,
Dance! Whirl! Whirl!
Till the quick day is done.
Rest at pale evening . . .
A tall, slim tree . . .
Night coming tenderly
    Black like me.

## Frosting

> Freedom
> Is just frosting
> On somebody else's
> Cake—
> And so must be
> Till we
> Learn how to
> Bake.

## Harlem Night Song

> Come,
> Let us roam the night together
> Singing.
>
> I love you.
>
> Across
> The Harlem roof-tops
> Moon is shining.
> Night sky is blue.
> Stars are great drops
> Of golden dew.
>
> Down the street
> A band is playing.
>
> I love you.
>
> Come,
> Let us roam the night together
> Singing.

## Harlem Sweeties

Have you dug the spill
Of Sugar Hill?
Cast your gims
On this sepia thrill:
Brown sugar lassie,
Caramel treat,
Honey-gold baby
Sweet enough to eat.
Peach-skinned girlie,
Coffee and cream,
Chocolate darling
Out of a dream.
Walnut tinted
Or cocoa brown,
Pomegranate lipped
Pride of the town.
Rich cream colored
To plum-tinted black,
Feminine sweetness
In Harlem's no lack.
Glow of the quince
To blush of the rose.
Persimmon bronze
To cinnamon toes.
Blackberry cordial,
Virginia Dare wine—
All those sweet colors
Flavor Harlem of mine!
Walnut or cocoa,
Let me repeat:
Caramel, brown sugar,
A chocolate treat.
Molasses taffy,
Coffee and cream,
Licorice, clove, cinnamon
To a honey-brown dream.
Ginger, wine-gold,

Persimmon, blackberry,
All through the spectrum
Harlem girls vary—
So if you want to know beauty's
Rainbow-sweet thrill,
Stroll down luscious,
Delicious, *fine* Sugar Hill.

## House in the World

I'm looking for a house
In the world
Where the white shadows
Will not fall.

*There is no such house,*
*Dark brothers,*
*No such house*
*At all.*

## Madam and the Rent Man

The rent man knocked.
He said, Howdy-do?
I said, What
Can I do for you?
He said, You know
Your rent is due.

I said, Listen,
Before I'd pay
I'd go to Hades
And rot away!

The sink is broke,
The water don't run,
And you ain't done a thing
You promised to've done.

Back window's cracked,
Kitchen floor squeaks,
There's rats in the cellar,
And the attic leaks.

He said, Madam,
It's not up to me.
I'm just the agent,
Don't you see?

I said, Naturally,
You pass the buck.
If it's money you want
You're out of luck.

He said, Madam,
I ain't pleased!
I said, Neither am I.

So we agrees!

## Mother to Son

Well, son, I'll tell you:
Life for me ain't been no crystal stair.
It's had tacks in it,
And splinters,
And boards torn up,
And places with no carpet on the floor—
Bare.
But all the time

I'se been a-climbin' on,
And reachin' landin's,
And turnin' corners,
And sometimes goin' in the dark
Where there ain't been no light.
So boy, don't you turn back.
Don't you set down on the steps
'Cause you finds it's kinder hard.
Don't you fall now—
For I'se still goin', honey,
I'se still climbin',
And life for me ain't been no crystal stair.

## Passing Love

Because you are to me a song
I must not sing you over-long.

Because you are to me a prayer
I cannot say you everywhere.

Because you are to me a rose—
You will not stay when summer goes.

## Personal

In an envelope marked:
    *Personal*
God addressed me a letter.
In an envelope marked:
    *Personal*
I have given my answer.

## Suicide's Note

The calm,
Cool face of the river
Asked me for a kiss.

## The Negro Speaks of Rivers

I've known rivers:
I've known rivers ancient as the world and older than the
    flow of human blood in human veins.

My soul has grown deep like the rivers.

I bathed in the Euphrates when dawns were young.
I built my hut near the Congo and it lulled me to sleep.
I looked upon the Nile and raised the pyramids above it.
I heard the singing of the Mississippi when Abe Lincoln went
    down to New Orleans, and I've seen its muddy bosom
    turn all golden in the sunset.

I've known rivers:
Ancient, dusky rivers.

My soul has grown deep like the rivers.

# Theme for English B

The instructor said,

> *Go home and write*
> *a page tonight.*
> *And let that page come out of you—*
> *Then, it will be true.*

I wonder if it's that simple?
I am twenty-two, colored, born in Winston-Salem.
I went to school there, then Durham, then here
to this college on the hill above Harlem.
I am the only colored student in my class.
The steps from the hill lead down into Harlem,
through a park, then I cross St. Nicholas,
Eighth Avenue, Seventh, and I come to the Y,
the Harlem Branch Y, where I take the elevator
up to my room, sit down, and write this page:

It's not easy to know what is true for you or me
at twenty-two, my age. But I guess I'm what
I feel and see and hear, Harlem, I hear you:
hear you, hear me—we two—you, me, talk on this page.
(I hear New York, too.) Me—who?
Well, I like to eat, sleep, drink, and be in love.
I like to work, read, learn, and understand life.
I like a pipe for a Christmas present,
or records—Bessie, bop, or Bach.
I guess being colored doesn't make me *not* like
the same things other folks like who are other races.
So will my page be colored that I write?
Being me, it will not be white.
But it will be
a part of you, instructor.
You are white—
yet a part of me, as I am a part of you.
That's American.
Sometimes perhaps you don't want to be a part of me.

Nor do I often want to be a part of you.
But we are, that's true!
As I learn from you,
I guess you learn from me—
although you're older—and white—
and somewhat more free.

This is my page for English B.

## Tower

Death is a tower
To which the soul ascends
To spend a meditative hour—
That never ends.

# COUNTEE CULLEN (1903–1946)

Countee Cullen, born in 1903, was raised in New York City, attending DeWitt Clinton High School in the Bronx and New York University, where he was graduated Phi Beta Kappa. Cullen excelled early as a student and by his undergraduate years was publishing accomplished, mature verse. He continued his studies at Harvard University, sharpening his formal craftsmanship under the poet Robert Hillyer. Cullen published his first volume of poetry, *Color* (1925), to critical acclaim while still at Harvard.

Cullen returned to New York City to work as an assistant editor for *Opportunity* magazine. His *Copper Sun* was published in 1927, a year that would prove very productive for him: he also published a special edition collection of poems, *The Ballad of the Brown Girl*, and an anthology of black poetry, *Caroling Dusk*, and he received a Guggenheim Fellowship. Cullen traveled with his fellowship money and in Paris produced *The Black Christ and Other Poems* (1929).

To support himself on returning to New York, Cullen took a position at Frederick Douglass Junior High School (where one of his students was James Baldwin), teaching English and French. By the time of this appointment, Cullen's career was suffering: like many other writers from the Harlem Renaissance, he found it difficult once the movement was over to connect with a consistently interested audience.

Cullen's poems at their best are a fluid coalescence of black life and English forms. His credo was to avoid propaganda while maintaining fidelity to the experiences of his people. Cullen's search for beauty was Keatsian, though his articulation of the human condition was entirely his own. His published works include *The Medea and Some Poems* (1935), *The Lost Zoo* (stories, 1940), *My Lives and How I Lost Them* (stories, 1942), *One Way to Heaven* (1932), and *On These I Stand*, a posthumous collection of his poetry. Cullen died in 1946.

## A Brown Girl Dead

> With two white roses on her breasts,
>     White candles at head and feet,
> Dark Madonna of the grave she rests;
>     Lord Death has found her sweet.
>
> Her mother pawned her wedding ring
>     To lay her out in white;
> She'd be so proud she'd dance and sing
>     To see herself tonight.

## Yet Do I Marvel

> I doubt not God is good, well-meaning, kind,
> And did He stoop to quibble could tell why
> The little buried mole continues blind,
> Why flesh that mirrors Him must some day die,
> Make plain the reason tortured Tantalus
> Is baited by the fickle fruit, declare
> If merely brute caprice dooms Sisyphus
> To struggle up a never-ending stair.
> Inscrutable His ways are, and immune
> To catechism by a mind too strewn
> With petty cares to slightly understand
> What awful brain compels His awful hand.
> Yet do I marvel at this curious thing:
> To make a poet black, and bid him sing!

# From the Dark Tower

*For Charles S. Johnson*

We shall not always plant while others reap
The golden increment of bursting fruit,
Not always countenance, abject and mute,
That lesser men should hold their brothers cheap;
Not everlastingly while others sleep
Shall we beguile their limbs with mellow flute,
Not always bend to some more subtle brute;
We were not made eternally to weep.

The night whose sable breast relieves the stark
White stars is no less lovely, being dark;
And there are buds that cannot bloom at all
In light, but crumple, piteous, and fall;
So in the dark we hide the heart that bleeds,
And wait, and tend our agonizing seeds.

# Uncle Jim

"White folks is white," says uncle Jim;
"A platitude," I sneer;
And then I tell him so is milk,
And the froth upon his beer.

His heart walled up with bitterness,
He smokes his pungent pipe,
And nods at me as if to say,
"Young fool, you'll soon be ripe!"

I have a friend who eats his heart
Away with grief of mine,
Who drinks my joy as tipplers drain
Deep goblets filled with wine.

I wonder why here at his side,
Face-in-the-grass with him,
My mind should stray the Grecian urn
To muse on uncle Jim.

## Death to the Poor

*(From the French of Baudelaire)*

In death alone is what consoles; and life
And all its end is death; and that fond hope
Whose music like a mad fantastic fife
Compels us up this ridged and rocky slope.
Through lightning, hail, and hurt of human look,
Death is the vibrant light we travel toward,
The mystic Inn forepromised in the Book
Where all are welcomed in to bed and board.

An angel whose star-banded fingers hold
The gift of dreams and calm, ecstatic sleep
In easier beds than those we had before,
Death is the face of God, the only fold
That pens content and ever-happy sheep,
To Paradise the only open door.

## Four Epitaphs

### I

*For My Grandmother*

This lovely flower fell to seed;
　　Work gently, sun and rain;
She held it as her dying creed
　　That she would grow again.

**2**

*For John Keats, Apostle of Beauty*

Not writ in water nor in mist,
     Sweet lyric throat, thy name;
Thy singing lips that cold death kissed
     Have seared his own with flame.

**3**

*For Paul Laurence Dunbar*

Born of the sorrowful of heart,
     Mirth was a crown upon his head;
Pride kept his twisted lips apart
     In jest, to hide a heart that bled.

**4**

*For a Lady I Know*

She even thinks that up in heaven
     Her class lies late and snores,
While poor black cherubs rise at seven
     To do celestial chores.

## Heritage

*For Harold Jackman*

What is Africa to me:
Copper sun or scarlet sea,
Jungle star or jungle track,
Strong bronzed men, or regal black
Women from whose loins I sprang
When the birds of Eden sang?

*One three centuries removed*
*From the scenes his fathers loved,*
*Spicy grove, cinnamon tree,*
*What is Africa to me?*

So I lie, who all day long
Want no sound except the song
Sung by wild barbaric birds
Goading massive jungle herds,
Juggernauts of flesh that pass
Trampling tall defiant grass
Where young forest lovers lie,
Plighting troth beneath the sky.
So I lie, who always hear,
Though I cram against my ear
Both my thumbs, and keep them there,
Great drums throbbing through the air.
So I lie, whose fount of pride,
Dear distress, and joy allied,
Is my somber flesh and skin,
With the dark blood dammed within
Like great pulsing tides of wine
That, I fear, must burst the fine
Channels of the chafing net
Where they surge and foam and fret.

Africa? A book one thumbs
Listlessly, till slumber comes.
Unremembered are her bats
Circling through the night, her cats
Crouching in the river reeds,
Stalking gentle flesh that feeds
By the river brink; no more
Does the bugle-throated roar
Cry that monarch claws have leapt
From the scabbards where they slept.
Silver snakes that once a year
Doff the lovely coats you wear,
Seek no covert in your fear

Lest a mortal eye should see;
What's your nakedness to me?
Here no leprous flowers rear
Fierce corollas in the air;
Here no bodies sleek and wet,
Dripping mingled rain and sweat,
Tread the savage measures of
Jungle boys and girls in love.
What is last year's snow to me,
Last year's anything? The tree
Budding yearly must forget
How its past arose or set—
Bough and blossom, flower, fruit,
Even what shy bird with mute
Wonder at her travail there,
Meekly labored in its hair.
*One three centuries removed*
*From the scenes his fathers loved,*
*Spice grove, cinnamon tree,*
*What is Africa to me?*

So I lie, who find no peace
Night or day, no slight release
From the unremittent beat
Made by cruel padded feet
Walking through my body's street.
Up and down they go, and back,
Treading out a jungle track.
So I lie, who never quite
Safely sleep from rain at night—
I can never rest at all
When the rain begins to fall;
Like a soul gone mad with pain
I must match its weird refrain;
Ever must I twist and squirm,
Writhing like a baited worm,
While its primal measures drip
Through my body, crying, "Strip!
Doff this new exuberance.

Come and dance the Lover's Dance!"
In an old remembered way
Rain works on me night and day.

Quaint, outlandish heathen gods
Black men fashion out of rods,
Clay, and brittle bits of stone,
In a likeness like their own,
My conversion came high-priced;
I belong to Jesus Christ,
Preacher of humility;
Heathen gods are naught to me.

Father, Son, and Holy Ghost,
So I make an idle boast;
Jesus of the twice-turned cheek,
Lamb of God, although I speak
With my mouth thus, in my heart
Do I play a double part.
Ever at Thy glowing altar
Must my heart grow sick and falter,
Wishing He I served were black,
Thinking then it would not lack
Precedent of pain to guide it,
Let who would or might deride it;
Surely then this flesh would know
Yours had borne a kindred woe.
Lord, I fashion dark gods, too,
Daring even to give You
Dark despairing features where,
Crowned with dark rebellious hair,
Patience wavers just so much as
Mortal grief compels, while touches
Quick and hot, of anger, rise
To smitten cheek and weary eyes.
Lord, forgive me if my need
Sometimes shapes a human creed.

*All day long and all night through,*
*One thing only must I do:*

*Quench my pride and cool my blood,*
*Lest I perish in the flood.*
*Lest a hidden ember set*
*Timber that I thought was wet*
*Burning like the dryest flax,*
*Melting like the merest wax,*
*Lest the grave restore its dead.*
*Not yet has my heart or head*
*In the least way realized*
*They and I are civilized.*

## Incident

*For Eric Walrond*

Once riding in old Baltimore,
    Heart-filled, head-filled with glee,
I saw a Baltimorean
    Keep looking straight at me.

Now I was eight and very small,
    And he was no whit bigger,
And so I smiled, but he poked out
    His tongue, and called me, "Nigger."

I saw the whole of Baltimore
    From May until December;
Of all the things that happened there
    That's all that I remember.

## A Negro Mother's Lullaby

*(After Visiting John Brown's Grave)*

Hushaby, hushaby, dark one at my knee;
Slumber you softly, nor pucker, nor frown;
Though some may be bonded, you shall be free,
Thanks to a man . . . Osawatamie Brown.
    His sons are high fellows,
    An Archangel is he,
    And they doff their bright haloes
    To none but the Three.

Hushaby, hushaby, sweet darkness at rest,
Two there have been who their lives laid down
That you might be beautiful here at my breast:
Our Jesus and . . . Osawatamie Brown.
    His sons are high fellows,
    An Archangel is he,
    And they doff their bright haloes
    To none but the Three.

Hushaby, hushaby, when a man, not a slave,
    With freedom for wings you go through the town,
    Let your love be dew on his evergreen grave;
    Sleep, in the name of Osawatamie Brown.
    Rich counsel he's giving
    Close by the throne,
    Tall he was living
    But now taller grown.
    His sons are high fellows,
    An Archangel is he,
    And they doff their bright haloes
    To none but the Three.

*Lake Placid, N.Y.*
*August 1941*

# Saturday's Child

Some are teethed on a silver spoon,
    With the stars strung for a rattle;
I cut my teeth as the black raccoon—
    For implements of battle.

Some are swaddled in silk and down,
    And heralded by a star;
They swathed my limbs in a sackcloth gown
    On a night that was black as tar.

For some, godfather and goddame
    The opulent fairies be;
Dame Poverty gave me my name,
    And Pain godfathered me.

For I was born on Saturday—
    "Bad time for planting a seed,"
Was all my father had to say,
    And, "One mouth more to feed."

Death cut the strings that gave me life,
    And handed me to Sorrow,
The only kind of middle wife
    My folks could beg or borrow.

# Scottsboro, Too, Is Worth Its Song

*(A Poem to American Poets)*

I said:
Now will the poets sing,—
Their cries go thundering
Like blood and tears
Into the nation's ears,

Like lightning dart
Into the nation's heart.
Against disease and death and all things fell,
And war,
Their strophes rise and swell
To jar
The foe smug in his citadel.

Remembering their sharp and pretty
Tunes for Sacco and Vanzetti,
I said:
Here too's a cause divinely spun
For those whose eyes are on the sun,
Here in epitome
Is all disgrace
And epic wrong,
Like wine to brace
The minstrel heart, and blare it into song.

Surely, I said,
Now will the poets sing.
   But they have raised no cry.
   I wonder why.

# ROBERT HAYDEN  *(1913–1980)*

Robert Hayden grew up in the area of Detroit known as Paradise Valley, raised from his birth in 1913 by stern foster parents he nevertheless considered his true family. Hayden, plagued by poor eyesight, could not play regularly with his peers, and his unusually large glasses made him an object of ridicule. He developed an early fondness for literature and the movies, both as intellectual sustenance and as an escape from the abject poverty of his surroundings.

Hayden earned his bachelor's degree from Detroit City College (now Wayne State University), majoring in Spanish and participating in local dramatic productions. After graduation he conducted extensive research on African American folk history at the Schomburg Center in New York City. This research would filter through Hayden's imagination to become the material for poems such as "Middle Passage."

Hayden returned to his home state to begin his graduate study under W. H. Auden at the University of Michigan. He considered Auden's influence a turning point in his career as a writer: he often remarked that, aside from the library, Auden was his only mentor. It was Auden whom he credited with fostering the precise and layered technique, as well as the strenuous discipline, of his best work.

While at Michigan, Hayden twice won the Hopwood Award for poetry. In 1936 he joined the Federal Writers' Project and researched local African American folklore and the history of the Underground Railroad in Michigan. In 1940 he released a volume of verse entitled *Heart-Shape in the Dust,* which he would later disavow as the work of an apprentice.

From 1946 to 1969 Hayden taught at Fisk University in Nashville, Tennessee, finding little time to write consistently. However, in 1962 he published his *Ballad of Remembrance,* which includes his Hopwood Award–winning poems, and in the following years he would publish *Selected Poems* (1966), *Words in the Mourning Time* (1970), *Angle of Ascent: New and Selected Poems* (1975), and *American Journal* (1978, 1980).

In 1970 Hayden joined the English faculty at the University of Michigan, the first African American so appointed. Six years later he was named consultant in poetry to the Library of Congress—the position that was to become the nation's poet laureateship. Hayden wore these distinctions with his noted reserve, preferring to think of himself as an artist before a public figure.

Hayden's faith in Baha'i, begun in 1967, became a major ordering principle of both his life and his work, and he served for many years as editor of the Baha'i journal *WorldOrder*.

With his consistently high level of accomplishment and his breadth of concern—from the historical narrative of poems like "Middle Passage" and "Runagate, Runagate," to the personal and existential musings of brief lyrics like "A Plague of Starlings" and "Ice Storm"—Hayden extended the boundaries of subject matter for African American poets. The careers of Michael Harper, Rita Dove, Yusef Komunyakaa, Carl Phillips, and Elizabeth Alexander are hard to imagine without Hayden's example. By the time of his death in 1980, Hayden had amassed a nearly flawless collection of poems regarded as among the finest by an American of this century.

## Ice Storm

Unable to sleep, or pray, I stand
by the window looking out
at moonstruck trees a December storm
has bowed with ice.

Maple and mountain ash bend
under its glassy weight,
their cracked branches falling upon
the frozen snow.

The trees themselves, as in winters past,
will survive their burdening,
broken thrive. And am I less to You,
my God, than they?

## Those Winter Sundays

Sundays too my father got up early
and put his clothes on in the blueblack cold,
then with cracked hands that ached
from labor in the weekday weather made
banked fires blaze. No one ever thanked him.

I'd wake and hear the cold splintering, breaking.
When the rooms were warm, he'd call,
and slowly I would rise and dress,
fearing the chronic angers of that house,

Speaking indifferently to him,
who had driven out the cold
and polished my good shoes as well.
What did I know, what did I know
of love's austere and lonely offices?

## A Plague of Starlings

*(Fisk Campus)*

Evenings I hear
the workmen fire
into the stiff
magnolia leaves,
routing the starlings
gathered noisy and
befouling there.

Their scissoring
terror like glass
coins spilling breaking
the birds explode
into mica sky

raggedly fall
to ground rigid
in clench of cold.

The spared return,
when the guns are through,
to the spoiled trees
like choiceless poor
to a dangerous
dwelling place,
chitter and quarrel
in the piercing dark
above the killed.

Mornings, I pick
my way past death's
black droppings:
on campus lawns
and streets
the troublesome
starlings
frost-salted lie,
troublesome still.

And if not careful
I shall tread
upon carcasses
carcasses when I
go mornings now
to lecture on
what Socrates,
the hemlock hour nigh,
told sorrowing
Phaedo and the rest
about the migratory
habits of the soul.

# October

### I

October—
its plangency, its glow

as of words in
the poet's mind,

as of God in
the saint's.

### II

I wept for your mother
in her pain, wept in
my joy when you were
born,
        Maia,
that October morning.
We named you
for a star a star-like
poem sang.
                I write this
for your birthday
and say I love you
and say October
like the phoenix sings you.

### III

This chiming
and tolling
        of lion
and phoenix
and chimera
        colors.
This huntsman's

horn, sounding
   mort for
quarry fleeing
through mirrors
   of burning
into deathless
   dying.


### IV

Rockweight
of surprising snow

crushed
the October trees,

broke
branches that

crashing set
the snow on fire.


## Frederick Douglass

When it is finally ours, this freedom, this liberty, this beautiful
and terrible thing, needful to man as air,
usable as earth; when it belongs at last to all,
when it is truly instinct, brain matter, diastole, systole,
reflex action; when it is finally won; when it is more
than the gaudy mumbo jumbo of politicians:
this man, this Douglass, this former slave, this Negro
beaten to his knees, exiled, visioning a world
where none is lonely, none hunted, alien,
this man, superb in love and logic, this man
shall be remembered. Oh, not with statues' rhetoric,
not with legends and poems and wreaths of bronze alone,

but with the lives grown out of his life, the lives
fleshing his dream of the beautiful, needful thing.


## Homage to the Empress of the Blues

Because there was a man somewhere in a candystripe silk shirt,
gracile and dangerous as a jaguar and because a woman moaned
for him in sixty-watt gloom and mourned him Faithless Love
Twotiming Love Oh Love Oh Careless Aggravating Love,

      She came out on the stage in yards of pearls, emerging like
      a favorite scenic view, flashed her golden smile and sang.

Because grey laths began somewhere to show from underneath
torn hurdygurdy lithographs of dollfaced heaven;
and because there were those who feared alarming fists of snow
on the door and those who feared the riot-squad of statistics,

      She came out on the stage in ostrich feathers, beaded satin,
      and shone that smile on us and sang.


## Paul Laurence Dunbar

        *For Herbert Martin*


        We lay red roses on his grave,
      speak sorrowfully of him
      as if he were but newly dead

        And so it seems to us
      this raw spring day, though years
      before we two were born he was
        a young poet dead.

Poet of our youth—
his "cri du coeur" our own,
his verses "in a broken tongue"

beguiling as an elder
brother's antic lore.
Their sad blackface lilt and croon
survive him like

The happy look (subliminal
of victim, dying man)
a summer's tintypes hold.

The roses flutter in the wind;
we weight their stems
with stones, then drive away.


## A Letter from Phillis Wheatley

*London, 1773*

Dear Obour
            Our crossing was without
event. I could not help, at times,
reflecting on that first—my Destined—
voyage long ago (I yet
have some remembrance of its Horrors)
and marvelling at God's Ways.
            Last evening, her Ladyship presented me
to her illustrious Friends.
I scarce could tell them anything
of Africa, though much of Boston
and my hope of Heaven. I read
my latest Elegies to them.
"O Sable Muse!" the Countess cried,
embracing me, when I had done.
I held back tears, as is my wont,
and there were tears in Dear

Nathaniel's eyes.
      At supper—I dined apart
like captive Royalty—
the Countess and her Güests promised
signatures affirming me
True Poetess, albeit once a slave.
Indeed, they were most kind, and spoke,
moreover, of presenting me
at Court (I thought of Pocahontas)—
an Honor, to be sure, but one,
I should, no doubt, as Patriot decline.
      My health is much improved;
I feel I may, if God so Wills,
entirely recover here.
Idyllic England! Alas, there is
no Eden without its Serpent. Under
the chiming Complaisance I hear him Hiss;
I see his flickering tongue
when foppish would-be Wits
murmur of the Yankee Pedlar
and his Cannibal Mockingbird.
      Sister, forgive th'intrusion of
my Sombreness—Nocturnal Mood
I would not share with any save
your trusted Self. Let me disperse,
in closing, such unseemly Gloom
by mention of an Incident
you may, as I, consider Droll:
Today, a little Chimney Sweep,
his face and hands with soot quite Black,
staring hard at me, politely asked:
"Does you, M'lady, sweep chimneys too?"
I was amused, but dear Nathaniel
(ever Solicitous) was not.
      I pray the Blessings of our Lord
and Saviour Jesus Christ be yours
Abundantly. In His Name,

               Phillis

# The Islands

*For Steve and Nancy, Allen and Magda*

Always this waking dream of palmtrees,
magic flowers—of sensual joys
like treasures brought up from the sea.

Always this longing, this nostalgia
for tropic islands we
have never known and yet recall.

We look for ease upon these islands named
to honor holiness; in their chromatic
torpor catch our breath.

Scorn greets us with promises of rum,
hostility welcomes us to bargain sales.
We make friends with Flamboyant trees.

Jamaican Cynthie, called alien by dese lazy
islanders—wo'k hahd, treated bad,
oh, mahn, I tellin you. She's full

of raucous anger. Nevertheless brings gifts of
scarlet hibiscus when she comes to clean,
white fragrant spider-lilies too sometimes.

The roofless walls, the tidy ruins
of sugar mill. More than cane
was crushed. But I am tired today

of history, its patina'd clichés
of endless evil. Flame trees.
The intricate sheen of waters flowing into sun.

I wake and see
the morning like a god
in peacock-flower mantle dancing

on opalescent waves—
and can believe my furies have
abandoned for a time their long pursuit.

# MARGARET WALKER (1915–1998)

**B**orn in Birmingham, Alabama, in 1915, Margaret Walker was the daughter of a Methodist minister. Her parents encouraged the zeal for literature that would take her to Northwestern University and on to the University of Iowa, from which she earned both master's and doctorate degrees. From 1936 to 1939 Walker worked for the Federal Writers' Project in Alabama, where she met Richard Wright.

In 1942 her first volume of verse, *For My People,* was published as the Yale University Younger Poets award winner. The title poem of the volume is an excellent example of the poet's strong and direct style, uniquely her own. One can see in her work a familiarity with the sonnet and the folk ballad, as well as her thematic concern with America's southern terrain.

Before retiring in 1979, Walker taught English at Livingston College, West Virginia State College, and Jackson State College (now University) in Jackson, Mississippi. She is also the author of a novel, *Jubilee* (1966), the biography *Richard Wright, Daemonic Genius* (1988), and two other volumes of verse, *Prophets for a New Day* and *October Journey.* She died in 1998.

## For My People

For my people everywhere singing their slave songs repeat-
    edly: their dirges and their ditties and their blues and
    jubilees, praying their prayers nightly to an unknown god,
    bending their knees humbly to an unseen power;

For my people lending their strength to the years, to the gone
    years and the now years and the maybe years, washing
    ironing cooking scrubbing sewing mending hoeing plow-
    ing digging planting pruning patching dragging along
    never gaining never reaping never knowing and never
    understanding.

For my playmates in the clay and dust and sand of Alabama
backyards playing baptizing and preaching and doctor
and jail and soldier and school and mama and cooking
and playhouse and concert and store and hair and Miss
Choomby and company;

For the cramped bewildered years we went to school to learn
to know the reasons why and the answers to and the
people who and the places where and the days when, in
memory of the bitter hours when we discovered we were
black and poor and small and different and nobody cared
and nobody wondered and nobody understood;

For the boys and girls who grew in spite of these things to be
Man and Woman, to laugh and dance and sing and play
and drink their wine and religion and success, to marry
their playmates and bear children and then die of con-
sumption and anemia and lynching;

For my people thronging 47th Street in Chicago and Lenox
Avenue in New York and Rampart Street in New Orleans,
lost disinherited dispossessed and happy people filling the
cabarets and taverns and other people's pockets needing
bread and shoes and milk and land and money and some-
thing—something all our own;

For my people walking blindly spreading joy, losing time
being lazy, sleeping when hungry, shouting when
burdened, drinking when hopeless, tied and shackled and
tangled among ourselves by the unseen creatures who
tower over us omnisciently and laugh;

For my people blundering and groping and floundering in
the dark of churches and schools and clubs and societies,
associations and councils and committees and conven-
tions, distressed and disturbed and deceived and devoured
by money-hungry glory-craving leeches, preyed on by
facile force of state and fad and novelty by false prophet
and holy believer;

For my people standing staring trying to fashion a better way
from confusion from hypocrisy and misunderstanding,
trying to fashion a world that will hold all the people, all
the faces, all the adams and eves and their countless gener-
ations;

Let a new earth rise. Let another world be born. Let a
bloody peace be written in the sky. Let a second genera-
tion full of courage issue forth; let a people loving free-
dom come to growth. Let a beauty full of healing and a
strength of final clenching be the pulsing in our spirits and
our blood. Let the martial songs be written, let the dirges
disappear. Let a race of men now rise and take control.

## Molly Means

Old Molly Means was a hag and a witch;
Chile of the devil, the dark, and sitch.
Her heavy hair hung thick in ropes
And her blazing eyes was black as pitch.
Imp at three and wench at 'leben
She counted her husbands to the number seben.
   O Molly, Molly, Molly Means
   There goes the ghost of Molly Means.

Some say she was born with a veil on her face
So she could look through unnatchal space
Through the future and through the past
And charm a body or an evil place
And every man could well despise
The evil look in her coal black eyes.
   Old Molly, Molly, Molly Means
   Dark is the ghost of Molly Means.

And when the tale begun to spread
Of evil and of holy dread:

Her black-hand arts and her evil powers
How she cast her spells and called the dead,
The younguns was afraid at night
And the farmers feared their crops would blight.
    Old Molly, Molly, Molly Means
    Cold is the ghost of Molly Means.

Then one dark day she put a spell
On a young gal-bride just come to dwell
In the lane just down from Molly's shack
And when her husband come riding back
His wife was barking like a dog
And on all fours like a common hog.
    O Molly, Molly, Molly Means
    Where is the ghost of Molly Means?

The neighbors come and they went away
And said she'd die before break of day
But her husband held her in his arms
And swore he'd break the wicked charms;
He'd search all up and down the land
And turn the spell on Molly's hand.
    O Molly, Molly, Molly Means
    Sharp is the ghost of Molly Means.

So he rode all day and he rode all night
And at the dawn he come in sight
Of a man who said he could move the spell
And cause the awful thing to dwell
On Molly Means, to bark and bleed
Till she died at the hands of her evil deed.
    Old Molly, Molly, Molly Means
    This is the ghost of Molly Means.

Sometimes at night through the shadowy trees
She rides along on a winter breeze.
You can hear her holler and whine and cry.
Her voice is thin and her moan is high,
And her cackling laugh or her barking cold

Bring terror to the young and old.
O Molly, Molly, Molly Means
Lean is the ghost of Molly Means.

## October Journey

Traveller take heed for journeys undertaken in the dark of the year.
Go in the bright blaze of Autumn's equinox.
Carry protection against ravages of a sun-robber, a vandal, a thief.
Cross no bright expanse of water in the full of the moon.
Choose no dangerous summer nights;
no heavy tempting hours of spring;
October journeys are safest, brightest, and best.

I want to tell you what hills are like in October
when colors gush down mountainsides
and little streams are freighted with a caravan of leaves.
I want to tell you how they blush and turn in fiery shame and joy,
how their love burns with flames consuming and terrible
until we wake one morning and woods are like a smoldering plain—
a glowing caldron full of jewelled fire;
the emerald earth a dragon's eye
the poplars drenched with yellow light
and dogwoods blazing bloody red.
Travelling southward earth changes from gray rock to green velvet.
Earth changes to red clay
with green grass growing brightly
with saffron skies of evening setting dully
with muddy rivers moving sluggishly.

In the early spring when the peach tree blooms
wearing a veil like a lavender haze
and the pear and plum in their bridal hair
gently snow their petals on earth's grassy bosom below
then the soughing breeze is soothing
and the world seems bathed in tenderness,

but in October
blossoms have long since fallen.
A few red apples hang on leafless boughs;
wind whips bushes briskly.
And where a blue stream sings cautiously
a barren land feeds hungrily.

An evil moon bleeds drops of death.
The earth burns brown.
Grass shrivels and dries to a yellowish mass.
Earth wears a dun-colored dress
like an old woman wooing the sun to be her lover,
be her sweetheart and her husband bound in one.
Farmers heap hay in stacks and bind corn in shocks
against the big breath of frost.

The train wheels hum, "I am going home, I am going home,
I am moving toward the South."
Soon cypress swamps and muskrat marshes
and black fields touched with cotton will appear.
I dream again of my childhood land
of a neighbor's yard with a redbud tree
the smell of pine for turpentine
and Easter dress, a Christmas Eve
and winding roads from the top of a hill.
A music sings within my flesh
I feel the pulse within my throat
my heart fills up with hungry fear
while hills and flatlands stark and staring
before my dark eyes sad and haunting
appear and disappear.

Then when I touch this land again
the promise of a sun-lit hour dies.
The greenness of an apple seems
to dry and rot before my eyes.
The sullen winter rains
are tears of grief I cannot shed.
The windless days are static lives.
The clock runs down

timeless and still.
The days and nights turn hours to years
and water in a gutter marks the circle of another world
hating, resentful, and afraid,
stagnant, and green, and full of slimy things.

# GWENDOLYN BROOKS  *(1917–   )*

The first African American to win the Pulitzer Prize in poetry, Gwendolyn Brooks was born in Topeka, Kansas, in 1917 and raised in Chicago. The terrain of Chicago's South Side would leave an indelible imprint on Brooks's imagination, providing the material for one of the more remarkable and sustained bodies of work of this century. Brooks's objective has been to give voice to the unique precincts of the "projects" and the black working and middle classes.

To this end she is a master of both form and free verse, urban folklore and classicism, accessing through these different modes of expression the variegated textures of character, place, and historical moment. Brooks's poetry reads as a continuous revelation of the poignancies of race and region, echoing and at times contending with the work of other regionalists like Edwin Arlington Robinson and Robert Frost. Her verse is marked by sharp images of people and place; her diction and careful irony, while emerging from contemplations on the African American experience, transcend these to universal relevance.

Brooks was graduated from Wilson Junior College in 1936. Her first volume of poetry, *A Street in Bronzeville,* was published in 1945. In 1950 her *Annie Allen* won the Pulitzer Prize, the first of many awards she would receive, including membership in the American Academy of Arts and Letters, and the state poet laureateship of Illinois.

Brooks's published works include a novel entitled *Maud Martha* (1953), a two-part autobiography, and numerous volumes of poetry, among them *The Bean Eaters* (1960), *Selected Poems* (1963), *In the Mecca* (1968), *Beckonings* (1975), and *Blacks* (1987). Brooks still resides in Chicago and remains a dedicated teacher and supporter of young African American poets.

Building on the innovations of poets such as Emily Dickinson, Carl Sandburg, and Langston Hughes, Brooks fashioned a new type of American poem—lushly romantic while epigrammatically terse, true to the minute specifics of a place and time yet musical and open to any reader. On continued reading her work begins to remind one more of Horace and Chaucer than does that of any of her American contemporaries. Brooks stands with Paul Laurence Dunbar, Sterling A. Brown, and Robert Hayden on the summit of the African American and American poetic traditions.

## The Bean Eaters

They eat beans mostly, this old yellow pair.
Dinner is a casual affair.
Plain chipware on a plain and creaking wood,
Tin flatware.

Two who are Mostly Good.
Two who have lived their day,
But keep on putting on their clothes
And putting things away.

And remembering . . .
Remembering, with twinklings and twinges,
As they lean over the beans in their rented back room that
        is full of beads and receipts and dolls and cloths,
            tobacco crumbs, vases and fringes.

## Sadie and Maud

Maud went to college.
Sadie stayed at home.
Sadie scraped life
With a fine-tooth comb.

She didn't leave a tangle in.
Her comb found every strand.
Sadie was one of the livingest chits
In all the land.

Sadie bore two babies
Under her maiden name.
Maud and Ma and Papa
Nearly died of shame.
Every one but Sadie
Nearly died of shame.

When Sadie said her last so-long
Her girls struck out from home.
(Sadie had left as heritage
Her fine-tooth comb.)

Maud, who went to college,
Is a thin brown mouse.
She is living all alone
In this old house.

## A Song in the Front Yard

I've stayed in the front yard all my life.
I want a peek at the back
Where it's rough and untended and hungry weed grows.
A girl gets sick of a rose.

I want to go in the back yard now
And maybe down the alley,
To where the charity children play.
I want a good time today.

They do some wonderful things.
They have some wonderful fun.
My mother sneers, but I say it's fine
How they don't have to go in at quarter to nine.
My mother, she tells me that Johnnie Mae
Will grow up to be a bad woman.
That George'll be taken to Jail soon or late
(On account of last winter he sold our back gate).

But I say it's fine. Honest, I do.
And I'd like to be a bad woman, too,
And wear the brave stockings of night-black lace
And strut down the streets with paint on my face.

# Of De Witt Williams on His Way to Lincoln Cemetery

He was born in Alabama.
He was bred in Illinois.
He was nothing but a
Plain black boy.

Swing low swing low sweet sweet chariot.
Nothing but a plain black boy.

Drive him past the Pool Hall.
Drive him past the Show.
Blind within his casket,
But maybe he will know.

Down through Forty-seventh Street:
Underneath the L,
And—Northwest Corner, Prairie,
That he loved so well.

Don't forget the Dance Halls—
Warwick and Savoy,
Where he picked his women, where
He drank his liquid joy.

Born in Alabama.
Bred in Illinois.
He was nothing but a
Plain black boy.

Swing low swing low sweet sweet chariot.
Nothing but a plain black boy.

## We Real Cool

            THE POOL PLAYERS.
            SEVEN AT THE GOLDEN SHOVEL.

    We real cool. We
    Left school. We

    Lurk late. We
    Strike straight. We

    Sing sin. We
    Thin gin. We

    Jazz June. We
    Die soon.

## The Mother

Abortions will not let you forget.
You remember the children you got that you did not get,
The damp small pulps with a little or with no hair,
The singers and workers that never handled the air.
You will never neglect or beat
Them, or silence or buy with a sweet.
You will never wind up the sucking-thumb
Or scuttle off ghosts that come.
You will never leave them, controlling your luscious sigh,
Return for a snack of them, with gobbling mother-eye.

I have heard in the voices of the wind the voices of my dim
    killed children.
I have contracted. I have eased
My dim dears at the breasts they could never suck.
I have said, Sweets, if I sinned, if I seized
Your luck

And your lives from your unfinished reach,
If I stole your births and your names,
Your straight baby tears and your games,
Your stilted or lovely loves, your tumults, your marriages,
    aches, and your deaths,
If I poisoned the beginnings of your breaths,
Believe that even in my deliberateness I was not deliberate.
Though why should I whine,
Whine that the crime was other than mine?—
Since anyhow you are dead.
Or rather, or instead,
You were never made.
But that too, I am afraid,
Is faulty: oh, what shall I say, how is the truth to be said?
You were born, you had body, you died.
It is just that you never giggled or planned or cried.

Believe me, I loved you all.
Believe me, I knew you, though faintly, and I loved, I loved you
All.

## To Be in Love

    To be in love
Is to touch things with a lighter hand.

In yourself you stretch, you are well.

You look at things
Through his eyes.
    A Cardinal is red.
    A sky is blue.
Suddenly you know he knows too.
He is not there but
You know you are tasting together
The winter, or light spring weather.

His hand to take your hand is overmuch.
Too much to bear.

You cannot look in his eyes
Because your pulse must not say
What must not be said.

When he
Shuts a door—
Is not there—
Your arms are water.

And you are free
With a ghastly freedom.

You are the beautiful half
Of a golden hurt.

You remember and covet his mouth,
To touch, to whisper on.

Oh when to declare
Is certain Death!

Oh when to apprize
Is to mesmerize,

To see fall down, the Column of Gold,
Into the commonest ash.

## Beverly Hills, Chicago

> *"and the people live till they have white hair"*
> —E. M. Price

The dry brown coughing beneath their feet,
(Only a while, for the handyman is on his way)
These people walk their golden gardens.
We say ourselves fortunate to be driving by today.

That we may look at them, in their gardens where
The summer ripeness rots. But not raggedly.
Even the leaves fall down in lovelier patterns here.
And the refuse, the refuse is a neat brilliancy.

When they flow sweetly into their houses
With softness and slowness touched by that everlasting gold,
We know what they go to. To tea. But that does not mean
They will throw some little black dots into some water and
    add sugar and the juice of the cheapest lemons that are
    sold,
While downstairs that woman's vague phonograph bleats,
    "Knock me a kiss."
And the living all to be made again in the sweatingest physi-
    cal manner
Tomorrow. . . . Not that anybody is saying that these people
    have no trouble.
Merely that it is trouble with a gold-flecked beautiful banner.

Nobody is saying that these people do not ultimately cease
    to be. And
Sometimes their passings are even more painful than ours.
It is just that so often they live till their hair is white.
They make excellent corpses, among the expensive
    flowers. . . .

Nobody is furious. Nobody hates these people.
At least, nobody driving by in this car.
It is only natural, however, that it should occur to us
How much more fortunate they are than we are.

It is only natural that we should look and look
At their wood and brick and stone
And think, while a breath of pine blows,
How different these are from our own.

We do not want them to have less.
But it is only natural that we should think we have not enough.
We drive on, we drive on.
When we speak to each other our voices are a little gruff.

## To an Old Black Woman, Homeless and Indistinct

### I.

Your every day is a pilgrimage.
A blue hubbub.
Your days are collected bacchanals of fear and self-troubling.

And your nights! Your nights.
When you put you down in alley or cardboard or viaduct,
your lovers are rats, finding your secret places.

### II.

When you rise in another morning,
you hit the street, your incessant enemy.

See? Here you are, in the so-busy world.
You walk. You walk.
You pass The People.
No. The People pass you.

Here's a Rich Girl marching briskly to her charms.
She is suede and scarf and belting and perfume.
She sees you not, she sees you very well.
At five in the afternoon Miss Rich Girl will go Home
to brooms and vacuum cleaner and carpeting,
two cats, two marble-top tables, two telephones,
shiny green peppers, flowers in impudent vases,
visitors.
Before all that there's luncheon to be known.
Lasagna, lobster salad, sandwiches.
All day there's coffee to be loved.
There are luxuries
of minor dissatisfaction, luxuries of Plan.


### III.

That's *her* story.
*You're* going to vanish, not necessarily nicely, fairly soon.
Although essentially dignity itself a death
is not necessarily tidy, modest or discreet.
When they find you
your legs may not be tidy nor aligned.
Your mouth may be all crooked or destroyed.


Black old woman, homeless, indistinct—
Your last and least adventure is Review.
   Folks used to celebrate your birthday!
Folks used to say "She's such a pretty little thing!"
Folks used to say "She draws such handsome horses, cows
   and houses,"
Folks used to say "That child is going far."

# The Blackstone Rangers

### I

## AS SEEN BY DISCIPLINES

There they are.
Thirty at the corner.
Black, raw, ready.
Sores in the city
that do not want to heal.

### II

## THE LEADERS

Jeff. Gene. Geronimo. And Bop.
They cancel, cure and curry.
Hardly the dupes of the downtown thing
the cold bonbon,
the rhinestone thing. And hardly
in a hurry.
Hardly Belafonte, King,
Black Jesus, Stokely, Malcolm X or Rap.
Bungled trophies.
Their country is a Nation on no map.

Jeff, Gene, Geronimo and Bop
in the passionate noon,
in bewitching night
are the detailed men, the copious men.
They curry, cure,
they cancel, cancelled images whose Concerts
are not divine, vivacious; the different tins
are intense last entries; pagan argument;
translations of the night.

The Blackstone bitter bureaus
(bureaucracy is footloose) edit, fuse

unfashionable damnations and descent;
and exulting, monstrous hand on monstrous hand,
construct, strangely, a monstrous pearl or grace.


### III

## GANG GIRLS

### *A Rangerette*

Gang Girls are sweet exotics.
Mary Ann
uses the nutrients of her orient,
but sometimes sighs for Cities of blue and jewel
beyond her Ranger rim of Cottage Grove.
(Bowery Boys, Disciples, Whip-Birds will
dissolve no margins, stop no savory sanctities.)

Mary is
a rose in a whiskey glass.

Mary's
Februaries shudder and are gone. Aprils
fret frankly, lilac hurries on.
Summer is a hard irregular ridge.
October looks away.
And that's the Year!
             Save for her bugle-love.
Save for the bleat of not-obese devotion.
Save for Somebody Terribly Dying, under
the philanthropy of robins. Save for her Ranger
bringing
an amount of rainbow in a string-drawn bag.
"Where did you get the diamond?" Do not ask:
but swallow, straight, the spirals of his flask
and assist him at your zipper; pet his lips
and help him clutch you.

Love's another departure.
Will there be any arrivals, confirmations?
Will there be gleaning?

Mary, the Shakedancer's child
from the rooming-flat, pants carefully, peers at
her laboring lover. . . .
                    Mary! Mary Ann!
Settle for sandwiches! settle for stocking caps!
for sudden blood, aborted carnival,
the props and niceties of non-loneliness—
the rhymes of Leaning.


## Mentors

For I am rightful fellow of their band.
My best allegiances are to the dead.
I swear to keep the dead upon my mind,
Disdain for all time to be overglad.
Among spring flowers, under summer trees,
By chilling autumn waters, in the frosts
Of supercilious winter—all my days
I'll have as mentors those reproving ghosts.
And at that cry, at that remotest whisper,
I'll stop my casual business. Leave the banquet.
Or leave the ball—reluctant to unclasp her
Who may be fragrant as the flower she wears,
Make gallant bows and dim excuses, then quit
Light for the midnight that is mine and theirs.

# BOB KAUFMAN  *(1925–1986)*

**B**ob Kaufman was born in 1925 in New Orleans, where he remained until he left junior high school to join the Merchant Marine. For the next twenty years he developed his interest in literature, and upon settling in San Francisco in the early sixties he found himself at the center of the Beat movement. His "Abomunist Manifesto" was published as a broadside in 1959 by City Lights, the press that had released Allen Ginsberg's "Howl" three years earlier. Kaufman's *Solitudes Crowded with Loneliness* followed in 1965.

Kaufman's poetry imbibes the pulse of urban life, particularly as accented and underscored by the tonal movements and rhetoric of American jazz. Though noted as an experimentalist, Kaufman wrestled as well with literary convention in a way that can infuse his work with a startling tension.

During the Vietnam War, Kaufman fell into a prolonged silence, which lifted briefly in the late 1970s. At times he had difficulty making a living and suffered regularly from dire poverty. The silences and the poverty punctuate his collected work, *The Ancient Rain: Poems 1956–1978*, which was published in 1986, the year of Kaufman's death in San Francisco.

## Battle Report

One thousand saxophones infiltrate the city,
Each with a man inside,
Hidden in ordinary cases,
Labeled FRAGILE.

A fleet of trumpets drops their hooks,
Inside at the outside.

Ten waves of trombones approach the city
Under blue cover
Of late autumn's neoclassical clouds.

Five hundred bassmen, all string feet tall,
Beating it back to the bass.

One hundred drummers, each a stick in each hand,
The delicate rumble of pianos, moving in.

The secret agent, an innocent bystander,
Drops a note in the wail box.

Five generals, gathered in the gallery,
Blowing plans.

At last, the secret code is flashed:
Now is the time, now is the time.

Attack: The sound of jazz.

The city falls.


## Grandfather Was Queer, Too


He was first seen in a Louisiana bayou,
Playing chess with an intellectual lobster.
They burned his linoleum house alive
And sent that intellectual off to jail.
He wrote home every day, to no avail.
Grandfather had cut out, he couldn't raise the bail.

Next seen, skiing on some dusty Texas road,
An intellectual's soul hung from his ears,
Discussing politics with an unemployed butterfly.
They hung that poor butterfly, poor butterfly.
Grandfather had cut out, he couldn't raise the bail.

Next seen on the Arizona desert, walking,
Applying soothing poultices to the teeth

Of an aching mountain.
Dentists all over the state brought gauze balls,
Bandaged the mountain, buried it at sea.
Grandfather had cut out, he couldn't raise the bail.

Next seen in California, the top part,
Arranging a marriage, mating trees,
Crossing a rich redwood and a black pine.
He was exposed by the Boy Scouts of America.
The trees were arrested on a vag charge.
Grandfather cut out, he couldn't raise the bail.

Now I have seen him here. He is beat.
His girlfriend has green ears;
She is twenty-three months pregnant.
I kissed them both:
Live happily ever after.


## Walking Parker Home


Sweet beats of jazz impaled on slivers of wind
Kansas Black Morning/ First Horn Eyes/
Historical sound pictures on New Bird wings
People shouts/ boy alto dreams/ Tomorrow's
Gold belled pipe of stops and future Blues Times
Lurking Hawkins/ shadows of Lester/ realization
Bronze fingers—brain extensions seeking trapped sounds
Ghetto thoughts/ bandstand courage/ solo flight
Nerve-wracked suspicions of newer songs and doubts
New York altar city/ black tears/ secret disciples
Hammer horn pounding soul marks on unswinging gates
Culture gods/ mob sounds/ visions of spikes
Panic excursions to tribal Jazz wombs and transfusions
Heroin nights of birth/ and soaring/ over boppy new ground.
Smothered rage covering pyramids of notes spontaneously exploding

Cool revelations/ shrill hopes/ beauty speared into greedy ears
Birdland nights on bop mountains, windy saxophone revolutions
Dayrooms of junk/ and melting walls and circling vultures/
Money cancer/ remembered pain/ terror flights/
Death and indestructible existence.

In that Jazz corner of life
Wrapped in a mist of sound
His legacy, our Jazz-tinted dawn
Wailing his triumphs of oddly begotten dreams
Inviting the nerveless to feel once more
That fierce dying of humans consumed
In raging fires of Love.

## Jail Poems

I

I am sitting in a cell with a view of evil parallels,
Waiting thunder to splinter me into a thousand me's.
It is not enough to be in one cage with one self;
I want to sit opposite every prisoner in every hole.
Doors roll and bang, every slam a finality, bang!
The junkie disappeared into a red noise, stoning out his hell.
The odored wino congratulates himself on not smoking,
Fingerprints left lying on black inky gravestones,
Noises of pain seeping through steel walls crashing
Reach my own hurt. I become part of someone forever.
Wild accents of criminals are sweeter to me than hum of cops,
Busy battening down hatches of human souls; cargo
Destined for ports of accusations, harbors of guilt.
What do policemen eat, Socrates, still prisoner, old one?

### 2

Painter, paint me a crazy jail, mad water-color cells.
Poet, how old is suffering? Write it in yellow lead.
God, make me a sky on my glass ceiling. I need stars now,
To lead through this atmosphere of shrieks and private hells,
Entrances and exits, in . . . out . . . up . . . down, the civic seesaw.
Here—me—now—hear—me—now—always here somehow.

### 3

In a universe of cells—who is not in jail? Jailers.
In a world of hospitals—who is not sick? Doctors.
A golden sardine is swimming in my head.
Oh we know some things, man, about some things
Like jazz and jails and God.
Saturday is a good day to go to jail.

### 4

Now they give a new form, quivering jelly-like,
That proves any boy can be president of Muscatel.
They are mad at him because he's one of Them.
Gray-speckled unplanned nakedness; stinking
Fingers grasping toilet bowl. Mr. America wants to bathe.
Look! On the floor, lying across America's face—
A real movie star featured in a million newsreels.
What am I doing—feeling compassion?
When he comes out of it, he will help kill me.
He probably hates living.

### 5

Nuts, skin bolts, clanking in his stomach, scrambled.
His society's gone to pieces in his belly, bloated.
See the great American windmill, tilting at itself,
Good solid stock, the kind that made America drunk.
Success written all over his street-streaked ass.
Successful-type success, forty home runs in one inning.

Stop suffering, Jack, you can't fool us. We know.
This is the greatest country in the world, ain't it?
He didn't make it. Wino in Cell 3.


### 6

There have been too many years in this short span of mine.
My soul demands a cave of its own, like the Jain god;
Yet I must make it go on, hard like jazz, glowing
In this dark plastic jungle, land of long night, chilled.
My navel is a button to push when I want inside out.
Am I not more than a mass of entrails and rough tissue?
Must I break my bones? Drink my wine-diluted blood?
Should I dredge old sadness from my chest?
Not again,
All those ancient balls of fire, hotly swallowed, let them lie.
Let me spit breath mists of introspection, bits of me,
So that when I am gone, I shall be in the air.


### 7

Someone whom I am is no one.
Something I have done is nothing.
Someplace I have been is nowhere.
I am not me.
What of the answers
I must find questions for?
All these strange streets
I must find cities for,
Thank God for beatniks.


### 8

All night the stink of rotting people,
Fumes rising from pyres of live men,
Fill my nose with gassy disgust,
Drown my exposed eyes in tears.

### 9

Traveling God salesmen, bursting my ear drum
With the dullest part of a good sexy book,
Impatient for Monday and adding machines.

### 10

Yellow-eyed dogs whistling in evening.

### 11

The baby came to jail today.

### 12

One more day to hell, filled with floating glands.

### 13

The jail, a huge hollow metal cube
Hanging from the moon by a silver chain.
Someday Johnny Appleseed is going to chop it down.

### 14

Three long strips of light
Braided into a ray.

### 15

I am apprehensive about my future;
My past has turned its back on me.

### 16

Shadows I see, forming on the wall,
Pictures of desires protected from my own eyes.

17

After spending all night constructing a dream,
Morning came and blinded me with light.
Now I seek among mountains of crushed eggshells
For the God damned dream I never wanted.

18

Sitting here writing things on paper,
Instead of sticking the pencil into the air.

19

The Battle of Monumental Failures raging,
Both hoping for a good clean loss.

20

Now I see the night, silently overwhelming day.

21

Caught in imaginary webs of conscience,
I weep over my acts, yet believe.

22

Cities should be built on one side of the street.

23

People who can't cast shadows
Never die of freckles.

24

The end always comes last.

### 25

We sat at a corner table,
Devouring each other word by word,
Until nothing was left, repulsive skeletons.

### 26

I sit here writing, not daring to stop,
For fear of seeing what's outside my head.

### 27

There, Jesus, didn't hurt a bit, did it?

### 28

I am afraid to follow my flesh over those narrow
Wide hard soft female beds, but I do.

### 29

Link by link, we forged the chain.
Then, discovering the end around our necks,
We bugged out.

### 30

I have never seen a wild poetic loaf of bread,
But if I did, I would eat it, crust and all.

### 31

From how many years away does a baby come?

### 32

Universality, duality, totality . . . one.

### 33

The defective on the floor, mumbling,
Was once a man who shouted across tables.

### 34

Come, help flatten a raindrop.

*Written in San Francisco City Prison*
*Cell 3, 1959*

# RAYMOND PATTERSON *(1929–   )*

**R**aymond Patterson was born in Harlem in 1929 and grew up in and around New York City. A graduate of Lincoln University, Patterson received a master's degree from New York University. He has taught for many years at the City University of New York and currently lives on Long Island.

In 1969 his volume *Twenty-six Ways of Looking at a Blackman* was published. The title poem, from its formal and textural nod to the Wallace Stevens masterpiece to its unique and original rendering of contemporary African American experience in the high modernist mode, is a stunning achievement of poetic practice. Its emotional resonance and the infinitely various, seamless shifts between philosophical contemplation and dark humor mark the poem as one of the more significant and subtle poetic evocations of the interior lives of blacks ever written.

## Twenty-six Ways of Looking at a Blackman

*For Boydie & Ama*

### I

On the road we met a blackman,
But no one else.

### II

Dreams are reunions. Who has not
On occasion entertained the presence
Of a blackman?

### III

From brown paper bags
A blackman fills the vacancies of morning
With orange speculations.

### IV

Always I hope to find
The blackman I know,
Or one who knows him.

### V

Devouring earthly possessions
Is one of a blackman's excesses.
Exaggerating their transiency
Is another.

### VI

Even this shadow has weight.
A cool heaviness.
Call it a blackman's ghost.

### VII

The possibilities of color
Were choices made by the eye
Looking inward.
The possibilities of rhythms
For a blackman are predetermined.

### VIII

When it had all been unravelled,
The blackman found that it had been
Entirely woven of black thread.

## IX

Children who loved him
Hid him from the world
By pretending he was a blackman.

## X

The fingerprints of a blackman
Were on her pillow. Or was it
Her luminous tears?
    . . . An absence, or a presence?
Only when it was darker
Would she know.

## XI

The blackman dipped water
From a well.
And when the well dried,
He dipped cool blackness.

## XII

We are told that the seeds
Of rainbows are not unlike
A blackman's tear.

## XIII

What is more beautiful than black flowers,
Or blackmen in fields
Gathering them?
    . . . The bride, or the wedding?

## XIV

When it was finished,
Some of the carvers of Destiny
Would sigh in relief,

But the blackman would sigh in intaglio,
Having shed vain illusions in mastering the stone.

## XV

Affirmation of negatives:
A blackman trembles
That his thoughts run toward darkness.

## XVI

The odor of a blackman derives
No less from the sweat of his apotheosis,
Than emanation of crushed apples
He carries in his arms.

## XVII

If I could imagine the shaping of Fate,
I would think of blackmen
Handling the sun.

## XVIII

Is it harvest time in the brown fields,
Or is it just a black man
Singing?

## XIX

There is the sorrow of blackmen
Lost in cities. But who can conceive
Of cities lost in a blackman?

## XX

A small boy lifts a seashell
To his listening ear.
It is the blackman again,
Whispering his sagas of drowned sailors.

## XXI

At the cradle of Justice were found
Three gifts: a pair of scales, a sword,
And a simple cloth. But the Magi had departed.
Several who were with us agreed
One of the givers must have been
A blackman.

## XXII

As vines grow towards light,
So roots grow towards darkness.
Back and forth a blackman goes,
Gathering the harvest.

## XXIII

By moonlight
We tossed our pebbles into the lake
And marveled
At the beauty of concentric sorrows.
You thought it was like the troubled heart
Of a blackman,
Because of the dancing light.

## XXIV

As the time of our leave taking drew near,
The blackman blessed each of us
By pronouncing the names of his children.

## XXV

As I remember it,
The only unicorn in the park
Belonged to a blackman
Who went about collecting bits
And torn scraps of afternoons.

## XXVI

At the center of Being
Said the blackman,
All is tangential.
Even this laughter, even your tears.

# DEREK WALCOTT *(1930– )*

**D**erek Walcott's poetic quest is to narrate the complexities of modern identity, in particular of African identity in the New World. His verse struggles beautifully against the bounds of time and place, echoing past events and poetic traditions while exploring modern landscapes ranging from the various coasts of the Caribbean archipelago to England and from the African veldt to the interstate highways of America's deep South. Walcott's rhetoric represents a unique and ever-changing fusion of influences that include Homer, Auden, Creole speech, and the English of the King James Bible. His best-known poems are marked by lush metaphor, careful characterization, and striking paradox.

Walcott was born in Castries, St. Lucia, in 1930. He was educated at St. Mary's College on St. Lucia and the University of the West Indies in Jamaica. From his youth Walcott displayed a keen interest not only in poetry but also in the visual arts and theater. His work in watercolors graces the covers of many of his volumes of verse. In Trinidad, Walcott founded a professional theater company. He has written numerous plays, including *Dream on Monkey Mountain* (1970) and *Remembrance and Pantomime* (1980). His published volumes of poetry include *The Castaway* (1965), *Another Life* (1973), *The Star-Apple Kingdom* (1979), *The Arkansas Testament* (1987), and *Omeros* (1990).

For the past two decades Walcott has split his time between the Caribbean and the United States. He has been awarded the Queen's Medal for poetry, and in 1992 the Nobel Prize in literature.

## God Rest Ye Merry, Gentlemen

Splitting from Jack Delaney's, Sheridan Square,
that winter night, stewed, seasoned in bourbon,
my body kindled by the whistling air
snowing the Village that Christ was reborn,
I lurched like any lush by his own glow
across towards Sixth, and froze before the tracks

of footprints bleeding on the virgin snow.
I tracked them where they led across the street
to the bright side, entering the wax-
sealed smell of neon, human heat,
some all-night diner with its wise-guy cook,
his stub thumb in my bowl of stew, and one
man's pulped and beaten face, its look
acknowledging all that, white-dark outside,
was possible: some beast prowling the block,
something fur-clotted, running wild
beyond the boundary of will. Outside,
more snow had fallen. My heart charred.
I longed for darkness, evil that was warm.
Walking, I'd stop and turn. What had I heard
wheezing behind my heel with whitening breath?
Nothing. Sixth Avenue yawned wet and wide.
The night was white. There was nowhere to hide.

# God Rest Ye Merry, Gentlemen
# Part II

> *I saw Jesus in the Project.*
> —Richard Pryor

Every street corner is Christmas Eve
in downtown Newark. The Magi walk
in black overcoats hugging a fifth
of methylated spirits, and hookers hook
nothing from the dark cribs of doorways.
A crazy king breaks a bottle in praise
of Welfare, "I'll kill the motherfucker,"
and for black blocks without work
the sky is full of crystal splinters.

A bus breaks out of the mirage of water,
a hippo in wet streetlights, and grinds on
in smoke; every shadow seems to stagger
under the fiery acids of neon—
wavering like a piss, some l tt rs miss-
ing, extinguished—except for two white
nurses, their vocation made whiter
in darkness. It's two days from elections.

Johannesburg is full of starlit shebeens.
It is anti-American to make such connections.
Think of Newark as Christmas Eve,
when all men are your brothers, even
these; bring peace to us in parcels,
let there be no more broken bottles in heaven
over Newark, let it not shine like spit
on a doorstep, think of the evergreen
apex with the gold star over it
on the Day-Glo bumper sticker a passing car sells.

Daughter of your own Son, Mother and Virgin,
great is the sparkle of the high-rise firmament
in acid puddles, the gold star in store windows,
and the yellow star on the night's moth-eaten sleeve
like the black coat He wore through blade-thin elbows
out of the ghetto into the cattle train
    from Warsaw; nowhere is His coming more immanent
than downtown Newark, where three lights believe
the starlit cradle, and the evergreen carols
to the sparrow-child: a black coat-flapping urchin
followed by a white star as a police car patrols.

# The Bounty

*For Alix Walcott*

*i*

Between the vision of the Tourist Board and the true
Paradise lies the desert where Isaiah's elations
force a rose from the sand. The thirty-third canto

cores the dawn clouds with concentric radiance,
the breadfruit opens its palms in praise of the bounty,
*bois-pain,* tree of bread, slave food, the bliss of John Clare,

torn, wandering Tom, stoat-stoker in his county
of reeds and stalk-crickets, fiddling the dank air,
lacing his boots with vines, steering glazed beetles

with the tenderest prods, knight of the cockchafer,
wrapped in the mists of shires, their snail-horned steeples
palms opening to the cupped pool—but his soul safer

than ours, though iron streams fetter his ankles.
Frost whitening his stubble, he stands in the ford
of a brook like the Baptist lifting his branches to bless

cathedrals and snails, the breaking of this new day,
and the shadows of the beach road near which my mother lies,
with the traffic of insects going to work anyway.

The lizard on the white wall fixed on the hieroglyph
of its stone shadow, the palms' rustling archery,
the souls and sails of circling gulls rhyme with:

*"In la sua volonta e nostra pace,"*
In His will is our peace. Peace in white harbours,
in marinas whose masts agree, in crescent melons

left all night in the fridge, in the Egyptian labours
of ants moving boulders of sugar, words in this sentence,
shadow and light, who live next door like neighbours,

and in sardines with pepper sauce. My mother lies
near the white beach stones, John Clare near the sea-almonds,
yet the bounty returns each daybreak, to my surprise,

to my surprise and betrayal, yes, both at once.
I am moved like you, mad Tom, by a line of ants;
I behold their industry and they are giants.

*ii*

There on the beach, in the desert, lies the dark well
where the rose of my life was lowered, near the shaken plants,
near a pool of fresh tears, tolled by the golden bell

of allamanda, thorns of the bougainvillea, and that is
their bounty! They shine with defiance from weed and flower,
even those that flourish elsewhere, vetch, ivy, clematis,

on whom the sun now rises with all its power,
not for the Tourist Board or for Dante Alighieri,
but because there is no other path for its wheel to take

except to make the ruts of the beach road an allegory
of this poem's career, of yours, that she died for the sake
of a crowning wreath of fresh laurel; so, John Clare, forgive me,

for this morning's sake, forgive me, coffee, and pardon me,
milk with two packets of artificial sugar,
as I watch these lines grow and the art of poetry harden me

into sorrow as measured as this, to draw the veiled figure
of Mamma entering the standard elegiac.
No, there is grief, there will always be, but it must not madden,

like Clare, who wept for a beetle's loss, for the weight
of the world in a bead of dew on clematis or vetch,
and the fire in these tinder-dry lines of this poem I hate

as much as I love her, poor rain-beaten wretch,
redeemer of mice, earl of the doomed protectorate
of cavalry under your cloak; come on now, enough!

*iii*

Bounty!
        In the bells of tree-frogs with their steady clamour
in the indigo dark before dawn, the fading morse
of fireflies and crickets, then light on the beetle's armour,

and the toad's too-late presages, nettles of remorse
that shall spring from her grave from the spade's heartbreak.
And yet not to have loved her enough is to love more,

if I confess it, and I confess it. The trickle of underground
springs, the babble of swollen gulches under drenched ferns,
loosening the grip of their roots, till their hairy clods

like unclenching fists swirl wherever the gulch turns
them, and the shuddering aftermath bends the rods
of wild cane. Bounty in the ant's waking fury,

in the snail's chapel stirring under wild yams,
praise in decay and process, awe in the ordinary
in wind that reads the lines of the breadfruit's palms

in the sun contained in a globe of the crystal dew,
bounty in the ants' continuing a line of raw flour,
mercy on the mongoose scuttling past my door,

in the light's parallelogram laid on the kitchen floor,
for Thine is the Kingdom, the Glory, and the Power,
the bells of Saint Clement's in the marigolds on the altar,

in the bougainvillea's thorns, in the imperial lilac
and the feathery palms that nodded at the entry
into Jerusalem, the weight of the world on the back

of an ass; dismounting, He left His cross there for sentry
and sneering centurion; then I believed in His Word,
in a widow's immaculate husband, in pews of brown wood,

when the cattle-bell of the chapel summoned our herd
into the varnished stalls, in whose rustling hymnals I heard
the fresh Jacobean springs, the murmur Clare heard

of bounty abiding, the clear language she taught us,
"as the hart panteth," at this, her keen ears pronged
while her three fawns nibbled the soul-freshening waters,

"as the hart panteth for the water-brooks" that belonged
to the language in which I mourn her now, or when
I showed her my first elegy, her husband's, and then her own.

### iv

But can she or can she not read this? Can you read this,
Mamma, or hear it? If I took the pulpit, lay-preacher
like tender Clare, like poor Tom, so that look, Miss!

the ants come to you like children, their beloved teacher
Alix, but unlike the silent recitation of the infants,
the choir that Clare and Tom heard in their rainy county,

we have no solace but utterance, hence this wild cry.
Snails move into harbour, the breadfruit plants on the *Bounty*
will be heaved aboard, and the white God is Captain Bligh.

Across white feathery grave-grass the shadow of the soul
passes, the canvas cracks open on the cross-trees of the *Bounty,*
and the Trades lift the shrouds of the resurrected sail.

All move in their passage to the same mother-country,
the dirt-clawing weasel, the blank owl or sunning seal.
Faith grows mutinous. The ribbed body with its cargo

stalls in its doldrums, the God-captain is cast adrift
by a mutinous Christian, in the wake of the turning *Argo*
plants bob in the ocean's furrows, their shoots dip and lift,

and the soul's Australia is like the New Testament
after the Old World, the code of an eye for an eye;
the horizon spins slowly and Authority's argument

diminishes in power, in the longboat with Captain Bligh.
This was one of your earliest lessons, how the Christ-Son
questions the Father, to settle on another island, haunted by
    Him,

by the speck of a raging deity on the ruled horizon,
diminishing in meaning and distance, growing more dim:
all these predictable passages that we first disobey

before we become what we challenged; but you never altered
your voice, either sighing or sewing, you would pray
to your husband aloud, pedalling the hymns we all heard

in the varnished pew: "There Is a Green Hill Far Away,"
"Jerusalem the Golden." Your melody faltered
but never your faith in the bounty which is His Word.

*v*

All of these waves crepitate from the culture of Ovid,
its sibilants and consonants; a universal metre
piles up these signatures like inscriptions of seaweed

that dry in the pungent sun, lines ruled by mitre
and laurel, or spray swiftly garlanding the forehead
of an outcrop (and I hope this settles the matter

of presences). No soul was ever invented,
yet every presence is transparent; if I met her
(in her nightdress ankling barefoot, crooning to the shallows),

should I call her shadow that of a pattern invented
by Graeco-Roman design, columns of shadows
cast by the Forum, Augustan perspectives—

poplars, casuarina-colonnades, the in-and-out light of almonds
made from original Latin, no leaf but the olive's?
Questions of pitch. Faced with seraphic radiance

(don't interrupt!), mortals rub their skeptical eyes
that hell is a beach-fire at night where embers dance,
with temporal fireflies like thoughts of Paradise;

but there are inexplicable instincts that keep recurring
not from hope or fear only, that are real as stones,
the faces of the dead we wait for as ants are transferring

their cities, though we no longer believe in the shining ones.
I half-expect to see you no longer, then more than half,
almost never, or never then—there I have said it—

but felt something less than final at the edge of your grave,
some other something somewhere, equally dreaded,
since the fear of the infinite is the same as death,

unendurable brightness, the substantial dreading
its own substance, dissolving to gases and vapours,
like our dread of distance; we need a horizon,

a dividing line that turns the stars into neighbours
though infinity separates them, we can think of only one sun:
all I am saying is that the dread of death is in the faces

we love, the dread of our dying, or theirs;
therefore we see in the glint of immeasurable spaces
not stars or falling embers, not meteors, but tears.

*vi*

The mango trees serenely rust when they are in flower,
nobody knows the name for that voluble cedar
whose bell-flowers fall, the pomme-arac purples its floor.

The blue hills in late afternoon always look sadder.
The country night waiting to come in outside the door;
the firefly keeps striking matches, and the hillside fumes

with a bluish signal of charcoal, then the smoke burns
into a larger question, one that forms and unforms,
then loses itself in a cloud, till the question returns.

Buckets clatter under pipes, villages begin at corners.
A man and his trotting dog come back from their garden.
The sea blazes beyond the rust roofs, dark is on us

before we know it. The earth smells of what's done,
small yards brighten, day dies and its mourners
begin, the first wreath of gnats; this was when we sat down

on bright verandahs watching the hills die. Nothing is trite
once the beloved have vanished; empty clothes in a row,
but perhaps our sadness tires them who cherished delight;

not only are they relieved of our customary sorrow,
they are without hunger, without any appetite,
but are part of earth's vegetal fury; their veins grow

with the wild mammy-apple, the open-handed breadfruit,
their heart in the open pomegranate, in the sliced avocado;
ground-doves pick from their palms; ants carry the freight

of their sweetness, their absence in all that we eat,
their savour that sweetens all of our multiple juices,
their faith that we break and chew in a wedge of cassava,

and here at first is the astonishment: that earth rejoices
in the middle of our agony, earth that will have her
for good: wind shines white stones and the shallow's voices.

*vii*

In spring, after the bear's self-burial, the stuttering
crocuses open and choir, glaciers shelve and thaw,
frozen ponds crack into maps, green lances spring

from the melting fields, flags of rooks rise and tatter
the pierced light, the crumbling quiet avalanches
of an unsteady sky; the vole uncoils and the otter

worries his sleek head through the verge's branches;
crannies, culverts, and creeks roar with wrist-numbing water.
Deer vault invisible hurdles and sniff the sharp air,

squirrels spring up like questions, berries easily redden,
edges delight in their own shapes (whoever their shaper).
But here there is one season, our viridian Eden

is that of the primal garden that engendered decay,
from the seed of a beetle's shard or a dead hare
white and forgotten as winter with spring on its way.

There is no change now, no cycles of spring, autumn, winter,
nor an island's perpetual summer; she took time with her;
no climate, no calendar except for this bountiful day.

As poor Tom fed his last crust to trembling birds,
as by reeds and cold pools John Clare blest these thin musicians,
let the ants teach me again with the long lines of words,

my business and duty, the lesson you taught your sons,
to write of the light's bounty on familiar things
that stand on the verge of translating themselves into news:

the crab, the frigate that floats on cruciform wings,
and that nailed and thorn-riddled tree that opens its pews
to the blackbird that hasn't forgotten her because it sings.

# ETHERIDGE KNIGHT *(1931–1991)*

Etheridge Knight was born in Corinth, Mississippi, in 1931. He served in the United States Army during the Korean War and was badly wounded. In 1960 Knight was arrested for armed robbery and sentenced to eight years in prison. While there he began to write poems displaying a deft sense of lyricism and rhetoric, and a strong ear for the rhythms, disappointments, and triumphs of everyday life for impoverished African Americans.

   *Poems from Prison* was published in 1968 by the poet Dudley Randall's Broadside Press. After his release from prison Knight became associated with the Black Arts Movement of the late 1960s and early 1970s. His *Belly Song and Other Poems* was published to great acclaim in 1973. Knight died of cancer in 1991.


## Haiku

### 1

Eastern guard tower
glints in sunset; convicts rest
like lizards on rocks.

### 2

The piano man
is stingy at 3 A.M.
his songs drop like plum.

### 3

Morning sun slants cell.
Drunks stagger like cripple flies
On jailhouse floor.

### 4

To write a blues song
is to regiment riots
and pluck gems from graves.

### 5

A bare pecan tree
slips a pencil shadow down
a moonlit snow slope.

### 6

The falling snow flakes
Cannot blunt the hard aches nor
Match the steel stillness.

### 7

Under moon shadows
A tall boy flashes knife and
Slices star bright ice.

### 8

In the August grass
Struck by the last rays of sun
The cracked teacup screams.

### 9

Making jazz swing in
Seventeen syllables AIN'T
No square poet's job.

# The Idea of Ancestry

## I

Taped to the wall of my cell are 47 pictures: 47 black
faces: my father, mother, grandmothers (1 dead), grand
fathers (both dead), brothers, sisters, uncles, aunts,
cousins (1st & 2nd), nieces, and nephews. They stare
across the space at me sprawling on my bunk. I know
their dark eyes, they know mine. I know their style,
they know mine. I am all of them, they are all of me;
they are farmers, I am a thief, I am me, they are thee.

I have at one time or another been in love with my mother,
1 grandmother, 2 sisters, 2 aunts (I went to the asylum),
and 5 cousins. I am now in love with a 7 yr old niece
(she sends me letters written in large block print, and
her picture is the only one that smiles at me).

I have the same name as 1 grandfather, 3 cousins, 3 nephews,
and 1 uncle. The uncle disappeared when he was 15, just took
off and caught a freight (they say). He's discussed each year
when the family has a reunion, he causes uneasiness in
the clan, he is an empty space. My father's mother, who is 93
and who keeps the Family Bible with everybody's birth dates
(and death dates) in it, always mentions him. There is no
place in her Bible for "whereabouts unknown."

## II

Each Fall the graves of my grandfathers call me, the brown
hills and red gullies of mississippi send out their electric
messages, galvanizing my genes. Last yr/ like a salmon quitting
the cold ocean—leaping and bucking up his birthstream/ I
hitchhiked my way from L.A. with 16 caps in my pocket and a
monkey on my back, and I almost kicked it with the kinfolks.
I walked barefoot in my grandmother's backyard/ I smelled the old

land and the woods /I sipped cornwhiskey from fruit jars with the
   men/
I flirted with the women/ I had a ball till the caps ran out
and my habit came down. That night I looked at my grandmother
and split/ my guts were screaming for junk/ but I was almost
contented/ I had almost caught up with me.
   The next day in Memphis I cracked a croaker's crib for a fix.

This yr there is a gray stone wall damming my stream, and when
the falling leaves stir my genes, I pace my cell or flop on my bunk
and stare at 47 black faces across the space. I am all of them,
they are all of me, I am me, they are thee, and I have no sons
to float in the space between.

## For Freckle-Faced Gerald

Now you take ol Rufus. He beat drums,
was free and funky under the arms,
fucked white girls, jumped off a bridge
(and thought nothing of the sacrilege),
he copped out—and he was over twenty-one.

Take Gerald. Sixteen years hadn't even done
a good job on his voice. He didn't even know
how to talk tough, or how to hide the glow
of life before he was thrown in as "pigmeat"
for the buzzards to eat.

Gerald, who had no memory or hope of copper hot lips—
of firm upthrusting thighs
to reinforce his flow,
let tall walls and buzzards change the course
of his river from south to north.

(No safety in numbers, like back on the block:
two's aplenty. three? definitely not.

four? "you're all muslims."
five? "you were planning a race riot."
plus, Gerald could never quite win
with his precise speech and innocent grin
the trust and fists of the young black cats.)

Gerald, sun-kissed ten thousand times on the nose
and cheeks, didn't stand a chance,
didn't even know that the loss of his balls
had been plotted years in advance
by wiser and bigger buzzards than those
who now hover above his track
and at night light upon his back.

## Dark Prophecy: I Sing of Shine

And, yeah, brothers
while white / america sings about the unsink-
able molly brown
(who was hustling the titanic
when it went down)
I sing to thee of Shine
the stoker who was hip enough to flee the fucking ship
and let the white folks drown
with screams on their lips
(jumped his black ass into the dark sea, Shine did,
broke free from the straining steel).
Yeah, I sing to thee of Shine
and how the millionaire banker stood on the deck
and pulled from his pockets a million dollar check
saying Shine Shine save poor me
and I'll give you all the money a black boy needs—
how Shine looked at the money and then at the sea
and said jump in mothafucka and swim like me—
And Shine swam on—Shine swam on—
and how the banker's daughter ran naked on the deck
with her pink tits trembling and her pants roun her neck

screaming Shine Shine save poor me
and I'll give you all the pussy a black boy needs—
how Shine said now pussy is good and that's no jive
but you got to swim not fuck to stay alive—
And Shine swam on Shine swam on—
How Shine swam past a preacher afloating on a board
crying save *me* nigger Shine in the name of the Lord—
and how the preacher grabbed Shine's arm and broke his stroke—
how Shine pulled his shank and cut the preacher's throat—
And Shine swam on—Shine swam on—
And when the news hit shore that the titanic had sunk
Shine was up in Harlem damn near drunk

# AMIRI BARAKA (LEROI JONES) *(1934–  )*

**A**miri Baraka began his literary career under his original name, LeRoi Jones. In 1952 Jones enrolled at Howard University and after graduating spent three years in the United States Air Force. In 1957 he moved to New York and joined the Beat movement then in full swing in Greenwich Village. He began writing regularly on jazz in the area's popular magazines. His poetry soon attracted interest as well; his *Preface to a Twenty Volume Suicide Note* was published in 1961. The poems from this volume display the author's quick wit and technical skill, in particular his mastery of the avant-garde poetics of William Carlos Williams and Charles Olson.

As the 1960s progressed Jones became increasingly politically active, eventually changing his name. Amiri Baraka has remained a prolific writer. His off-Broadway play *Dutchman* was immensely popular. He has continued to write poetry, espousing a new "Black Aesthetic," the goal of which is to achieve a black nationalist consciousness through a Marxist sense of art as political action.

Baraka is the author of one novel, numerous volumes of verse, a collection of short stories, an autobiography, and many plays. He is the founder of the Black Repertory Arts Theatre in Harlem and Spirit House in Newark. His poetry is largely invested in the cadences and spontaneity of jazz music, his sense of line and meter well-suited for public performance. Baraka currently lives in Newark, New Jersey, and teaches at the State University of New York at Stony Brook.

## Preface to a Twenty Volume Suicide Note

*For Kellie Jones, born 16 May 1959*

Lately, I've become accustomed to the way
The ground opens up and envelops me
Each time I go out to walk the dog.
Or the broad edged silly music the wind
Makes when I run for a bus . . .

Things have come to that.

And now, each night I count the stars,
And each night I get the same number.
And when they will not come to be counted,
I count the holes they leave.

Nobody sings anymore.

And then last night, I tiptoed up
To my daughter's room and heard her
Talking to someone, and when I opened
The door, there was no one there . . .
Only she on her knees, peeking into

Her own clasped hands.


## *from* Hymn to Lanie Poo: Each Morning

### 4

Each morning
I go down
to Gansevoort St.
and stand on the docks.
I stare out
at the horizon
until it gets up
and comes to embrace
me. I
make believe
it is my father.
This is known
as genealogy.

## A Short Speech to My Friends

A political art, let it be
tenderness, low strings the fingers
touch, or the width of autumn
climbing wider avenues, among the virtue
and dignity of knowing what city
you're in, who to talk to, what clothes
—even what buttons—to wear. I address
                              /the society
                              the image, of
                              common utopia.
                                 /The perversity
                                 of separation, isolation,
after so many years of trying to enter their kingdoms,
now they suffer in tears, these others, saxophones whining
through the wooden doors of their less than gracious homes.
The poor have become our creators. The black. The thoroughly
ignorant.
           Let the combination of morality
and inhumanity
begin.


                              2.

Is power, the enemy? (Destroyer
of dawns, cool flesh of valentines, among
the radios, pauses, drunks
of the 19th century. I see it,
as any man's single history. All the possible heroes
dead from heat exhaustion

                         at the beach,
                         or hiding for years from cameras
only to die cheaply in the pages
of our daily lie.
           One hero
has pretensions toward literature
one toward the cultivation of errors, arrogance,
and constantly changing disguises, as trucker, boxer,

valet, barkeep, in the ageing taverns of memory. Making love
to those speedy heroines of masturbation. Or kicking literal evil
continually down filmy public stairs.

A compromise
would be silence. To shut up, even such risk
as the proper placement
of verbs and nouns. To freeze the spit
in mid-air, as it aims itself
at some valiant intellectual's face.
There would be someone
who would understand, for whatever
fancy reason. Dead, lying, Roi, as your children
came up, would also rise. As George Armstrong Custer
these 100 years, has never made
a mistake.


## Three Modes of History and Culture


Chalk mark sex of the nation, on walls we drummers
know
as cathedrals. Cathedra, in a churning meat milk.

Women glide through looking for telephones. Maps
weep
and are mothers and their daughters listening to

music teachers. From heavy beginnings. Plantations,
learning
America, as speech, and a common emptiness. Songs knocking

inside old women's faces. Knocking through cardboard trunks.
Trains
leaning north, catching hellfire in windows, passing through

the first ignoble cities of missouri, to illinois, and the panting
Chicago.
And then all ways, we go where flesh is cheap. Where factories

sit open, burning the chiefs. Make your way! Up through fog and
history
Make your way, and swing the general, that it come flash open

and spill the innards of that sweet thing we heard, and gave theory
to.
Make your way, and swing the general, that it come flash open

and spill the innards of that sweet thing we heard, and gave theory
to.
Breech, bridge, and reach, to where all talk is energy. And there's

enough, for anything singular. All our lean prophets and rhythms.
Entire
we arrive and set up shacks, hole cards, Western hearts at the edge

of saying. Thriving to balance the meanness of particular skies.
Race
of madmen and giants.

Brick songs. Shoe songs. Chants of open weariness.
Knife wiggle early evenings of the wet mouth. Tongue
dance midnight, any season shakes our house. Don't
tear my clothes! To doubt the balance of misery

ripping meat hug shuffle fuck. The Party of Insane
Hope, I've come from there too. Where the dead told lies
about clever social justice. Burning coffins voted
and staggered through cold white streets listening
to Willkie or Wallace or Dewey through the dead face
of Lincoln. Come from there, and belched it out.

I think about a time when I will be relaxed.
When flames and non-specific passion wear themselves
away. And my eyes and hands and mind can turn

and soften, and my songs will be softer
and lightly weight the air.


## Black Art

                Poems are bullshit unless they are
                teeth or trees or lemons piled
                on a step. Or black ladies dying
                of men leaving nickel hearts
                beating them down. Fuck poems
                and they are useful, wd they shoot
                come at you, love what you are,
                breathe like wrestlers, or shudder
                strangely after pissing. We want live
                words of the hip world live flesh &
                coursing blood. Hearts Brains
                Souls splintering fire. We want poems
                like fists beating niggers out of Jocks
                or dagger poems in the slimy bellies
                of the owner-jews. Black poems to
                smear on girdlemamma mulatto bitches
                whose brains are red jelly stuck
                between 'lizabeth taylor's toes. Stinking
                Whores! We want "poems that kill."
                Assassin poems, Poems that shoot
                guns. Poems that wrestle cops into alleys
                and take their weapons leaving them dead
                with tongues pulled out and sent to Ireland. Knockoff
                poems for dope selling wops or slick halfwhite
                politicians Airplane poems, rrrrrrrrrrrrrrrr
                rrrrrrrrrrrrrrr . . . tuhtuhtuhtuhtuhtuhtuhtuhtuh
                . . . rrrrrrrrrrrrrrrr . . . Setting fire and death to
                whities ass. Look at the Liberal
                Spokesman for the jews clutch his throat
                & puke himself into eternity . . . rrrrrrrr
                There's a negroleader pinned to

a bar stool in Sardi's eyeballs melting
in hot flame Another negroleader
on the steps of the white house one
kneeling between the sheriff's thighs
negotiating coolly for his people.
Agggh . . . stumbles across the room . . .
Put it on him, poem. Strip him naked
to the world! Another bad poem cracking
steel knuckles in a jewlady's mouth
Poem scream poison gas on beasts in green berets
Clean out the world for virtue and love,
Let there be no love poems written
until love can exist freely and
cleanly. Let Black People understand
that they are the lovers and the sons
of lovers and warriors and sons
of warriors Are poems & poets &
all the loveliness here in the world

We want a black poem. And a
Black World.
Let the world be a Black Poem
And Let All Black People Speak This Poem
Silently
or LOUD


## Black Bourgeoisie,

      has a gold tooth, sits long hours
      on a stool thinking about money.
      sees white skin in a secret room
      rummages his sense for sense
      dreams about Lincoln (s)
      conks his daughter's hair
      sends his coon to school
      works very hard

grins politely in restaurants
has a good word to say
never says it
does not hate ofays
hates, instead, him self
him black self

## Clay

Killed
by a white woman
on a subway
in 1964.
he rose
      to be the first negro congressman
      from missouri.
      we're not saying
      that being dead
      is the pre
      requisite
      for this honor
      but it certainly helped make him
      what he is
      today.

# AUDRE LORDE *(1934–1992)*

Audre Lorde strove in both her life and her art to embrace, rather than turn from, the complexities of her various identities—as an American, Caribbean, feminist, lesbian, mother, poet, theorist, essayist. Lorde's expansive free verse allowed her in her finest work to merge her collective senses of self, place, and responsibility.

Born in New York City in 1934, Lorde graduated from Hunter College. She continued her education at Columbia University, earning a master's degree in library science. She went on to teach at Tougaloo College in Mississippi, and throughout the City University of New York system. Her volumes of poetry include *From a Land Where Other People Live* (1973), a nominee for the National Book Award; *Coal* (1976); *The Black Unicorn* (1978); *Undersong: Chosen Poems, Old and New* (1992); and *The Collected Poems of Audre Lorde* (1997). She is also the author of *Sister Outsider: Essays and Speeches* (1984), a seminal feminist text. Lorde died in St. Croix of cancer in 1992.

## Separation

The stars dwindle
and will not reward me
even in triumph.

It is possible
to shoot a man
in self defense
and still notice
how his red blood
decorates the snow.

## But What Can You Teach My Daughter

What do you mean
no no no no
you don't have the right
to know
how often
have we built each other
as shelters
against the cold
and even my daughter knows
what you know
can hurt you
she says her nos
and it hurts
she says
when she talks of liberation
she means freedom
from that pain
she knows
what you know
can hurt
but what you do
not know
can kill.

## Revolution Is One Form of Social Change

When the man is busy
making niggers
it doesn't matter much
what shade
you are.

If he runs out of one
particular color

he can always switch
to size
and when he's finished
off the big ones
he'll just change
to sex
which is
after all
where it all began.

# SONIA SANCHEZ  *(1934–  )*

Sonia Sanchez was born in Birmingham, Alabama, in 1934 and raised in Harlem. She graduated from Hunter College in 1955 and went on to work for the Congress of Racial Equality. In the 1960s Sanchez became a vocal political activist in her own right, associated through her teaching and writing with the Black Arts Movement.

Sanchez's poetry is consistently political and, at its best, expresses this deeply felt vision in the context of her personal experience. Beginning with *Homecoming* (1969), her numerous writings—verse, essays, drama, children's stories—are imbued with a lyricism that invokes the vernacular. Sanchez has performed her work around the world. She currently resides in Philadelphia, where she is professor of African American studies at Temple University.

## Reflections After the June 12th March for Disarmament

I have come to you tonite out of the depths
    of slavery
    from white hands peeling black skins over
    america;
I have come out to you from reconstruction eyes
    that closed on black humanity
    that reduced black hope to the dark
    huts of america;
I have come to you from the lynching years,
    the exploitation of black men and women by
    a country that allowed the swinging of
    strange fruits from southern trees;
I have come to you tonite thru the
    delaney years, the du bois years, the
    b. t. washington years, the robeson

years, the garvey years, the
depression years, the you can't eat
or sit or live just die here years,
the civil rights years, the black power
years, the black nationalist years, the
affirmative action years, the liberal
years, the neo-conservative years;
I have come to say that those years
were not in vain, the ghosts of our
ancestors searching this american dust for
rest were not in vain, black women
walking their lives in clots were not
in vain, the years walked
sideways in a forsaken land were not
in vain;
I have come to you tonite as an equal,
as a comrade, as a black woman
walking down a corridor of tears,
looking neither to the left or the right,
pulling my history with bruised
heels,
beckoning to the illusion of america
daring you to look me in the eyes to
see these faces, the exploitation of a
people because of skin pigmentation;
I have come to you tonite because no people
have been asked to be modern day people
with the history of slavery, and still
we walk, and still we talk, and
still we plan, and still we hope and
still we sing;
I have come to you tonite because there are
inhumanitarians in the world. they are not
new. they are old. they go back into history.
they were called explorers, soldiers, mercenaries,
imperialists, missionaries, adventurers,
but they looked at the world for what
it would give up to them and they violated
the land and the people, they looked

at the land and sectioned it up for
private ownership, they looked at the
people and decided how to manipulate
them thru fear and ignorance, they looked
at the gold and began to hoard and
worship it;
I have come to you because it is time
for us all to purge capitalism from
our dreams, to purge materialism
from our eyes, from the planet earth
to deliver the earth again into the hands
of the humanitarians;
I have come to you tonite not just for the stoppage
of nuclear proliferation, nuclear
plants, nuclear bombs, nuclear
waste, but to stop the proliferation
of nuclear minds, of nuclear generals,
of nuclear presidents, of nuclear scientists,
who spread human and nuclear waste
over the world;
I come to you because the world needs to be
saved for the future generations who must
return the earth to peace, who will not
be startled by a man's/woman's skin color;
I come to you because the world needs sanity
now, needs men and women who will
not work to produce nuclear weapons,
who will give up their need for excess
wealth and learn how to share the
world's resources, who will never
again as scientists invent again just
for the sake of inventing;
I come to you because we need to turn our
eyes to the beauty of this planet, to the
bright green laughter of trees, to the beautiful
human animals waiting to smile their unprostituted smiles;
I have come to you to talk about our inexperience
at living as human beings, thru death marches and camps,
thru middle passages and slavery
and thundering countries raining hungry faces;

I am here to move against
    leaving our shadows implanted on the
    earth while our bodies disintegrate in
    nuclear lightning;
I am here between the voices of our ancestors
    and the noise of the planet,
    between the surprise of death and life;
I am here because I shall not give the
    earth up to non-dreamers and earth molesters;
I am here to say to you:
    my body is full of veins
    like the bombs waiting to burst
    with blood.
    we must learn to suckle life not
    bombs and rhetoric
    rising up in redwhiteandblue patriotism;
I am here. and my breath/our breaths
    must thunder across this land
    arousing new breaths. new life.
    new people, who will live in peace
    and honor.

# LUCILLE CLIFTON  (*1936–*  )

Lucille Clifton's is the provocative voice of an artist unafraid of self-reflection in the public sphere. Clifton poeticizes many of her most private concerns in a stark yet elegant free verse; her poetry, primarily short lyrics, has been widely praised for its lucid portraiture of the interior dimensions of African American life.

Born in Depew, New York, in 1936, Clifton attended both Howard University and Fredonia State Teachers College. Her work, including her acclaimed children's books, has appeared consistently throughout the past four decades. Among Clifton's volumes of poetry are *Good News About the Earth* (1972), *Two Headed Woman* (1980), and *Quilting* (1991). She currently lives in Baltimore.

## miss rosie

when i watch you
wrapped up like garbage
sitting, surrounded by the smell
of too old potato peels
or
when i watch you
in your old man's shoes
with the little toe cut out
sitting, waiting for your mind
like next week's grocery
i say
when i watch you
you wet brown bag of a woman
who used to be the best looking gal in georgia
used to be called the Georgia Rose
i stand up
through your destruction
i stand up

## the lost baby poem

the time i dropped your almost body down
down to meet the waters under the city
and run one with the sewage to the sea
what did i know about waters rushing back
what did i know about drowning
or being drowned

you would have been born into winter
in the year of the disconnected gas
and no car      we would have made the thin
walk over genesee hill into the canada wind
to watch you slip like ice into strangers' hands
you would have fallen naked as snow into winter
if you were here i could tell you these
and some other things

if i am ever less than a mountain
for your definite brothers and sisters
let the rivers pour over my head
let the sea take me for a spiller
of seas      let black men call me stranger
always      for your never named sake


## light on my mother's tongue

light
on my mother's tongue
breaks through her soft
extravagant hip
into life.
lucille
she calls the light,
which was the name

of the grandmother
who waited by the crossroads
in virginia
and shot the whiteman off his horse,
killing the killer of sons.
light breaks from her life
to her lives . . .
mine already is
an afrikan name.

## to ms. ann

i will have to forget
your face
when you watched me breaking
in the fields,
missing my children.

i will have to forget
your face
when you watched me carry
your husband's
stagnant water.

i will have to forget
your face
when you handed me
your house
to make a home,

and you never called me sister
then, you never called me sister
and it has only been forever and
i will have to forget your face.

## why some people be mad at me sometimes

they ask me to remember
but they want me to remember
their memories
and i keep on remembering
mine.

## to my friend, jerina

listen,
when i found there was no safety
in my father's house
i knew there was none anywhere.
you are right about this,
how i nurtured my work
not my self, how i left the girl
wallowing in her own shame
and took on the flesh of my mother.
but listen,
the girl is rising in me,
not willing to be left to
the silent fingers in the dark,
and you are right,
she is asking for more than
most men are able to give,
but she means to have what she
has earned,
sweet sighs, safe houses,
hands she can trust.

# white lady

*a street name for cocaine*

wants my son
wants my niece
wants josie's daughter
holds them hard
and close as slavery
what will it cost
to keep our children
what will it cost
to buy them back.

white lady
says i want you
whispers
let me be your lover
whispers
run me through your
fingers
feel me smell me taste me
love me
nobody understands you like
white lady

white lady
you have chained our sons
in the basement
of the big house
white lady

you have walked our daughters
out into the streets
white lady
what do we have to pay
to repossess our children
white lady

what do we have to owe
to own our own at last


## 4/30/92 for Rodney King

                    so
                    the body
                    of one black man
                    is rag and stone
                    is mud
                    and blood
                    the body of one
                    black man
                    contains no life
                    worth loving
                    so the body
                    of one black man
                    is nobody
                    mama
                    mama
                    mamacita
                    is there no value
                    in this skin
                    mama
                    mama
                    if we are nothing
                    why
                    should we spare
                    the neighborhood
                    mama
                    mama
                    who will be next and
                    why should we save
                    the pictures

# slaveship

loaded like spoons
into the belly of Jesus
where we lay for weeks      for months
in the sweat and stink of our own
breathing
Jesus
why do you not protect us
chained to the heart of the Angel
where the prayers we never tell
are hot and red as our bloody ankles
Jesus
Angel
can these be men
who vomit us out from ships
called Jesus      Angel      Grace of God
onto a heathen country
Jesus
Angel
ever again
can this tongue speak
can this bone walk
Grace of God
can this sin live

jesus and angel and grace of god were the names of slaveships

# JAY WRIGHT  *(1935–  )*

Jay Wright's vision of America is among the most far-reaching of
any contemporary American poet. Wright seeks through history, a
range of myth (from West African to Mesoamerican), and personal
reflection to chart not only this country's but the continent's jour-
ney into modernity. In this poetic effort to trace the dense geologic
layering of a nation's soul, he continues to expand the boundaries
of the African American tradition. His literary ancestors include
Robert Hayden, W. E. B. Du Bois, Benjamin Banneker, Ralph Elli-
son, Hart Crane, Rainer Maria Rilke, and Wole Soyinka, though
Wright's meditative tone and delicately crafted language are
uniquely his own. Like Hayden, Wright is equally adept at the short
lyric and the dense, multipart epic.

Wright was born in Albuquerque, New Mexico, in 1935 and
was educated at the University of California at Berkeley and Rut-
gers. He has received both Guggenheim and MacArthur fellow-
ships. He is the author of nine volumes of poetry, including *Selected
Poems of Jay Wright* (1987), edited by Robert B. Stepto. Wright
currently resides in New Hampshire.

## Journey to the Place of Ghosts

> *Wolbe dich, Welt:*
> *Wenn die Totenmuschel heranschwimmt,*
> *will es hier lauten.*
>
> *Vault over, world:*
> *when the seashell of death washes up*
> *there will be a knelling.*
> > —Paul Celan, *Stimmen* (Voices)

Death knocks all night at my door.
The soul answers,
and runs from the water in my throat.

Water will sustain me when I climb
                    the steep hill
that leads to a now familiar place.
I began, even as a child, to learn water's order,  ·
and, as I grew intact, the feel of its warmth
in a new sponge, of its weight in a virgin towel.
I have earned my wine in another's misery,
when rum bathed a sealed throat
and cast its seal on the ground.
I will be bound, to the one who leads me away,
by the ornaments on my wrists, the gold dust
in my ears, below my eye and tied to my
                    loin cloth in a leather pouch.
They dress me now in my best cloth,
and fold my hands, adorned with silk,
                    against my left cheek.
Gold lies with me on my left side.
Gold has become the color of distance,
                    and of your sorrow.

Sorrow lies, red clay on my brow.
Red pepper caresses my temples.
I am adorned in the russet-brown message
the soul brings from its coming-to-be.
There is a silken despair in my body
that grief shakes from it,
a cat's voice, controlled by palm-wine
                    and a widow's passion.
It is time to feed the soul
  —a hen, eggs, mashed yams—
and encourage the thirst resting
near the right hand I see before me.
                Always I think of death.
                    I cannot eat.
            I walk in sadness, and I die
Yet life is the invocation sealed in the coffin,
and will walk through our wall,
passing and passing and passing,
                until it is set down,
to be lifted from this body's habitation.

I now assume the widow's pot,
the lamp that will lead me through solitude,
to the edge of my husband's journey.
I hold three stones upon my head,
darkness I will release when I run
from the dead,
with my eyes turned away
                toward another light.

This is the day of rising.
A hut sits in the bush, sheltered by summe,
standing on four forked ends.
We have prepared for the soul's feast
with pestle, mortar, a strainer, three
hearthstones, a new pot and new spoon.
Someone has stripped the hut's body
and dressed it with the edowa.
Now, when the wine speaks
and the fire has lifted its voice,
the dead will be clothed in hair,
                the signs of our grief.
Sun closes down on an intensity of ghosts.
It is time to close the path.
It is time for the snail's pace
of coming again into life,
                with the world swept clean,
                the crying done,
and our ordinary garments decent in the dead one's eyes.

Boleros 19

### CLIO—KHU

In my Binu shrine, the sogo altars pull me home.
The stone I lay upon on Teo found itself
in a dance of stones,
four sisters turning near a brown pond,

each a promise of the sea within me.
For years now, Bamako has been dry.
Millstones,
                which held Nommo's
                        and the rain god's gifts,
fade into the bilious doors.
Nevertheless,
the bilu still whisper in spirit ears,
and my father seeds my spirit
                with the first fruits of autumn,
pots that address the dead in me.
Yet I know myself an "intangible ethereal casing,"
lucent intelligence,
heavenbound by being bound to the emblems
                                of my person.

Clio call me,
scroll of the brave,
with one foot in the bush,
                one foot in the city,
a human tongue fit for taunting
the pretensions of pure love,
and an ear for the wind sound of a woman
riding a seashell into this desert desolation.
Though I have second sight,
my creations wither and die.
The balance I found easy escapes from my gardens.
I continue to weave my checkerboard,
cloth of the Word,
healing music of the head,
my soul's improvisation.


*(Art Tatum)*


When I sit at the piano,
I don't count the keys.
I see you looking at my eyes;
you wonder what I see.
What I see is in my touch,
and in the assurance
that the sound will be right there.

Some cats always carp.
They say the music isn't mine,
keep asking me for "an original."
So I lay two notes in the bar ahead,
diminish a major,
tunnel through the dark
of the brightest minor,
and come out on the right side of the song.
I pick the composer's pocket,
and lay the hidden jewels out there.
This wired, hammering woman
wants her fortune told.
Hammer and anvil guide the music of my house,
smithy of the ear's anticipation, forge
of the mind in what it denies
              and what it fulfills.
On the terrace,
altars resonate with the water sound
of goatskin over hollow wood,
and the frog pitch of the mudbanks
within the house
             answer.
I dream of the smith music within me,
and hear its cithara voice in the dyeli's craft.

## The Healing Improvisation of Hair

If you undo your do you would
be strange. Hair has been on my mind.
I used to lean in the doorway
and watch my stony woman wind
the copper through the black, and play
with my understanding, show me she could
take a cup of river water,
and watch it shimmy, watch it change,
turn around and become ash bone.
Wind in the cottonwoods wakes me

to a day so thin its breastbone
shows, so paid out it shakes me free
of its blue dust. I will arrange
that river water, bottom juice.
I conjure my head in the stream
and ride with the silk feel of it
as my woman bathes me, and shaves
away the scorn, sponges the grit
of solitude from my skin, laves
the salt water of self-esteem
over my feathering body.
How like joy to come upon me
in remembering a head of hair
and the way water would caress
it, and stress beauty in the flair
and cut off the only witness
to my dance under sorrow's tree.
   This swift darkness is spring's first hour.

I carried my life, like a stone,
in a ragged pocket, but I
had a true weaving song, a sly
way with rhythm, a healing tone.

## The Albuquerque Graveyard

It would be easier
to bury our dead
at the corner lot.
No need to wake
before sunrise,
take three buses,
walk two blocks,
search at the rear
of the cemetery,
to come upon the familiar names
with wilted flowers and patience.

But now I am here again.
After so many years
of coming here,
passing the sealed mausoleums,
the pretentious brooks and springs,
the white, sturdy limestone crosses,
the pattern of the place is clear to me.
I am going back
to the Black limbo,
an unwritten history
of our own tensions.
The dead lie here
in a hierarchy of small defeats.
I can almost see the leaders smile,
ashamed now of standing
at the head of those
who lie tangled
at the edge of the cemetery
still ready to curse and rage
as I do.
Here, I stop by the imitative cross
of one who stocked his parlor
with pictures of Robeson,
and would boom down the days,
dreaming of Othello's robes.
I say he never bothered me,
and forgive his frightened singing.
Here, I stop by the simple mound
of a woman who taught me
spelling on the sly,
parsing my tongue
to make me fit for her own dreams.
I could go on all day,
unhappily recognizing small heroes,
discontent with finding them here,
reproaches to my own failings.
Uneasy, I search the names
and simple mounds I call my own,
abruptly drop my wilted flowers,
and turn for home.

## Love in the Weather's Bells

Snow hurries
the strawberries
from the bush.
Star-wet water rides
you into summer,
into my autumn.
Your cactus hands
are at my heart again.
Lady, I court
my dream of you
in lilies and in rain.
I vest myself
in your oldest memory
and in my oldest need.
And in my passion
you are the deepest blue
of the oldest rose.
Star circle me an axe.
I cannot cut myself
from any of your emblems.
It will soon be cold here,
and dark here;
the grass will lie flat
to search for its spring head.
I will bow again
in the winter of your eyes.
If there is music,
it will be the weather's bells
to call me to the abandoned chapel
of your simple body.

# Meta-A and the A of Absolutes

I write my God in blue.
I run my gods upstream on flimsy rafts.
I bathe my goddesses in foam, in moonlight.
I take my reasons from my mother's snuff breath,
or from an old woman, sitting with a lemonade,
at twilight, on the desert's steps.
Brown by day and black by night,
my God has wings that open to no reason.
He scutters from the touch of old men's eyes,
scutters from the smell of wisdom, an orb
of light leaping from a fire.
Press him he bleeds.
When you take your hand to sacred water,
there is no sign of any wound.
And so I call him supreme, great artist,
judge of time, scholar of all living event,
the possible prophet of the possible event.
Blind men, on bourbon, with guitars,
blind men with their scars dulled by kola,
blind men seeking the shelter of a raindrop,
blind men in corn, blind men in steel,
reason by their lights that our tongues
are free, our tongues will redeem us.
Speech is the fact, and the fact is true.
What is moves, and what is moving is.
We cling to these contradictions.
We know we will become our contradictions,
our complex body's-own desire.
Yet speech is not the limit of our vision.
The ear entices itself with any sound.
The skin will caress whatever tone
or temperament that rises or descends.
The bones will set themselves to a dance.
The blood will argue with a bird in flight.
The heart will scale the dew from an old chalice,
brush and thrill to an old bone.

And yet there is no sign to arrest us
                            from the possible.
We remain at rest there, in transit
from our knowing to our knowledge.
So I would set a limit where I meet my logic.
I would clamber from my own cave
into the curve of sign, an alphabet
of transformation, the clan's cloak of reason.
I am good when I am in motion,
when I think of myself at rest
in the knowledge of my moving,
when I have the vision of my mother at rest,
in moonlight, her lap the cradle of my father's head.
I am good when I trade my shells,
and walk from boundary to boundary,
unarmed and unafraid of another's speech.
I am good when I learn the world
through the touch of my present body.
I am good when I take the cove of a cub
                            into my care.
I am good when I hear the changes in my body
echo all my changes down the years,
when what I know indeed is what I would
                            know in deed.
I am good when I know the darkness of all light,
and accept the darkness, not as sign, but as my body.
This is the A of absolutes,
the logbook of judgments,
the good sign.


## The Lake in Central Park


It should have a woman's name,
something to tell us how the green skirt of land
                            has bound its hips.
When the day lowers its vermilion tapestry over the west ridge,
the water has the sound of leaves shaken in a sack,

and the child's voice that you have heard below

                                  sings of the sea.

By slow movements of the earth's crust,
or is it that her hip bones have been shaped
by a fault of engineering?
Some coquetry cycles this blue edge,
a spring ready to come forth to correct

                                  love's mathematics.

Saturday rises immaculately.
The water's jade edge plays against corn colored
picnic baskets, rose and lemon bottles, red balloons,
dancers in purple tights, a roan mare out of its field.
It is not the moment to think of Bahia
and the gray mother with her water explanation.
Not far from here, the city, a mass of swift water
in its own depression, licks its sores.

Still, I would be eased by reasons.
Sand dunes in drifts.
Lava cuts its own bed at a mountain base.
Blindness enters where the light refuses to go.
In Loch Lomond, the water flowers with algae
and a small life has taken the name of a star.

You will hear my star-slow heart
empty itself with a light-swift pitch
where the water thins to a silence.
And the woman who will not be named
screams in the birth of her fading away.

## Desire's Persistence

> Yo ave del agua floreciente duro en fiesta.
> "Deseo de persistencia,"
> *Poesia Náhuatl*

### I

In the region of rain and cloud,
I live in shade,
under the moss mat of days bruised
            purple with desire.
My dominion is a song in the wide ring of water.
There, I run to and fro,
braiding the logical act
            in the birth of an Ear of Corn,
polychromatic story I will now tell
in the weaving, power's form in motion,
a devotion to the unstressed.
Once, I wreathed around a king,
became a fishing-net, a maze,
            "a deadly wealth of robe."
Mothers who have heard me sing take heart;
I always prick them into power.

### 2

> Y vengo alzando al viento la roja flor de invierno.
> I lift the red flower of winter into the wind.
> *Poesia Náhuatl*

### I

Out of the ninth circle,
a Phoenician boat rocks upward into light
and the warmth of a name—given to heaven—
that arises in the ninth realm.
Earth's realm discloses the Egyptian

on the point of invention,
               deprived of life and death,
heart deep in the soul's hawk,
a thymos shadow knapping the tombed body.
Some one or thing is always heaven bound.
Some flowered log doubles my bones.
The spirit of Toltec turtledoves escapes.
A sharp, metaphorical cry sends me
               into the adorned sepulchre,
and the thing that decays learns
             how to speak its name.

*Lift*

Down Hidalgo,
past Alvarado and Basurto,
I walk a straight line
to the snailed Paseo Los Berros.
Here, at noon, the sun,
     a silver bead,
veils what the dawn has displayed.
Even so,
   I have taken up the morning's bond again
   —the lake with its pendulum leg
   shining in the distance,
   the boy in white
   hauling his bottle of chalky milk home.

I know I sit in the deep of a city
with its brocade of hills,
where a thin rain is an evening's fire.
I have heard the women sing
near their gas lamps,
when the rose end of day lights a hunger
for the garlanded soups and meat they prepare.
Often, I have taken the high ground
by the pond, over a frog's voice
             dampened by lilies,
and been exalted by the soothsayer

who knows I'm not at home.
I am the arcane body,
raised at the ninth hour,
to be welcomed by the moonlight
              of such spirited air.
I am the Dane of degrees
who realizes how the spirit glows
              even as it descends.

## Red

The heart, catalectic though it be, does glow,
responds to every midnight bell within you.
This is a discourse on reading heat,
the flushed char of burned moments one sees
after the sexton's lamp flows
over the body's dark book.
There is suspicion
here that violet
traces of
sacrifice
stand
bare.

## Flower

This marble dust recalls that sunset
with the best burgundy, and the way,
after the charm of it, the peacocks
escaped their cages on the green.
I would now embellish the flame
that ornaments you,
even as it once in that moment
                        did.

I carry you blossomed,
cream and salt of a high crown.
You *must* flare,
          stream forth,

blister and scale me,
even as you structure the enveloping kiss,
        sporophore of our highest loss.

*Winter*

Under the evergreens,
the grouse have gone under the snow.
Women who follow their fall flight
tell us that, if you listen, you can hear
their dove's voices ridge the air,
a singing that follows us to a bourne
        released from its heat sleep.
We have come to an imagined line,
        celestial,
that binds us to the burr of a sheltered thing
and rings us with a fire that will not dance,
        in a horn that will not sound.
We have learned, like these birds,
to publish our decline,
when over knotted apples and straw-crisp leaves,
the slanted sun welcomes us once again
to the arrested music in the earth's divided embrace.

*Wind*

Through winter,
harmattan blacks the air.
My body fat with oil,
I become another star at noon,
when the vatic insistence
of the dog star's breath clings to me.
Though I am a woman,
I turn south,
toward the fire,
and hear the spirits in the bush.
But this is my conceit:
water will come from the west,
and I will have my trance,
        be reborn,

perhaps in a Mediterranean air,
the Rhone delta's contention
with the eastern side of rain.
In all these disguises,
I follow the aroma of power.
So I am charged in my own field,
to give birth to the solar wind,
particles spiraling around the line
                              of my body,
moving toward the disruption,
the moment when the oil of my star at noon
                              is a new dawn.


3


I shall go away, I shall disappear,
I shall be stretched on a bed of yellow roses
and the old women will cry for me.
So the Toltecas wrote: their books are finished,
but your heart has become perfect.

# MICHAEL S. HARPER  *(1938–     )*

Michael S. Harper was born in 1938 in Brooklyn, New York, and moved with his family to Los Angeles at the age of thirteen. He was educated at California State University at Los Angeles and the University of Iowa. A chance correspondence with Gwendolyn Brooks, who had enthusiastically read his manuscript, led to the publication of *Dear John, Dear Coltrane* in 1970.

Harper's distinct poetic voicings are inflected throughout with the tonal qualities of jazz and the blues, though firmly placed in the Western tradition by their comprehensive vision of the textures and complexities of history. He has steadily expanded his reach to encompass more of the American and world landscape, tracing personal and family linkages and creating a dense, allusive mosaic of soul and race.

Harper is the author of *History Is Your Own Heartbeat* (1971), *Song: I Want a Witness* (1972), *Images of Kin* (1977), and *Honorable Amendments* (1995), among others. He has taught at Brown University since 1970; his other teaching positions have included Harvard, Yale, Colgate, and NYU.

## Dear John, Dear Coltrane

*a love supreme, a love supreme*
*a love supreme, a love supreme*


Sex fingers toes
in the marketplace
near your father's church
in Hamlet, North Carolina—
witness to this love
in this calm fallow
of these minds,
there is no substitute for pain:
genitals gone or going,

seed burned out,
you tuck the roots in the earth,
turn back, and move
by river through the swamps,
singing: *a love supreme, a love supreme;*
what does it all mean?
Loss, so great each black
woman expects your failure
in mute change, the seed gone.
You plod up into the electric city—
your song now crystal and
the blues. You pick up the horn
with some will and blow
into the freezing night:
*a love supreme, a love supreme—*

Dawn comes and you cook
up the thick sin 'tween
impotence and death, fuel
the tenor sax cannibal
heart, genitals and sweat
that makes you clean—
*a love supreme, a love supreme—*
*Why you so black?*
*cause I am*
*why you so funky?*
*cause I am*
*why you so black?*
*cause I am*
*why you so sweet?*
*cause I am*
*why you so black?*
*cause I am*
*a love supreme, a love supreme:*

So sick
you couldn't play *Naima,*
so flat we ached
for song you'd concealed
with your own blood,

your diseased liver gave
out its purity,
the inflated heart
pumps out, the tenor kiss,
tenor love:
*a love supreme, a love supreme—*
*a love supreme, a love supreme—*


## For Bud


Could it be, Bud
that in slow galvanized
fingers beauty seeped
into *bop* like Bird
*weed* and Diz clowned—
Sugar waltzing
back into dynamite,
sweetest left hook you
ever dug, baby;
could it violate violence
Bud, like Leadbelly's
chaingang chuckle,
the candied yam
twelve string clutch
of all blues:
there's no rain
anywhere, soft
enough for you.

*for Bud Powell*

# We Assume: On the Death of Our Son, Reuben Masai Harper

We assume
that in 28 hours,
lived in a collapsible isolette,
you learned to accept pure oxygen
as the natural sky;
the scant shallow breaths
that filled those hours
cannot, did not make you fly—
but dreams were there
like crooked palmprints on
the twin-thick windows of the nursery—
in the glands of your mother.

We assume
the sterile hands
drank chemicals in and out
from lungs opaque with mucus,
pumped your stomach,
*eeked* the bicarbonate in
crooked, green-winged veins,
out in a plastic mask;

A woman who'd lost her first son
consoled us with an angel gone ahead
to pray for our family—
gone into that sky
seeking oxygen,
gone into autopsy,
a fine brown powdered sugar,
a disposable cremation:

We assume
you did not know we loved you.

# Here Where Coltrane Is

Soul and race
are private dominions,
memories and modal
songs, a tenor blossoming,
which would paint suffering
a clear color but is not in
this Victorian house
without oil in zero-degree
weather and a forty-mile-an-hour wind;
it is all a well-knit family:
*a love supreme*.
Oak leaves pile up on walkway
and steps, catholic as apples
in a special mist of clear white
children who love my children.
I play "Alabama"
on a warped record player
skipping the scratches
on your faces over the fibrous
conical hairs of plastic
under the wooden floors.

Dreaming on a train from New York
to Philly, you hand out six
notes which become an anthem
to our memories of you:
oak, birch, maple,
apple, cocoa, rubber.
For this reason Martin is dead;
for this reason Malcolm is dead;
for this reason Coltrane is dead;
in the eyes of my first son are the browns
of these men and their music.

# Last Affair: Bessie's Blues Song

Disarticulated
arm torn out,
large veins cross
her shoulder intact,
her tourniquet
her blood in all-white big bands:

*Can't you see*
*what love and heartache's done to me*
*I'm not the same as I used to be*
*this is my last affair*

Mail truck or parked car
in the fast lane,
afloat at forty-three
on a Mississippi road,
Two-hundred-pound muscle on her ham bone,
'nother nigger dead 'fore noon:

*Can't you see*
*what love and heartache's done to me*
*I'm not the same as I used to be*
*this is my last affair*

Fifty-dollar record
cut the vein in her neck,
fool about her money
toll her black train wreck,
white press missed her fun'ral
in the same stacked deck:

*Can't you see*
*what love and heartache's done to me*
*I'm not the same as I used to be*
*this is my last affair*

Loved a little blackbird
heard she could sing,
Martha in her vineyard
pestle in her spring,
Bessie had a bad mouth
made my chimes ring:

*Can't you see*
*what love and heartache's done to me*
*I'm not the same as I used to be*
*this is my last affair*

## Br'er Sterling and the Rocker

Any fool knows a Br'er in a rocker
is a boomerang incarnate; look at the blade
of the rocker, that wondrous crescent
rockin' in harness as poem.

To speak of poetry is the curled line straightened;
to speak of doubletalk, the tongue
gone pure, the stoic line a trestle
whistlin', a man a train comin' on:

Listen Br'er Sterling
steel-drivin' man, folk-said, folk-sayin',
that chair's a blues-harnessed star
turnin' on its earthy axis;

Miss Daisy, latch on that star's arc,
hold on sweet mama; Br'er Sterling's rocker glows.

## Nightmare Begins Responsibility

I place these numbed wrists to the pane
watching white uniforms whisk over
him in the tube-kept
prison
fear what they will do in experiment
watch my gloved stickshifting gasolined hands
breathe *boxcar-information-please* infirmary tubes
distrusting white-pink mending paperthin
silkened end hairs, distrusting tubes
shrunk in his *trunk-skincapped*
shaven head, in thighs
*distrusting-white-hands-picking-baboon-light*
on this son who will not make his second night
of this wardstrewn intensive airpocket
where his father's asthmatic
hymns of *night-train,* train done gone
his mother can only know that he has flown
up into essential calm unseen corridor
going boxscarred home, *mamaborn, sweetsonchild*
*gonedowntown into researchtestingwarehousebatteryacid*
*mama-son-done-gone*/me telling her 'nother
train tonight, no music, no breathstroked
heartbeat in my infinite distrust of them:

and of my distrusting self
*white-doctor-who-breathed-for-him-all-night*
say it for two sons gone,
say nightmare, say it loud
panebreaking heartmadness:
nightmare begins responsibility.

## In Hayden's Collage

Van Gogh would paint the landscape
green—or somber blue;
if you could see the weather
in Amsterdam in June, or August,
you'd cut your lobe too,
perhaps simply on heroin,
the best high in the world,
instead of the genius of sunflowers,
blossoming trees. The Japanese
bridge in Hiroshima,
precursor to the real impression,
modern life, goes to Windsor, Ontario,
or Jordan, or the Natchez
Trace. From this angle, earless,
a torsioned Django Rhinehart
accompanies Josephine. You know
those rainbow children couldn't
get along in this *ole worl'*.

Not over that troubled water;
and when the band would play once
too often in Arkansas, or Paris,
you'd cry because the sunset was too
bright to see the true colors,
the first hue, and so nearsighted
you had to touch the spiderman's
bouquet; you put your arcane colors
to the spatula and cook
to force the palate in the lion's
den—to find God in all the light
the paintbrush would let in—
the proper colors,
the corn, the wheat, the valley,
dike, the shadows, and the heart
of self—minnow of the universe,
your flaccid fishing pole,
pieced together, never broken, never end.

# Angola (Louisiana)

Three-fourths Mississippi
River, one-fourth rattlesnakes,
and for company, razorwire
fences, experiments from South
Africa, aging behind bars,
all in their seventies,
with no parole; perhaps
2500 natural life sentences,
30-year lifers behind bars.

Still, the roads have flowers;
and in the prison hospital
the Lifers Association creed
is in full bloom, technical
supernovas of the TV world:
you avoid mirrors as you can't
avoid hard labor, false teeth,
high blood pressure, rape:
all this in the prison magazine.

Wheelchair has transcended mirrors;
he dreams about theft and harassment
as a prison underwater,
decompression channels of the bends,
cheap guards in scuba tanks,
for he is never coming up;
it is "too exotic," he says,
and you hunger for the fields
you were broken in;
you hunger for your white neighbors,
dragon deputies, the KKK,
as you count the gray hairs
on the sideview of your mustache.

After three heart attacks
you can stand gospel music,
sports, violence, drugs,

for deathrow education
is bimonthly books,
the old folks' home on this shuttle.

I was born on False River:
tell my story in amplitude
from one slavery to another;
give me the pure medicine
for rape, murder, the nectar
in balm for the barroom fight:
teach me to read, and write.

*For Ernest J. Gaines*


## Psalm

Strange
that a harp
of a thousand
strings
should stay
in tune
so long

*Katherine Johnson Harper, 1913–1988*
*in memoriam*


## Release

*Kind of Blue*

Miles (being ahead)
came in early

with the sketches
he did not mention Japanese

visual art
though Bill Evans did

his liner notes
stretching each brushstroke

as metaphor
for playing together

Because you cannot go back
resonance builds

new material
at a recording session

only once
in a lifetime

For these players
five settings

and a figure
who asked of us

to do this
perfectly

as if to play *live*
alone in a group

Miles asked
we answered

# The Ghost of Soul-making

*"On that day it was decreed who shall live and who shall die."*
—Yom Kippur prayer

*"Art in its ultimate always celebrates the victory."*


The ghost appears in the dark of winter,
sometimes in the light of summer, in the light
of spring, confronts you behind the half-door
in the first shock of morning,
often after-hours, with bad memories to stunt
your day, whines in twilight, whines in the umbrella of trees.

He stands outside the locked doors, rain or shine;
he constructs the stuntwork of allegiances
in the form of students, in the form of the half-measure
of blankets—he comes to parade rest in the itch of frost
on the maple, on the cherry caught in the open field
of artillery; he remembers the battlefields of the democratic
order; he marks each accent through the gates of the orchard
singing in the cadences of books—
you remember books burned, a shattering of crystals,
prayers for now, and in the afterlife, Germany of the northern
lights of Kristallnacht, the ashes of synagogues.

The ghost turns to your mother as if he believed
in penance, in wages earned, in truth places these flowers
you have brought with your own hands,
irises certainly, and the dalmatian rose,
whose fragrance calms every hunger in religious feast or fast.
Into her hands, these blossoms, her fragrant palms.
There is no wedding ring in the life of ghosts,
no sacred asp on the wrist in imperial cool,
but there is a bowl on the reception table,
offerings of Swiss black licorice.
On good days the bowl would entice the dream
of husband, children, and grandchildren;

on good days one could build a synagogue in one's own city,
call it *city of testimony, conscious city of words.*
In this precinct male and female, the ghost commences, the ghost
    disappears.

What of the lady in the half-door of the enlightenment:
tact, and a few scarves, a small indulgence for a frugal
woman; loyalty learned in the lost records of intricate relations:
how to remember, how to forget the priceless injuries
on a steno tablet, in the tenured cabinets of the files.
At birth, and before, the ghost taught understanding:
that no history is fully a record, for the food we will eat
is never sour on the tongue, lethal, or not, as a defenseless
scapegoat, the tongue turned over, as compost is turned over,
to sainthood which makes the palate sing. These are jewels
in the service of others; this is her song. She reaps
the great reward of praise, where answers do not answer,
when the self, unleashed from the delicate bottle,
wafts over the trees at sunrise and forgives the dusk.

*For Ruth Oppenheim*

## My Father's Face

### *Schomburg Archives*

Over his fastidious hands
his voice breaks,
and because he had executed
the bequest
(typing the book lists
sermons in manuscript
& unlisted artifacts)
on his son's birthday
in the Brooklyn brownstone,
this is a double loss,
unbeknownst, even to him,

at this late date
in the March snow,
*how much the past costs;*
how much the health
of one's nation
as neighborhood,
is stored in the family,
the archives,
the handwriting
of our saints & sinners,
and the forgiveness
of sin's remembering.
(As for the saints)
For now the ancient folders
are enough for the sorrow,
which is grief over my mother's
life, and the grand thematics
of a little girl,
polishing her jacks
on her grandfather's marble
steps, too close, even for him,
to the Germantown governors
who account for the meal
and his till.

We are here on the edge
of another parade,
a huge mural
as a gate,
east and west,
in honor of Nat Cole's walk,
as if his majesty
on the keyboard,
the lilt of his Montgomery
voice,
was a memorial to running water,
to stone, and the masonry
of singing on the stone,
which was his pledge,
which was his right.

This is the penmanship
of song; we are journalists
for the race this Saturday,
in honor of Saturday's child,
a sacred seat with the father.

# ISHMAEL REED *(1938– )*

Ishmael Reed was born in Chattanooga, Tennessee, in 1938 and raised in Buffalo, New York. He attended the State University of New York at Buffalo before moving to New York City, where he wrote his novel *Mumbo Jumbo* (1972), which won him international acclaim. Reed has since published consistently, establishing a formidable reputation as a poet, novelist, essayist, and general supporter of the arts.

Reed's poetry, like his prose, uses parody and satire as vehicles for the investigation of African and African American folk experience as read against the grain of both popular culture and myth. Reed is the recipient of a MacArthur Award. He has taught at Harvard, Yale, and Dartmouth, and currently teaches at the University of California at Berkeley.

## Dualism

### *In Ralph Ellison's* Invisible Man

I am outside of
history. i wish
i had some peanuts, it
looks hungry there in
its cage

i am inside of
history. its
hungrier than i
thot

.05

If i had a nickel
For all the women who've
Rejected me in my life
I would be the head of the
World Bank with a flunkie
To hold my derby as i
Prepared to fly chartered
Jet to sign a check
Giving India a new lease
On life.

If i had a nickel for
All the women who've loved
Me in my life i would be
The World Bank's assistant
Janitor and wouldn't need
To wear a derby
All i'd think about would
Be going home

## Paul Laurence Dunbar in the Tenderloin

Even at 26, the hush when
you unexpectedly walked
into a theatre. One year
after *The History of Cakewalk*.

Desiring not to cause
a fuss, you sit alone
in the rear, watching a re
hearsal.
The actors are impressed. Wel
don Johnson, so super at des
cription, jots it all down.

I don't blame you for
disliking Whitman, Paul.
He lacked your style, like
your highcollared mandalaed
portrait in hayden's
*Kaleidoscope;* unobserved,
Death, the uncouth critic
does a first draft on your
              breath.


# I Am a Cowboy in the Boat of Ra

*The devil must be forced to reveal any such physical evil (potions,
charms, fetishes, etc.) still outside the body and these must be burned.*
      —*Rituale Romanum,* published 1947, endorsed by the coat-of-
      arms and introductory letter from Francis Cardinal Spellman


I am a cowboy in the boat of Ra,
sidewinders in the saloons of fools
bit my forehead      like      O
the untrustworthiness of Egyptologists
who do not know their trips. Who was that
dog-faced man? they asked, the day I rode
from town.

School marms with halitosis cannot see
the Nefertiti fake chipped on the run by slick
germans, the hawk behind Sonny Rollins' head or
the ritual beard of his axe; a longhorn winding
its bells thru the Field of Reeds.

I am a cowboy in the boat of Ra. I bedded
down with Isis, Lady of the Boogaloo, dove
down deep in her horny, stuck up her Wells-Far-ago
in daring midday getaway. "Start grabbing the
blue," I said from top of my double crown.

I am a cowboy in the boat of Ra. Ezzard Charles
of the Chisholm Trail. Took up the brass but they
blew off my thumb. Alchemist in ringmanship but a
sucker for the right cross.

I am a cowboy in the boat of Ra. Vamoosed from
the temple i bide my time. The price on the wanted
poster was a-going down, outlaw alias copped my stance
and moody greenhorns were making me dance;
   while my mouth's
shooting iron got its chambers jammed.

I am a cowboy in the boat of Ra. Boning-up in
the ol West i bide my time. You should see
me pick off these tin cans whippersnappers. I
write the motown long plays for the comeback of
Osiris. Make them up when stars stare at sleeping
steer out here near the campfire. Women arrive
on the backs of goats and throw themselves on
my Bowie.

I am a cowboy in the boat of Ra. Lord of the lash,
the Loup Garou Kid. Half breed son of Pisces and
Aquarius. I hold the souls of men in my pot. I do
the dirty boogie with scorpions. I make the bulls
keep still and was the first swinger to grape the taste.

I am a cowboy in his boat. Pope Joan of the
Ptah Ra. C/mere a minute willya doll?
Be a good girl and
bring me my Buffalo horn of black powder
bring me my headdress of black feathers
bring me my bones of Ju-Ju snake
go get my eyelids of red paint.
Hand me my shadow
I'm going into town after Set

I am a cowboy in the boat of Ra

look out Set     here i come Set
to get Set     to sunset Set
to unseat Set     to Set down Set

usurper of the Royal couch
—imposter RAdio of Moses' bush
party pooper O hater of dance
vampire outlaw of the milky way

## The Reactionary Poet

If you are a revolutionary
Then I must be a reactionary
For if you stand for the future
I have no choice but to
Be with the past

Bring back suspenders!
Bring back Mom!
Homemade ice cream
Picnics in the park
Flagpole sitting
Straw hats
Rent parties
Corn liquor
The banjo
Georgia quilts
Krazy Kat
Restock

The syncopation of
Fletcher Henderson
The Kiplingesque lines
of James Weldon Johnson
Black Eagle
Mickey Mouse
The Bach Family

Sunday School
Even Mayor La Guardia
Who read the comics
Is more appealing than
Your version of
What Lies Ahead

In your world of
Tomorrow Humor
Will be locked up and
The key thrown away
The public address system
Will pound out headaches
All day
Everybody will wear the same
Funny caps
And the same funny jackets
Enchantment will be found
Expendable, charm, a
Luxury
Love and kisses
A crime against the state
Duke Ellington will be
Ordered to write more marches
"For the people," naturally

If you are what's coming
I must be what's going

Make it by steamboat
I likes to take it real slow

# AL YOUNG  (1939–        )

Al Young was born in Ocean Springs, Mississippi, in 1939 and educated at the University of Michigan. He has taught at a number of universities, among them Stanford and Rice, the University of California at Berkeley, and the University of Washington. He currently resides in Palo Alto, California.

Young's poems find their distinctly American texture in a successful merging of the Romantic musings of a learned poet with the dazzling cadences and sharp allusions of a jazzman. His phrasing combines lyricism with direct address; he presents his themes of music, love, history, and personal struggle with an at times startling honesty. Young's publishing career thus far includes over ten volumes of verse, fiction, anthologies, and memoirs, as well as screenplays.

## Dance of the Infidels

*In memory of Bud Powell*

The smooth smell of Manhattan taxis,
Parisian taxis, it doesn't matter, it's
the feeling that modern man is all youve
laid him out to be in those tinglings & rushes;
the simple touch of your ringed fingers
against a functioning piano.

The winds of Brooklyn
still mean a lot to me. The way certain chicks
formed themselves & their whole lives around
a few notes, an attitude more than anything.
I know about the being out of touch, bumming
nickels & dimes worth of this & that off

him & her here & there—everything but
hither & yon.

Genius does not grow on trees.

I owe
you a million love dollars & so much more than
thank-you for re-writing the touch & taste & smell
of the world for me those city years when I could
very well have fasted on into oblivion.

Ive just
been playing the record you made in Paris with Art
Blakey & Lee Morgan. The european audience
is applauding madly. I think of what Ive heard
of Buttercup's flowering on the Left Bank & days
you had no one to speak to. Wayne Shorter is
beautifying the background of sunlight with
children playing in it & shiny convertibles
& sedans parked along the blocks as I blow.

Grass
grows. Negroes. Women walk. The world, in case
youre losing touch again, keeps wanting the same
old thing.

You gave me some of it; beauty I sought
before I was even aware how much I needed it.

I know
this world is terrible & that one must, above all,
hold onto the heart & the hearts of others.

I love *you*

## How the Rainbow Works

*For Jean Cook, on learning of her
mother's death*

Mostly we occupy ocular zones, clinging
only to what we think we can see.
We can't see wind or waves of thought,
electrical fields or atoms dancing;
only what they do or make us believe.

Look on all of life as color—
vibratile movement, heart-centered,
from invisibility to the merely visible.
Never mind what happens when one of us dies.
Where are you before you even get born?
Where am I and all the unseeable souls
we love at this moment, or loathed
before birth? Where are we right now?

Everything that ever happened either
never did or always will with variations.
Let's put it another way: Nothing ever
happened that wasn't dreamed, that wasn't
sketched from the start with artful surprises.
Think of the dreamer as God, a painter,
a ham, to be sure, but a divine old master
whose medium is light and who sidesteps
tedium by leaving room both inside and outside
this picture for subjects and scenery to wing it.

Look on death as living color too: the dyeing
of fabric, submersion into a temporary sea,
a spectruming beyond the reach of sensual
range which, like time, is chained to change;
the strange notion that everything we've
ever done or been up until now is past
history, is gone away, is bleached, bereft,

perfect, leaving the scene clean to freshen
with pigment and space and leftover light.

# The Blues Don't Change

> *Now I'll tell you about the*
> *Blues. All Negroes like Blues.*
> *Why? Because they was born with*
> *the Blues. And now everybody*
> *have the Blues. Sometimes they*
> *don't know what it is.*
> —Leadbelly

And I was born with you, wasn't I, Blues?
Wombed with you, wounded, reared and forwarded
from address to address, stamped, stomped
and returned to sender by nobody else but you,
Blue Rider, writing me off every chance you
got, you mean old grudgeful-hearted, table-
turning demon, you, you sexy soul-sucking gem.

Blue diamond in the rough, you *are* forever.
You can't be outfoxed don't care how they cut
and smuggle and shine you on, you're like a
shadow, too dumb and stubborn and necessary
to let them turn you into what you ain't
with color or theory or powder or paint.

That's how you can stay in style without sticking
and not getting stuck. You know how to sting
where I can't scratch, and you move from frying
pan to skillet the same way you move people
to go to wiggling their bodies, juggling their
limbs, loosening that goose, upping their voices,
opening their pores, rolling their hips and lips.

They can shake their bodies but they can't shake *you*.

## How Stars Start

I don't ask to be forgiven
nor do I wish to be given up,
not entirely, not yet, not while
pain is shooting clean through
the only world I know: this one.
There is no Mal Waldron song or
Marlene Dietrich epic in black
& white where to scrawl against
the paradigms of time is to mean
something benign, like dismissing
present actions or behavior because
I know & understand deep down
inside & beyond that life itself
is acting all of this out; this
kamikaze drama, cosmic if you
will, but certainly comic, in a style
so common as to invite confusion.

Who am I now? What have I become?
Where do we draw the line between being
who I am and what I ought to be?
Need is a needle, nosing its sticky load
into my grief, spilling into veins
that can't be sewn, transforming their dark
cells in lighted semblances of relief.
The stomach is involved; flesh itself;
memories of an island doom that leaves
no room for senses or sensitive
assessments of truth about myself.
Which is the me that never changes?

All roads lead back to starts, to where
I started out, to stars: the fiery
beginnings of our ends & means; our
meanness and our meanings. There never
was a night begun in darkness,
nor a single day begun in light.

## From Bowling Green

The prompt sadness of Schumann or Tchaikovsky
is the wistfulness of Basho or Bukowski
in a furnished apartment that happens
to hold me now in January-glacial splendor.
As love condenses into ice and snow
forms the steam that bleeds from molten lava,
so music and its poetry will ooze
with sweet symphonic arias and blues.
Getting used to appearing in a poem or song
means becoming comfortable with life. The long
way around usually ends up being the shortcut.

## Leaving Syracuse

All these girls licking & sucking
their own twitchy fingers free of chocolate
were winos once on well-policed benches,
or smoking in urine-lined johns.

The lyrical light of Greyhound,
its bright snowiness the color of Rip
Van Winkle's beard, erect with winter,
lushes up the loveliest of valleys.
Those trucks & barns & frozen

slopes as up-and-down as chimney smoke
give you plenty to shine on.

Joy is with us all the time
we're being bused from one universe
to the next. Dappled or evenly iced over,
these subtle imitations of life keep
on the move. Good morning, Rochester,
have you heard the news?

# TOI DERRICOTTE  *(1940–      )*

Toi Derricotte was born in Detroit, Michigan, in 1941. She was educated at Wayne State and New York University, and has taught at numerous universities, among them George Mason, N.Y.U., and Old Dominion.

In her poetry Derricotte displays a quiet, understated lyricism, a perfect vehicle for her explorations of loneliness and loss in the modern world. She is interested in the often painful bonds and the small tendernesses of family and of love, as well as in the obstacles and possibilities inherent in being a woman and black. Her work is equally unafraid of horror or celebration, seeing in the balance of human experience the path toward healing and understanding.

Toi Derricotte has published several volumes of poetry, including *Captivity* (1989) and *Tender* (1997), as well as a well-noted work of nonfiction prose, *The Black Notebooks*. She currently teaches at the University of Pittsburgh.

## Before Making Love

I move my hands over your face,
closing my eyes, as if blind;
the cheek bones, broadly spaced,
the wide thick nostrils of the African,
the forehead whose bones push
at both sides as if the horns
of fallen angels lie just under,
the chin that juts forward with pride.
I think of the delicate skull of the Tuang child—
earliest of human beings
emerged from darkness—whose geometry
brings word of a small town of dignity
that all the bloody kingdoms rest on.

# On the Turning Up of Unidentified Black Female Corpses

Mowing his three acres with a tractor,
a man notices something ahead—a mannequin—
he thinks someone threw it from a car. Closer
he sees it is the body of a black woman.

The medics come and turn her with pitchforks.
Her gaze shoots past him to nothing. Nothing
is explained. How many black women
have been turned up to stare at us blankly,

in weedy fields, off highways,
pushed out in plastic bags,
shot, knifed, unclothed partially, raped,
their wounds sealed with a powdery crust.

Last week on TV, a gruesome face, eyes bloated shut.
No one will say, "She looks like she's sleeping," ropes
of blue-black slashes at the mouth. Does anybody
know this woman? Will anyone come forth? Silence

like a backwave rushes into that field
where, just the week before, four other black girls
had been found. The gritty image hangs in the air
just a few seconds, but it strikes me,

a black woman, there is a question being asked
about my life. How can I
protect myself? Even if I lock my doors,
walk only in the light, someone wants me dead.

Am I wrong to think
if five white women had been stripped,
broken, the sirens would wail until
someone was named?

Is it any wonder I walk over these bodies
pretending they are not mine, that I do not know
the killer, that I am just like any woman—
if not wanted, at least tolerated.

Part of me wants to disappear, to pull
the earth on top of me. Then there is this part
that digs me up with this pen
and turns my sad black face to the light.

## Invisible Dreams

> *La poesie vit d'insomnie perpetuelle*
> —Rene Char

There's a sickness in me. During
the night I wake up & it's brought

a stain into my mouth, as if
an ocean has risen & left back

a stink on the rocks of my teeth.
I stink. My mouth is ugly, human

stink. A color like rust
is in me. I can't get rid of it.

It rises after I
brush my teeth, a taste

like iron. In the
night, left like a dream,

a caustic light
washing over the insides of me.

What to do with my arms? They
coil out of my body

like snakes.
They branch & spit.

I want to shake myself
until they fall like withered

roots; until
they bend the right way—

until I fit in them,
or they in me.

I have to lay them down as
carefully as an old wedding dress,

I have to fold them
like the arms of someone dead.

The house is quiet; all
night I struggle. All

because of my arms,
which have no peace.


I'm a martyr, a girl who's been dead
two thousand years. I turn

on my left side, like one comfortable
after a long, hard death.

The angels look down
tenderly. "She's sleeping," they say

& pass me by. But
all night, I am passing

in & out of my body
on my naked feet.


I'm awake when I'm sleeping & I'm
sleeping when I'm awake, & no one

knows, not even me, for my eyes
are closed to myself.

I think I am thinking I see
a man beside me, & he thinks

in his sleep that I'm awake
writing. I hear a pen scratch

a paper. There is some idea
I think is clever: I want to

capture myself in a book.


I have to make a
place for my body in

my body. I'm like a
dog pawing a blanket

on the floor. I have to
turn & twist myself

like a rag until I
can smell myself in myself.

I'm sweating; the water is
pouring out of me

like silver. I put my head
in the crook of my arm

like a brilliant moon.


The bones of my left foot
are too heavy on the bones

of my right. They
lie still for a little while,

sleeping, but soon they
bruise each other like

angry twins. Then
the bones of my right foot

command the bones of my left
to climb down.

# HAKI MADHUBUTI (DON L. LEE) *(1942–     )*

Haki Madhubuti was born Don L. Lee in Little Rock, Arkansas, in 1942 and raised primarily in Chicago. Madhubuti became involved in the Black Power revolution of the 1960s and has remained deeply committed to the African American community, devoting great amounts of time and money to helping young people.

Madhubuti's direct and oftentimes explosive verse engages the themes and issues of contemporary black experience in uniquely forthright and honest ways. His meter is free; his poetics, by turns wrenching and humorous, lean toward the projective verse made popular in the poetic experiments of the late 1960s and early 1970s.

A publisher and essayist as well as a poet, Madhubuti has continued to live on Chicago's South Side. His *GroundWork: New and Selected Poems of Don L. Lee/Haki Madhubuti, from 1966–1996* was published by Third World Press in 1996.

## We Walk the Way of the New World

I.

we run the dangercourse.
the way of the stocking caps & murray's grease.
(if u is modern u used duke greaseless hair pomade)
jo jo was modern/ an international nigger
                     born: jan. 1, 1863 in new york, mississippi.
his momma was mo militant than he was/is
jo jo bes no instant negro
his development took all of 106 years
& he was the first to be stamped "made in USA"
where he arrived bow-legged a curve ahead of the 20th
          century's new weapon: television.
which invented, "how to win and influence people"
& gave jo jo is how/ever look: however u want me.

we discovered that with the right brand of cigarettes
that one, with his best girl,
cd skip thru grassy fields in living color
& in slow-motion: Caution: niggers, cigarette smoking
       will kill u & yr/health.
& that the breakfast of champions is: blackeyed peas & rice.
& that God is dead & Jesus is black and last seen on 63rd
     street in a gold & black dashiki, sitting in a pink
      hog speaking swahili with a pig-latin accent.
& that integration and coalition are synonymous,
& that the only thing that really mattered was:
   who could get the highest on the least or how to expand
   & break one's mind.


in the coming world
new prizes are
to be given
we *ran* the dangercourse.
now, it's a silent walk/ a careful eye
jo jo is there
to his mother he is unknown
(she accepted with a newlook: what wd u do if someone
   loved u?)
jo jo is back
& he will catch all the new jo jo's as they wander in & out
and with a fan-like whisper say: you ain't no
           tourist
           and Harlem ain't for
           sight-seeing, brother.


### 2.

Start with the itch and there will be no scratch. Study
  yourself.
Watch yr/every movement as u skip thru-out the southside of
   chicago.
be hip to yr/actions.

our dreams are realities
traveling the nature-way.

we meet them
at the apex of their utmost
meanings/means;
we walk in cleanliness
down state st/or Fifth Ave.
& wicked apartment buildings shake
as their windows announce our presence
as we jump into the interior
& cut the day's evil away.

We walk in cleanliness
the newness of it all
becomes us
our women listen to us
and learn.
We teach our children thru
our actions.

We'll become owners of the                 New World
the New World.
will run it as unowners
for
we will live in it too
& will want to be remembered
as        realpeople.


## the self-hatred of don l. lee

(9/22/63)

        i,
        at one time,
        loved
        my
        color—
        it
        opened sMALL

doors of
tokenism
&
acceptance.
          (doors called, "the only one" & "our negro")
after painfully
struggling
thru Du Bois,
Rogers, Locke
Wright & others,
my blindness
was vanquished
by pitchblack
paragraphs of
"us, we, me, i"
awareness.


i
began
to love
only a
part of
me—
my inner
self which
is all
black—
&
developed a
vehement
hatred of
my light
brown
outer.

# SHERLEY ANNE WILLIAMS *(1944–1999)*

**S**herley Anne Williams was born in Bakersfield, California, in 1944
and raised in Fresno. She earned her B.A. from California State
University at Fresno and her M.A. from Brown University. She is
the author of two volumes of poetry, a book of criticism, and two
novels, the second of which, *Dessa Rose* (1986), won wide critical
acclaim. Her poetry covers an extraordinary range of styles at a
consistently high level—from the elegant, precise formalism of
works like "Letters from a New England Negro" to the true, earthy
(though at the same time modernist) blues expression of works like
"The Peacock Poems." Many of her poems are concerned with
history, the blues, and the sisterhood of black women. Williams was
professor of English for many years at the University of California
at San Diego. She died in 1999.

## Letters from a New England Negro

> *. . . and every member rejoiced*
> *in a single segment made whole*
> *with the circle*
> *in the recognition*
> *of a single voice . . .*

Mrs. Josiah Harris
No. 5 The Grange Street
Newport, Rhode Island

August 25, 1867

Dear Miss Nettie,

The School is in a spinney
down behind the old Quarters
where many of the freedmen

live. The teachers, myself
included, live in the Big
House, which—thus far!—has stirred
little comment among the
local whites.

The School is the largest
public building in which blacks
and whites can safely congregate.
Sunday services are held there
and many of the freedmen
attend. Miss Esther introduced
me to several as "the
herald of Emancipation's
new day."

They murmured discreetly
among themselves, the women
smiling quickly, the men
nodding or cutting their
eyes toward me. Finally an
older man stepped forward, "I'm is
Peter, Miss Patient Herald,"
he said, pumping my hand. Then,
with great satisfaction,
"Lotsa room in the Big House.

                              Now."


Mr. Edward Harris
5 The Grange Street
Newport, Rhode Island


    August 25, 1867

Edward, I do know *some* of
whom they speak, especially
the ones now dead, Pope and Homer,
though I cannot read the Greek;
such discussions are the dreams

I dreamed myself in that one
short year at school. But Homer,
as you warned, does not so often
figure in conversation
as I had supposed.

I nod
and smile as Miss Nettie bade
me, but my silence is more
noticeable here than at
her table. I have told my
tale of meeting Emerson
while a servant for the Straights;
they have marveled at that lucky
fate. And only after the
moment passes do I
remember the humorous
exchange between some children
or my comical fright at
walking through the spinney.

2

August 25, 1867

We sit on the veranda
most evenings and sometimes Beryl
consents to play for us. The
Old Nights gather then in this
southern dusk: Mistress at the
piano, light from twin
candelabra bringing
color to her cheeks, French doors
open to the darkness;
listeners sitting quietly
in the heat.

Now and then
beneath the country airs that

are Beryl's specialty comes a
snatch of melody such as
no mistress ever played and
I am recalled to the present
place. *Free*dmen sing here and now. It
is Cassie or Miss Esther who
turns the music's page. Or myself.

Miss Ann Spencer
Lyme on Eaton
New Strowbridge, Connecticut

    August 30, 1867

Dear Ann,

Caution is not so necessary
here as in some other parts
of the state, but we hear of
the "night-riding" and terror
and so are careful. Yet, Miss
Esther's bearing is such that
she is accorded grudging
civility by even
rabid Rebels and though there
was at first some muttering
at young white women teaching
"nigras," Cassie and Beryl are
likewise accepted; thus the
School escapes reprisals.

And,
if the local ladies lift
their skirts aside as I pass—
Well, perhaps I *should* smirch them.
If my cast-off clothes are
thought unsuited to my station,
my head held too high as I
step back to let the meanest white
go before me, why—What then

is a concert in Newport
or a day in Boston compared
to the chance to be arrogant
amongst so many southerners!

   September 9, 1867

Dear Edward,

The children, I am told, had
little notion of order
and none of *school*. The first months
here, by all accounts, were
hectic. New students came daily
and changed their names almost
as often, or came and went
at will and those that stayed, talked
throughout the lesson.

They sit
now as prim as Topsy must
have done when first confronted
with Miss Ophelia, hands
folded neatly, faces lit
with pious expectancy.
We teach them to read and write
their names, some basic sums and
talk to them of Douglass and
Tubman and other heroes
of the race.

They are bright
enough—as quick as any
I taught in Newport. Yet behind
their solemn stares, I sense a
game such as I played with those
mistresses who tried to teach
me how best to do the very
task for which I had been
especially recommended,

and so suspect that what we
call learning is in them mere
obedience to some rules.

*October 22, 1867*

The girls are bold, fingering
our dresses, marveling at
our speech. They cluster around
us at recess, peppering
us with questions about the
North and ourselves. Today, one
asked why I did not cover
my head or at least braid my
hair as is decent around
white folk. We do not speak of
hair in the north, at least in
public, and I answered sharply,
It is not the custom in
the North and I am from the
North—meaning, of course, that I
am freeborn.

I know how
chancy freedom is among
us and so have never
boasted of my birth. And
they were as much stung by my
retort as I by their question.
But in the moment of my
answer the scarves worn by the
women seemed so much a symbol
of our slavery that I would
have died before admitting
my childhood's longing for just
such patient plaiting of my
tangled hair or cover now
my wild and sullen head.

November 10, 1867

Dear Miss Nettie,

My group numbers twenty, aged
four through sixteen, now that
harvest is done. There are no
grades, of course, and Tuesday
nights I take a group of grown-ups
over the lessons I give the
youngsters the following week.

The
grown-ups are more shy with me
than with Miss Esther and the
others, seldom speaking unless
I have done so first and then
without elaboration.

I did not expect immediate
kinship as Beryl chides: I am
as stiff with them as they with
me; yet, in unguarded moments,
I speak as they do, softly
a little down in the throat
muting the harsh gutturals and
strident diphthongs on my tongue.

*November 24, 1867*

There was in Warwick Neck, at
the time we lived there, a black
woman named Miss Girt whose aunt
had bought her out of slavery
in the District some fifty
years before. She was a
familiar and striking figure
in that town where there were few
negroes; of that color we
called smoothblack—a dense and

even tone that seems to drink
the light. The strawberry pink
of her mouth spilled over onto
the darkness of her lips and
a sliver of it seemed to
cut the bottom one in two.

She kept a boarding house for
negroes, mostly men who worked
at odd jobs up and down the
Coast. The white children whispered
about it—though the house
differed only in being
set in a larger plot with
two or three vacant ones between
it and its nearest neighbors.
It was the closest thing to
a haunted house the town provided
and on idle afternoons
the white children "dared
the boogey man"—though they seldom
got close enough to disturb
Miss Girt or her boarders with
their rude calls and flourishes—
and withdrew giggling and
pushing at the slightest
movement or noise.

We went also,
on our infrequent trips
to town, to see the boogey
man and sometimes heard a strain
of music, a sudden snatch
of laughter. Or watched the white
children from a distance. Once
George Adam called out, "Here She
come," sending them into clumsy
flight and us into delighted
laughter. Once Miss Girt herself

came round the corner on the
heels of their cry, "Nigger!"

"And
a free one, too," she called and
laughed at their startled silence.
They fled in disorder,
routed, so George said, by the
boldness of this sally, and,
I thought, by the hot pink in
the laughing dark of Miss Girt's face.

December 15, 1867

Edward dearest,

They persist in calling me
Patient though I have tried to
make it clear that neither
Emancipation nor Patience
is part of my given name.
They understand the Herald
part and laugh at Peter who
says he could not then understand
that New England talk. The
following week, I am again
Miss Patient Hannah. I tell
myself, it is not so important
and truly have ceased to argue,
have come indeed to still any
impulse to retort almost
as it is born.

Tonight my
old devil tongue slipped from
me after weeks of careful
holding. I answered roughly
some harmless question, My name
is Hannah. Hannah. There is
no Patience to it.

"Hannah
our name for the sun," Stokes said
in the silence that followed
my remark. "You warm us like
she do, but you are more patient
wid us when we come to learn."

   *December 27, 1867*

The men play their bodies like
drums, their mouths and noses like
wind instruments, creating
syncopated rhythms, wild
melodies that move the people
to wordless cries as they dance.
There are true musicians—Givens
who plays the banjo, Lloyd the
fiddler, many singers. Even
the tamborinists and those
who shake the bones coax beauty
from nothingness and desire.
Yet it is the music of
those who play themselves, that tone
half voice, half instrument that
echoes in my head. Tonight at
Stokes' wedding I was moved by
this to moan and dance myself.

   *January 5, 1868*

My dear,

Beryl sees the poverty of my
childhood as a dim reflection
of the slavery in which
Pansy lived, sees in her, as
indeed in all, some vestige
of my former self that teaching
frees me of.

I see in her,
too, some other Pansy, some
Other, not my self and not
so simple as we thought her.

We have come among Christians
for whom Dance is the crossing
of the feet; what they do not
know of the world is learnable.
It is this I have come to
teach. Beryl has no eye for such
distinctions, seeing only
frenzy where I have been taught
the speech of walk and shout.

   January 12, 1868

Dear Miss Nettie,

The school stands now where the praise
grove was; the grass then was worn
away by bended knees, the
dirt packed hard by shouting feet.

"Go wid Massa, Lawd; go wid
Massa."
Pansy mimics the
old prayer, torso going
in one direction, limbs in
some other. There is laughter,
murmurs of "Do, Lawd" and "Amen."
But it is memory she
dances; the praise grove was gone
before the War, closed by the
Masters' fears.

"Dey ain trus mo'n
one darky alone wid Chris;
two darkies togetha need
a *live* white man near."

Pansy's
mother and many others
gathered then in twos and threes
in secret clearings in the
woods, quiet witness that
our Savior lives.

"Go wid
Massa, Jesus. Go *wid* dis
white man.

"And Mista Lincoln
                            did."

Their triumph is renewed
in our laughter, yet there are
some—Pansy I think is one—
who scoff at white men's ways and
gather now in the same hushed
harbors to worship and to
whisper of the new jesus
in the old praise grove's heart.

   *January 21, 1868*

She comes grudgingly
to know the world
within the printed
page yet rejoices
in Stokes' progress

She trusts the power
of the word only
as speech and sets me
riddles whose answers
I cannot speak

How
do the white man school
you
*Give a nigga*
*a hoe*

How do he
control you
*Put a*
*mark on some paper*
*turn our chi'ren to*

*noughts*
How do master
tell darkies apart
*By looking at the*
*lines and dots*

I tell
myself it is the
catechism of
unlettered negroes
that one dance has made

me Darky; pagan
and half wild.
She is
as black and lovely
as her namesake's heart
and teases me about
my "learnin"
She would
row my head with seed
plaits And prays I have
not been ruined by

this white man's schooling.

February 7, 1868

Edward,

I may attend prayer meetings
in the Quarters, go now
and then to the services "Singing"
Johnson leads. If such as
Sister Jones or Mrs. Casper from
the town ask, I may go to
gatherings in their homes. And
I am free to go wherever
Cassie and Beryl are invited.
Thus my need for company
is understood and addressed;
so, I am not to go to
play parties in the Quarters
nor go there of an evening
to Stokes' and Pansy's to talk
and listen at the music and
the tales. Miss Esther is shocked
that I would even consider
such actions without seeking
advice from Beryl or Cassie
or go without asking leave
of herself. It is a stalemate:
she will not give her permission;
I go and ask no one's consent.

February 15, 1868

I know you are not wholly
knowledgeable of all I
write you, dearest Ann, yet your
own eccentricity at
times allows you to apprehend
what most would miss. And I do
not expect answers or advice.
We stand outside each other's
lives and are enchanted with this

unlikely meeting: the blue-
stockinged white lady, the smart
colored girl. I stand now
outside the life I know as
negro. Sometimes, as I try
to make sensible all that
I would tell you, I see my
self as no more than a
recorder and you a listening
ear in some future house.

March 3, 1868

Dearest One,

I have no clear recall of
how I came to be at the
door of my first mistress, kept
little of that beginning, save
that through bargaining I fixed
my wage and worked extra for
room and board. I cannot now
remember all the helping
hands I passed through before the
Harrises took me in. There are
things I tell no one and have
ceased to tell myself. I have
grown to womanhood with my past
almost a blank.

I do not
recall, yet the memory
colors all that I am. I
know only that I was a
servant; now my labor is
returned to me and all my
waiting is upon myself.

# MARILYN NELSON   *(1946–        )*

Marilyn Nelson was born in Cleveland, Ohio, in 1946. She received her bachelor's degree from the University of California at Davis and her master's and doctorate degrees respectively from the University of Pennsylvania and the University of Minnesota. She currently teaches at the University of Connecticut.

Nelson's third volume of verse, *The Homeplace* (1985), was nominated for the National Book Award, as was her most recent book, *The Fields of Praise* (1997). She is also the author of three other volumes.

Nelson's poems are intelligent and thoughtful, combining delicate phrasing and carefully chosen imagery with a fluid range of themes—though she finds her inspiration most often in the particularities of family life. Her father's experiences as a member of the first group of African Americans allowed to fly in the United States Army provide the background for one of Nelson's finest and best-known poems, "Tuskegee Airfield."


## My Grandfather Walks in the Woods

Somewhere
in the light above the womb,
black trees
and white trees
populate a world.

It is a March landscape,
the only birds around are small
and black.
What do they eat,
sitting in the birches
like warnings?

The branches of the trees
are black and white.
Their race is winter.
They thrive in cold.

There is my grandfather
walking among the trees.
He does not notice
his fingers are cold.
His black felt hat
covers his eyes.

He is knocking on each tree,
listening to their voices
as they answer slowly
deep, deep from their roots.
I am John, he says,
are you my father?

They answer
with voices like wind
blowing away from him.


## Emily Dickinson's Defunct

She used to
pack poems
in her hip pocket.
Under all the
gray old lady
clothes she was
dressed for action.
She had hair,
imagine,
in certain places, and
believe me
she smelled human

on a hot summer day.
Stalking snakes
or counting
the thousand notes
in sunlight
she walked just
like an Indian.
She was New England's
favorite daughter,
she could pray
like the devil.
She was a
two-fisted woman,
this babe.
All the flies
just stood around
and buzzed
when she died.

## Tuskegee Airfield

*For the Tuskegee Airmen*

These men,
these proud black men:
our first to touch
their fingers to the sky.

The Germans learned to call them
*Die Schwarzen Vogelmenschen.*
They call themselves
*The Spookwaffe.*

Laughing.
And marching to class under officers
whose thin-lipped ambition
was to *was the niggers out.*

Sitting at attention
for lectures about ailerons, airspeed, altimeters
from boring lieutenants who believed
*you monkeys ain't meant to fly.*

Oh, there were parties,
cadet-dances, guest appearances
by the Count
and the lovely Lena.

There was the embarrassing
adulation of Negro civilians.
A woman approached my father in a bar
where he was drinking with his buddies.
*Hello, Airmen.* She held out her palm.
*Will you tell me my future?*

There was that,
like a breath of pure oxygen.
But first,
they had to earn wings.

    There was this one instructor
    who was pretty nice.
    I mean, we just sat around
    and *talked* when a flight had gone well.

    But he was from Minnesota,
    and he made us sing
    the Minnesota Fight Song
    before we took off.

    If you didn't sing it,
    your days were numbered.
    "Minnesota, hats off to thee . . ."
    That bastard!

    One time I had a check-flight
    with an instructor from Louisiana.

As we were about to head for base,
he chopped the power.

*Forced landing, nigger.*
There were trees everywhere I looked.
Except on that little island . . .
I began my approach.

The instructor said, *Pull up.*
*That was an excellent approach.*
Real surprised.
*But where would you have taken off, wise guy?*

I said, *Sir,*
*I was ordered*
*to land the plane.*
*Not take off.*

The instructor grinned.
*Boy, if your ass*
*is as hard as your head,*
*you'll go far in this world.*

# YUSEF KOMUNYAKAA  *(1947–     )*

**Y**usef Komunyakaa, currently professor of creative writing at Princeton University, was the 1994 winner of the Pulitzer Prize in poetry for *Neon Vernacular*. Born in Bogalusa, Louisiana, in 1947, Komunyakaa earned his B.A. from the University of Colorado and continued his studies at Colorado State and the University of California at Irvine. A war correspondent in Vietnam, he won the Bronze Star for his work with the military newspaper *The Southern Cross*. He is the author of eight volumes of poetry, including *Lost in the Bonewheel Factory* (1979), *Copacetic* (1984), *February in Sydney* (1989), and *Thieves of Paradise* (1998). He is also the coeditor of *The Jazz Poetry Anthology* (1991).

Komunyakaa's poems take as their subject his experiences growing up in the South and the divergent paths of his life since then. Often the transcendental qualities of music and love which provide the satisfying resonances and surprising resolutions of his melancholy-hued poetics of the retrieval of experience.

## Untitled Blues

*After a Photograph by Yevgeni Yevtushenko*

I catch myself trying
to look into the eyes
of the photo, at a black boy
behind a laughing white mask
he's painted on. I
could've been that boy
years ago.
Sure, I could say everything's copacetic,
listen to a Buddy Bolden cornet
cry from one of those coffin-
shaped houses called
shotgun. We could

meet in Storyville,
famous for quadroons,
with drunks discussing God
around a honky-tonk piano.
We could pretend we can't
see the kitchen help
under a cloud of steam.
Other lurid snow jobs:
night & day, the city
clothed in her see-through
French lace, as pigeons
coo like a beggar chorus
among makeshift studios
on wheels—Vieux Carré
belles have portraits painted
twenty years younger.
We could hand jive
down on Bourbon & Conti
where tap dancers hold
to their last steps,
mammy dolls frozen
in glass cages. The boy
locked inside your camera,
perhaps he's lucky—
he knows how to steal
laughs in a place
where your skin
is your passport.

## Elegy for Thelonious

Damn the snow.
Its senseless beauty
pours a hard light
through the hemlock.
Thelonious is dead. Winter
drifts in the hourglass;

notes pour from the brain cup.
Damn the alley cat
wailing a muted dirge
off Lenox Ave.
Thelonious is dead.
Tonight's a lazy rhapsody of shadows
swaying to blue vertigo
& metaphysical funk.
Black trees in the wind.
*Crepuscule with Nellie*
plays inside the bowed head.
"Dig the Man Ray of piano!"
O Satisfaction,
hot fingers blur
on those white rib keys.
*Coming on the Hudson.*
*Monk's Dream.*
The ghost of bebop
from 52nd Street,
footprints in the snow.
Damn February.
Let's go to Minton's
& play "modern malice"
till daybreak. Lord,
there's Thelonious
wearing that old funky hat
pulled down over his eyes.

## Between Days

Expecting to see him anytime
coming up the walkway
through blueweed & bloodwort,
she says, "That closed casket
was weighed down with stones."
The room is as he left it
fourteen years ago, everything

freshly dusted & polished
with lemon oil. The uncashed
death check from Uncle Sam
marks a passage in the Bible
on the dresser, next to the photo
staring out through the window.
"Mistakes. Mistakes. Now,
he's gonna have to give them this
money back when he gets home.
But I wouldn't. I would
let them pay for their mistakes.
They killed his daddy. & Janet,
she & her three children
by three different men, I hope
he's strong enough to tell her
to get lost. Lord, mistakes."
His row of tin soldiers
lines the window sill. The sunset
flashes across them like a blast.
She's buried the Silver Star
& flag under his winter clothes.
The evening's first fireflies
dance in the air like distant tracers.
Her chair faces the walkway
where she sits before the TV
asleep, as the screen dissolves
into days between snow.

## Facing It

My black face fades,
hiding inside the black granite.
I said I wouldn't,
dammit: No tears.
I'm stone. I'm flesh.
My clouded reflection eyes me
like a bird of prey, the profile of night

slanted against morning. I turn
this way—the stone lets me go.
I turn that way—I'm inside
the Vietnam Veterans Memorial
again, depending on the light
to make a difference.
I go down the 58,022 names,
half-expecting to find
my own in letters like smoke.
I touch the name Andrew Johnson;
I see the booby trap's white flash.
Names shimmer on a woman's blouse
but when she walks away
the names stay on the wall.
Brushstrokes flash, a red bird's
wings cutting across my stare.
The sky. A plane in the sky.
A white vet's image floats
closer to me, then his pale eyes
look through mine. I'm a window.
He's lost his right arm
inside the stone. In the black mirror
a woman's trying to erase names:
No, she's brushing a boy's hair.

## February in Sydney

Dexter Gordon's tenor sax
plays "April in Paris"
inside my head all the way back
on the bus from Double Bay.
*Round Midnight,* the '50s,
cool cobblestone streets
resound footsteps of Bebop
musicians with whiskey-laced voices
from a boundless dream in French.
Bud, Prez, Webster, & The Hawk,

their names run together riffs.
Painful gods jive talk through
bloodstained reeds & shiny brass
where music is an anesthetic.
Unreadable faces from the human void
float like torn pages across the bus
windows. An old anger drips into my throat,
& I try thinking something good,
letting the precious bad
settle to the salty bottom.
Another scene keeps repeating itself:
I emerge from the dark theatre,
passing a woman who grabs her red purse
& hugs it to her like a heart attack.
Tremolo. Dexter comes back to rest
behind my eyelids. A loneliness
lingers like a silver needle
under my black skin,
as I try to feel how it is
to scream for help through a horn.

## Euphony

Hands make love to thigh, breast, clavicle,
Willed to each other, to the keyboard—
Searching the whole forest of compromises
Till the soft engine kicks in, running

On honey. Dissonance worked
Into harmony, even-handed
As Art Tatum's plea to the keys.
Like a woman & man who have lived

A long time together, they know how
To keep the song alive. Wordless
epics into the cold night, keepers
Of the fire—the right hand lifts

Like the ghost of a sparrow
& the left uses every motionless muscle.
Notes divide, balancing each other,
Love & hate tattooed on the fingers.

## My Father's Love Letters

On Fridays he'd open a can of Jax
After coming home from the mill,
& ask me to write a letter to my mother
Who sent postcards of desert flowers
Taller than men. He would beg,
Promising to never beat her
Again. Somehow I was happy
She had gone, & sometimes wanted
To slip in a reminder, how Mary Lou
Williams' "Polka Dots & Moonbeams"
Never made the swelling go down.
His carpenter's apron always bulged
With old nails, a claw hammer
Looped at his side & extension cords
Coiled around his feet.
Words rolled from under the pressure
Of my ballpoint: Love,
Baby, Honey, Please.
We sat in the quiet brutality
Of voltage meters & pipe threaders,
Lost between sentences . . .
The gleam of a five-pound wedge
On the concrete floor
Pulled a sunset
Through the doorway of his toolshed.
I wondered if she laughed
& held them over a gas burner.
My father could only sign
His name, but he'd look at blueprints
& say how many bricks

Formed each wall. This man,
Who stole roses & hyacinth
For his yard, would stand there
With eyes closed & fists balled,
Laboring over a simple word, almost
Redeemed by what he tried to say.

# NATHANIEL MACKEY  *(1948–    )*

Nathaniel Mackey was born in Miami, Florida, in 1948 and raised in California. He received his B.A. from Princeton University and his Ph.D. from Stanford. Mackey is the author of two chapbooks of verse, *Four for Trane* (1978) and *Septet for the End of Time* (1983). His first full-length collection of poems, *Eroding Witness* (1985), was selected by Michael S. Harper for the National Poetry Series; his second collection, *School of Udhra,* was published in 1993.

Also an essayist, critic, editor, and prose writer, Mackey has since childhood explored literature's analogies with music. His poetry, paying particular homage to the equation of myth with music in black cultures, is exploratory, ornate, and ambitious. In 1993 Mackey coedited an anthology, *Moment's Notice: Jazz in Poetry and Prose,* and released a collection of essays, *Discrepant Engagement: Dissonance, Cross-Culturality, and Experimental Writing.* At present he teaches at the University of California at Santa Cruz.

## Winged Abyss

*For Olivier Messiaen*

I wake up dreaming I'm forty years in
      back of the times,     hear talk of a
Bright Star converging on Egypt.

                                  This on day
      two of this my thirty-fifth year,
forty years out in front that I
      even hear of it at all . . .

Such abrupt
fallings away of the ground, such obstructions
like a cello with one string gone.
An avalanche of
light. An old out-of-tune upright, some of
whose keys keep getting stuck . . .
A creaking door makes me dream of colors,
caught up in whose warp a knotted
stick
leaned on by the sun . . .


A war camp quartet for the end of time
heard with ears whose time has yet to
begin . . .
An unlikely music I hear makes a world
break
beyond its reach . . .


So I wake up handed a book
by an angel whose head has a rainbow
behind it.
I wake up holding a book announcing the
end of time.
A lullaby of wings, under-
neath whose auspices, obedient, asleep

with only one eye shut, not the
end of
the world but a bird at whose feet I hear
time
dissolve . . .


A free-beating fist, each tip of wing turned
inward. Battered gate of a City said to be
of the Heart.
Held me up as if to cleanse me
with fire, neither more nor less alive
than when
I wasn't there . . .

I hear talk.
Out of touch
with the times, I wake up asking what
bird
would make so awkward a
sound


## Black Snake Visitation

*for Jimi Hendrix*


A black tantric
snake I dream
two days to the

morning I die
slipping up
thru my throat,

slithers out
like the vomit I'll
be choked by

can't, gigantic
seven-headed
snake, sticks out

one head at a
time. Must
be this hiss my

guitar's been
rehearsing
sits me down by

where the salt
water crosses the
sweet. Self-

searching twitch,
the scrawny
light of its

carriage, broken
sealit stark-
ness, furtive

sea of regrets.
But not re-
duced by what

I knew would not
matter, woke
to see no one

caress the arisen
wonder's dreamt-of
thigh. Death

enters a slack
circle whispering,
slapping hands,

beauty baited
like a hook, hurt
muse at whose

feet whatever
fruit I'd give goes
abruptly bad.

*Must be this*
*hiss my*
*guitar's*

been rehearsing,
lizardquick
tongues like

they were
licking the sky.

Must be this
hiss my
guitar's been

rehearsing, these
lizardquick tongues
like they

were licking
the sky.

Down on my
knees testing
notes with

my teeth, always
knew a day'd
come I'd

put my wings out
and fly.

# GAYL JONES  *(1949–     )*

Gayl Jones was born in Kentucky in 1949 and educated at Connecticut College and Brown University. She is a talented novelist, poet, and literary critic, displaying in all genres an unmatched ear for sonority and rhythm. Her work is concerned primarily with the private lives of African American women—their struggles with the limitations put on them by both white society and black community and kin. Her striking ability to create the fully fleshed voices of a wide range of characters is perhaps connected to her early love of Chaucer and Joyce. Her mastery of rhythm at times, as in the poem "Deep Song," can give her work an incantatory quality.

Jones has taught at Wellesley College and the University of Michigan. She is the author of *Corregidora* (1975), *Eva's Man* (1976), and *Liberating Voices: Oral Traditions in African-American Literature* (1991). Her most recent novel, *The Healing* (1998), was nominated for the National Book Award. Her collections of poetry include *The Hermit Women* (1983) and *Xarque and Other Poems* (1985).

## Deep Song

*For B.H.*

The blues calling my name.
She is singing a deep song.
She is singing a deep song.
I am human.
He calls me crazy.
He says, "You must be
crazy."
I say, "Yes, I'm crazy."
He sits with his knees apart.
His fly is broken.
She is singing a deep song.

He smiles.
She is singing a deep song.
"Yes, I'm crazy."
I care about you.
I care.
I care about you.
I care.
He lifts his eyebrows.
The blues is calling my name.
I tell him he'd better
do something about his fly.
He says something softly.
He says something so softly
that I can't even hear him.
He is a dark man.
Sometimes he is a good dark man.
Sometimes he is a bad dark man.
I love him.

# C. S. GISCOMBE  (*1950–*    )

**C.** S. Giscombe's poetry constitutes a unique vision of the
post–World War II African American experience—recounting the
cultural and existential disjunctions attending the Great Migration
from South to North, the Rust Belt's loss of manufacturing, and the
interweaving of place and memory into the complex present. His
delicate, lyrical tracings of landscape, kinship, and collective loss in
the postmodern world evoke Ezra Pound, Charles Olson, and
James Wright, among others.

Giscombe was born in Dayton, Ohio, in 1950. He studied at the
State University of New York at Albany and Cornell University,
was a longtime professor at Illinois State University, and currently
teaches at Cornell. His volumes of poetry include *Postcards* (1977),
*At Large* (1989), *Here* (1994), *Two Selections from Giscombe
Road* (1995), and *Giscombe Road* (1998). His "All (Facts, Stories,
Chance)" appeared in *The Best American Poetry 1996* (edited by
Adrienne Rich). Giscombe has received numerous awards, includ-
ing a Fulbright Research Award and fellowships from both the
National Endowment for the Arts and the Illinois Arts Council.

## Dayton, O., the 50's & 60's

### 1.

Sat through stories

right through them as they were told

& I sat through confluence & allegory
through metaphor

through old movies repeated on TV, through leaping blue light
all around the couch

through dinners

*through* chance

(through unexpected moments, intimations
of sex & music

(through bus trips downtown across the bridge
into downtown Dayton over
the Great Miami

through ceremony kept simple, in
& back

### 2.

By the 50's & 60's we'd been well-ensconced for years
all along the road from Cincinnati Gateway City
to the South, had pushed in down Germantown hill

in fact as far as the Miami to the east, Wolf Creek
to the north,

Dunbar's house on Summit overlooked Wolf Creek,
grandly misnamed Riverview Av across the bridge

### 3.

I'd simply value the humidity

of land alongside water

the steep sides
even the levees downtown

(though it's boundaries
(even then

            —sat through a repetition
of the natcheral confluences

the fact divided finally out of that

self w/ self, self on the surface
of other

not mine, thanks

4.

Out abroad of an evening in 1960-something, way
across Wolf Creek w/ a white boy my age
the 2 of us—waiting for buses—reclined
on some lawn, at
some intersection:

nothing happened
my bus came first
it was a warm clear night among the dark houses
this far up in
(myself this present in

the set-up, the sequence
of description, not its demand

5.

How I've *wanted* to see myself

at the moment of crossing into downtown
over the 3rd St bridge,

in traffic, a pistol
loaded & unhidden on the dashboard or passenger seat,

the radio blaring

—to be at odds w/ nothing in my life
at loggerheads w/ no man or woman
to have no ritual, no quantity of value *here*
or over *there*

no gift
at something or for
anyone

but approaching as if from
close in
as if from far away, either one
(visible

6.

Or simply at large

passionate along the drift of streets
through the chant
of things continuing
rhetorical drone of the real doing
for the long stare out of town

*back* south

(or ahead/ at this?

### 7. *To Sam Stoloff*

In a dream years later we weren't Black/ hadn't been Black

we were Jews in a made-for-TV movie called "Jews"
set near the end of WW2
liberation drawing near:

some of us busted out of camp ahead of the gas
—*how many? what percentage?*—escaping
over hills surprisingly green for a war zone, hiding in them
above the lights of hostile countryside:

how far up can you creep, we wondered
how far up on the other?

Tenuous days in which the war was winding down
in which we had to stay between the Germans
to keep moving between them & the barbaric Soviets, "the
    advancing
& retreating armies":

                            we were nowhere

we were fluid, the moveable heart circling

we *set out,* then moved in circles
through the same scenes:

when we got to a big firebombed city w/ no name it was really
    Dayton,
I recognized it

# RITA DOVE  (1952–    )

Now the Commonwealth Professor of English at the University of Virginia, Rita Dove served as poet laureate of the United States from 1993 to 1995, the youngest poet ever so appointed. She has authored six volumes of poetry, a novel, a collection of short stories, and a play.

A graduate of Miami University in Ohio, Tübingen University in Germany, and the University of Iowa, Dove tirelessly explores the nuances of history in her work. In her Pulitzer Prize–winning *Thomas and Beulah* (1986), she presents a poem sequence at once biographical and imaginary, culture-specific and universal. Her talent for disclosing vibrant inner images in elegant phrasing gives her lines their force and balance, ranking Dove's poems as among the finest of her era.

## "Teach Us to Number Our Days"

In the old neighborhood, each funeral parlor
is more elaborate than the last.
The alleys smell of cops, pistols bumping their thighs,
each chamber steeled with a slim blue bullet.

Low-rent balconies stacked to the sky.
A boy plays tic-tac-toe on a moon
crossed by TV antennae, dreams

he has swallowed a blue bean.
It takes root in his gut, sprouts
and twines upward, the vines curling
around the sockets and locking them shut.

And this sky, knotting like a dark tie?
The patroller, disinterested, holds all the beans.

August. The mums nod past, each a prickly heart on a sleeve.

# Banneker

What did he do except lie
under a pear tree, wrapped in
a great cloak, and meditate
on the heavenly bodies?
*Venerable,* the good people of Baltimore
whispered, shocked and more than
a little afraid. After all it was said
he took to strong drink.
Why else would he stay out
under the stars all night
and why hadn't he married?

But who would want him! Neither
Ethiopian nor English, neither
lucky nor crazy, a capacious bird
humming as he penned in his mind
another enflamed letter
to President Jefferson—he imagined
the reply, polite and rhetorical.
Those who had been to Philadelphia
reported the statue
of Benjamin Franklin
before the library

his very size and likeness.
A wife? No, thank you.
At dawn he milked
the cows, then went inside
and put on a pot to stew
while he slept. The clock
he whittled as a boy
still ran. Neighbors
woke him up
with warm bread and quilts.
At nightfall he took out
his rifle—a white-maned
figure stalking the darkened

breast of the Union—and
shot at the stars, and by chance
one went out. Had he killed?
*I assure thee, my dear Sir!*
Lowering his eyes to fields
sweet with the rot of spring, he could see
a government's domed city
rising from the morass and spreading
in a spiral of lights. . . .

# Parsley

## 1. *The Cane Fields*

There is a parrot imitating spring
in the palace, its feathers parsley green.
Out of the swamp the cane appears

to haunt us, and we cut it down. El General
searches for a word; he is all the world
there is. Like a parrot imitating spring,

we lie down screaming as rain punches through
and we come up green. We cannot speak an R—
out of the swamp, the cane appears

and then the mountain we call in whispers *Katalina.*
The children gnaw their teeth to arrowheads.
There is a parrot imitating spring.

El General has found his word: *perejil.*
Who says it, lives. He laughs, teeth shining
out of the swamp. The cane appears

in our dreams, lashed by wind and streaming.
And we lie down. For every drop of blood
there is a parrot imitating spring.
Out of the swamp the cane appears.

## 2. *The Palace*

The word the general's chosen is parsley.
It is fall, when thoughts turn
to love and death; the general thinks
of his mother, how she died in the fall
and he planted her walking cane at the grave
and it flowered, each spring stolidly forming
four-star blossoms. The general

pulls on his boots, he stomps to
her room in the palace, the one without
curtains, the one with a parrot
in a brass ring. As he paces he wonders
Who can I kill today. And for a moment
the little knot of screams
is still. The parrot, who has traveled

all the way from Australia in an ivory
cage, is, coy as a widow, practising
spring. Ever since the morning
his mother collapsed in the kitchen
while baking skull-shaped candies
for the Day of the Dead, the general
has hated sweets. He orders pastries
brought up for the bird; they arrive

dusted with sugar on a bed of lace.
The knot in his throat starts to twitch;
he sees his boots the first day in battle
splashed with mud and urine
as a soldier falls at his feet amazed—
how stupid he looked!—at the sound
of artillery. *I never thought it would sing*
the soldier said, and died. Now

the general sees the fields of sugar
cane, lashed by rain and streaming.
He sees his mother's smile, the teeth
gnawed to arrowheads. He hears

the Haitians sing without R's
as they swing the great machetes:
*Katalina,* they sing, *Katalina,*

*mi madle, mi amol en muelte.* God knows
his mother was no stupid woman; she
could roll an R like a queen. Even
a parrot can roll an R! In the bare room
the bright feathers arch in a parody
of greenery, as the last pale crumbs
disappear under the blackened tongue. Someone

calls out his name in a voice
so like his mother's, a startled tear
splashes the tip of his right boot.
*My mother, my love in death.*
The general remembers the tiny green sprigs
men of his village wore in their capes
to honor the birth of a son. He will
order many, this time, to be killed

for a single, beautiful word.


## The Event

Ever since they'd left the Tennessee ridge
with nothing to boast of
but good looks and a mandolin,

the two Negroes leaning
on the rail of a riverboat
were inseparable: Lem plucked

to Thomas' silver falsetto.
But the night was hot and they were drunk.
They spat where the wheel

churned mud and moonlight,
they called to the tarantulas
down among the bananas

to come out and dance.
*You're so fine and mighty; let's see
what you can do,* said Thomas, pointing

to a tree-capped island.
Lem stripped, spoke easy: *Them's chestnuts,
I believe.* Dove

quick as a gasp. Thomas, dry
on deck, saw the green crown shake
as the island slipped

under, dissolved
in the thickening stream.
At his feet

a stinking circle of rags,
the half-shell mandolin.
Where the wheel turned the water

gently shirred.


## Weathering Out

She liked the mornings the best—Thomas gone
to look for work, her coffee flushed with milk,

outside autumn trees blowsy and dripping.
Past the seventh month she couldn't see her feet

so she floated from room to room, houseshoes flapping,
navigating corners in wonder. When she leaned

against a door jamb to yawn, she disappeared entirely.

Last week they had taken a bus at dawn
to the new airdock. The hangar slid open in segments

and the zeppelin nosed forward in its silver envelope.
The men walked it out gingerly, like a poodle,

then tied it to a mast and went back inside.
Beulah felt just that large and placid, a lake;

she glistened from cocoa butter smoothed in
when Thomas returned every evening nearly

in tears. He'd lean an ear on her belly
and say: *Little fellow's really talking,*

though to her it was more the *pok-pok-pok*
of a fingernail tapping with a thick cream lampshade.

Sometimes during the night she woke and found him
asleep there and the child sleeping, too.

The coffee was good but too little. Outside
everything shivered in tinfoil—only the clover

between the cobblestones hung stubbornly on,
green as an afterthought. . . .

## The Great Palace of Versailles

*Nothing nastier than a white person!*
She mutters as she irons alterations
in the backroom of Charlotte's Dress Shoppe.
The steam rising from a cranberry wool
comes alive with perspiration

and stale Evening of Paris.
*Swamp she born from, swamp*
*she swallow, swamp she got to sink again.*

The iron shoves gently
into a gusset, waits until
the puckers bloom away. Beyond
the curtain, the white girls are all
wearing shoulder pads to make their faces
delicate. That hair would be Autumn,
tossing her hair in imitation of Bacall.

Beulah had read in the library
how French ladies at court would tuck
their fans in a sleeve
and walk in the gardens for air. Swaying
among lilies, lifting shy layers of silk,
they dropped excrements as daintily
as handkerchieves. Against all rules

she had saved the lining from a botched coat
to face last year's gray skirt. She knows
whenever she lifts a knee
she flashes crimson. That seems legitimate;
but in the book she had read
how the *cavaliere* amused themselves
wearing powder and perfume and spraying
yellow borders knee-high on the stucco
of the *Orangerie.*

A hanger clatters
in the front of the shoppe.
Beulah remembers how
even Autumn could lean into a settee
with her ankles crossed, sighing
*I need a man who'll protect me*
while smoking her cigarette down to the very end.

# Canary

*For Michael S. Harper*

Billie Holiday's burned voice
had as many shadows as lights,
a mournful candelabra against a sleek piano,
the gardenia her signature under that ruined face.

(Now you're cooking, drummer to bass,
magic spoon, magic needle.
Take all day if you have to
with your mirror and your bracelet of song.)

Fact is, the invention of women under siege
has been to sharpen love in the service of myth.

If you can't be free, be a mystery.

# THYLIAS MOSS *(1954– )*

Thylias Moss was born in Cleveland, Ohio, in 1954 and educated at Oberlin College. She is the author of *Hosiery Seams on a Bowlegged Woman* (1983), *Pyramid of Bone* (1988), *Rainbow Remnants in Rock Bottom Ghetto Sky* (1991), *Small Congregations: New and Selected Poems* (1993), and *Last Chance for the Tarzan Holler* (1998).

Moss's poetry displays a witty intelligence, a delight in surprising the reader. Her tone can shift subtly and masterfully from light playfulness to dark contemplation. Her work was included in the recent *The Best of the Best American Poetry: 1988–1997* (1998), selected by Harold Bloom.

## A Reconsideration of the Blackbird

Let's call him *Jim Crow*.

Let's call him *Nigger* and see if he rises
faster than when we say *abracadabra*.

*Guess who's coming to dinner?*
Score ten points if you said blackbird.
Score twenty points if you were more specific, as in the first line.

What do you find *from here to eternity*?
Blackbirds.

*Who never sang for my father?*
The blackbirds who came, one after the other, landed on the roof
and pressed it down, burying us alive.
Why didn't we jump out the windows? Didn't we have enough
    time?
We were outnumbered (13 on the clothesline, 4 & 20 in the pie).
We were holding hands and hugging like never before.
You could say the blackbirds did us a favor.

Let's not say that however. Instead let the crows speak.
Let them use their tongues or forfeit them.

Problem: What would we do with 13 little black tongues?

Solution: Give them away. Hold them for ransom. Make belts.
Little nooses for little necks.

Problem: The little nooses fit only fingers.

Solution: Get married.

Problem: No one's in love with the blackbirds.

Solution: Paint them white, call them visions, everyone will want
one.


## Landscape with Saxophonist

The usual is there,
nondescript trees opened like umbrellas,
pessimists always expecting rain,
chickadees whose folding and unfolding wings
suggest the shuffling and reshuffling
of the cardsharp's deck;
nothing noteworthy except the beginning saxophonist
blowing with the efficacy of wolves addicted to pigs,
blowing down those poorly built houses,
the leaves off the trees, the water in
another direction, the ace of spades
into the ground with the cardsharp's bad intentions.
The discord and stridency set off landslides
and avalanches; his playing moves the earth
not lovers who are satisfied too quickly
and by the wrong things.

## Lessons from a Mirror

Snow White was nude at her wedding, she's so white
the gown seemed to disappear when she put it on.

Put me beside her and the proximity is good
for a study of chiaroscuro, not much else.

Her name aggravates me most, as if I need to be told
what's white and what isn't.

Judging strictly by appearance there's a future for me
forever at her heels, a shadow's constant worship.

Is it fair for me to live that way, unable
to get off the ground?

Turning the tables isn't fair unless they keep turning.
Then there's the danger of Russian roulette

and my disadvantage: nothing falls from the sky
to name me.

I am the empty space where the tooth was, that my tongue
rushes to fill because I can't stand vacancies.

And it's not enough. The penis just fills another
gap. And it's not enough.

When you look at me,
know that more than white is missing.


## The Undertaker's Daughter Feels Neglect

Tonight, a beautiful redhead
whose hair he's combed six times.

It is always the same. He never finds
his way to my room. My mother played dead
the night I was conceived.
Like him I'm attracted
to things that can't run away from me.
I spit-shine aluminum pans.

It's been years since the mailman came, years
since I woke in the middle of the night
thinking a party was going on downstairs,
thinking my father was a magician
and all those scantily clad women his assistants,
wondering why no one could hear me,
why I was made to disappear permanently in the box.
I seldom wake at all anymore.

# CORNELIUS EADY *(1954–     )*

**B**orn in Rochester, New York, in 1954, Cornelius Eady studied at Empire State College and the M.F.A. program at Warren Wilson College. He is currently director of the Poetry Center at the State University of New York at Stony Brook. His volumes of verse include *Kartunes* (1980), *Victims of the Latest Dance Craze* (1985, 1997), *BOOM BOOM BOOM* (1988), *The Gathering of My Name* (1991), *You Don't Miss Your Water* (1995), and *The Autobiography of a Jukebox* (1997).

Eady is a poet of the city, capturing the metropolis's raucousness, its muted ironies and clashing cultures, with a verve akin to that of a practiced jazz musician. His work is contemplative, and his sense of the rhetorical power of the blues is strong.

## Crows in a Strong Wind

Off go the crows from the roof.
The crows can't hold on.
They might as well
Be perched on an oil slick.

Such an awkward dance,
These gentlemen
In their spotted-black coats.
Such a tipsy dance,

As if they didn't know where they were.
Such a humorous dance,
As they try to set things right,
As the wind reduces them.

Such a sorrowful dance.
How embarrassing is love
When it goes wrong

In front of everyone.

# Leadbelly

You can actually hear it in his voice:
Sometimes the only way to discuss it
Is to grip a guitar as if it were
Somebody's throat
And pluck. If there were

A ship off of this planet,
An ark where the blues could show
Its other face,

A street where you could walk,
Just walk without dogged air at
Your heels, at your back, don't
You think he'd choose it?
Meanwhile, here's the tune:
Bad luck, empty pockets,
Trouble walking your way
With his tin ear.


# Muddy Waters & the Chicago Blues

Good news from the windy city: Thomas Edison's
Time on the planet has been validated. The guitars
And harps begin their slow translation
Of the street, an S.O.S. of what you need
And what you have. The way this life
Tries to roar you down, you have to fight

Fire with fire: the amplified power
Of a hip rotating in an upstairs flat
Vs. the old indignities; the static
Heat of *nothing, nowhere,*

*No how* against this conversation
Of fingers and tongues, this
Rent party above the
Slaughter-house.

## Radio

There is the woman
Who will not listen
To music. There is the man
Who dreams of kissing the lips
Attached to the voice.
There is the singer
Who reinvents the world
In musical notation.
There is the young couple
Who dance slowly on the sidewalk,
As if the rest of the street
Didn't exist.
There is the school boy
Whose one possession
Is an electric box
That scrambles the neighborhood.
There is the young girl
Who locks her bedroom door,
And lip-syncs in the mirror.
There is the young beau
Who believes in the songs so much,
He hears them
Even when
He isn't kissing someone.
There is the mother
Who absent-mindedly sways to the beat,
But fears the implications
For her daughter.
There is the man
Who carries one in his

Breast pocket
And pretends it's a Luger.
There are the two young punks
Who lug one into our car
On the stalled D train,
Who, as we tense for the assault,
Tune in a classical music station,
As if this were
Saturday night
On another world.

## Travelin' Shoes

And at last, I get the phone call. The blues rolls into
my sleepy ears at five A.M., a dry, official voice from
my father's hospital. A question, a few quick facts,
and my daddy's lying upstate on the coolin' floor.

Death, it seems, was kinder to him in his last hour
than life was in his last four months.

Death, who pulls him to a low ebb, then slowly
floods over his wrecked body like a lover.

*Cardio-vascular collapse,* the polite voice is telling
me, but later my cousin tells me, he arrives on the
ward before they shut my father's eyes and mouth to
see the joy still resting on his face from the moment
my daddy finally split his misery open.

# CARL PHILLIPS  *(1958–    )*

Carl Phillips studied classics at Harvard University and earned an M.A.T. in Latin at the University of Massachusetts and an M.F.A. at Brown University. An elegant craftsman, Phillips finds his themes in love and loss in their various (at times dizzyingly so) incarnations—carnal, fraternal, ancestral, intellectual. His tender voicings of personal, private spaces gather momentum in his longer poems toward the creation of a world of their own—a world at once jubilant with the satisfaction of its creation and harboring a near-elegiac recognition of its potential desolation.

Phillips's poems have appeared frequently in *The Best American Poetry* annual series as well as in numerous journals, including *The Kenyon Review* and *The Paris Review*. He is the author of three volumes of verse, *In the Blood* (1992), *Cortege* (1995), and *From the Devotions* (1998).

## Cortege

> *Do not imagine you can abdicate*
> —Auden

### *Prologue*

If the sea could dream, and if the sea
were dreaming now, the dream
would be the usual one: Of the Flesh.
The letter written in the dream would go
something like: *Forgive me—love, Blue.*

### *I. The Viewing (A Chorus)*

*O what, then, did he look like?*
                              He had a good body.

*And how came you to know this?*

His body was naked.

*Say the sound of his body.*

His body was quiet.

*Say again—quiet?*

He was sleeping.

*You are sure of this? Sleeping?*

Inside it, yes. Inside it.

## II. Pavilion

Sometimes, a breeze: a canvas
flap will rise and, inside,
someone stirs; *a bird? a flower?*

One is thinking *Should there be
thirst, I have only to reach
for the swollen bag of skin*

*beside me, I have only to touch
my mouth that is meant for a flower
to it, and drink.*

One is for now certain he is
one of those poems that stop only;
they do not end.

One says without actually saying it
*I am sometimes a book of such poems,
I am other times a flower and lovely*

*pressed like so among them, but
always they forget me.
I miss my name.*

They are all of them heat-
weary, anxious for evening as for
some beautiful to the bone

messenger to come. They will open
again for him. His hands are good.
His message is a flower.

### III. The Tasting (A Chorus)

*O what, then, did he taste like?*
                    He tasted of sorrow.

*And how came you to know this?*
                    My tongue still remembers.

*Say the taste that is sorrow.*
                    Game, fallen unfairly.

*And yet, you still tasted?*
                    Still, I tasted.

*Did you say to him something?*
                    I could not speak, for hunger.

### IV. Interior

And now,
the candle blooms gorgeously away
from his hand—

and the light has made
blameless all over
the body of him (mystery,

mystery), twelvefold
shining, by grace of twelve
mirrors the moth can't stop

attending. Singly, in no order,
it flutters against, beats
the glass of each one,

as someone elsewhere
is maybe beating upon
a strange door now,

somebody knocks
and knocks at a new
country, of which

nothing is understood—
no danger occurs
to him, though

danger could be any
of the unusually wild
flowers

that, either side of the road,
spring.
When he slows, bends down and

closer, to see or
to take one—it is as if
he knows something to tell it.

### V. The Dreaming (A Chorus)

*O what, then, did it feel like?*
> I dreamed of an arrow.

*And how came you to know him?*
> I dreamed he was wanting.

*Say the dream of him wanting.*
> A swan, a wing folding.

*Why do you weep now?*
> I remember.

*Tell what else you remember.*
> The swan was mutilated.


### *Envoi*

And I came to where was nothing but drowning
and more drowning, and saw to where the sea—
besides flesh—was, as well, littered with boats,
how each was blue but trimmed with white, to each
a name I didn't know, and then, recalling,
did. And ignoring the flesh that, burning, gives
more stink than heat, I dragged what boats I could
to the shore and piled them severally in a tree—
less space, and lit a fire that didn't take
at first—the wood was wet—and then, helped by
the wind, became a blaze so high the sea
itself, along with the bodies in it, seemed
to burn. I watched as each boat fell to flame:
*Vincent* and *Matthew* and, last, what bore your name.


## Aubade for Eve Under the Arbor


To the buzz and drowse of flies coupling over and over,
I wake, find your body still here, and remember it can
be this way always, us in abundance, visitors few,
behind everything a suggestion of more, ready or not,
where that came from.

> In those spaces of the world that
the trees, bending aside, give onto, I watch small game
settle and move on, barely long enough for me to assign
them their various names: bush-fowl, blue raven, peahen
with her dull hand of a tail scribbling onto the wet grass

behind her the questions I still can't understand: how
long, when is too much not enough—what price desire?

It is easier for me to believe I came from dirt, having seen
what a little spit and a couple of fingers can do, given
the chance, than that anything torn from my side gave rise
to you, despite evenings when, still awake after turning
from you, I have run my hands up my own body and come
close to saying yes, something's missing. . . . I wonder,

this morning, can you say what it is. I roll over, intending
to ask, but can't wake you, seeing you this quiet, and the sun,
through vines that hold back the sky, throwing shadows, in
thin snakes, across you—look, there is one now, at your ear:
tell me, it seems to say, what can you know of the world?

# ANTHONY WALTON  *(1960–    )*

Anthony Walton was born in 1960 in Aurora, Illinois, and received his B.A. from the University of Notre Dame and his M.F.A. from Brown University. Like his chief influences, he is a poet deeply rooted in the blues—using it almost as an etymology unto itself and an enabling pattern of life.

His work has appeared in *The New York Times* and *The Oxford American,* among other publications. He is the author of *Mississippi: An American Journey* (1996) and numerous articles and essays, and in 1998 he received a Whiting Writers' Award. Walton is a longtime resident of Brunswick, Maine, where he teaches at Bowdoin College.

## Dissidence

### *In Memoriam Thelonious Monk*

You have to be able to hear past the pain, the obvious
minor-thirds and major-sevenths, the merely beautiful

ninths; you have to grow deaf to what you imagine
are the sounds of loneliness; you have to learn indifference

to static, and welcome noise like rain, acclimate
to another kind of silence; you have to be able to sleep

in the city, taxis and trucks careening through your dreams
and back again, hearing the whines and sirens and shrieks

as music; you must be a mathematician, a magician
of algebra, overtone and acoustics, mapping the splintered

intervals of time, tempo, harmony, stalking or sluicing blues
scales; you have to be unafraid of redundance, and aware

that dissonance-driven explorations of dissonance
may circle back to the crowded room of resolution;

you have to disagree with everything except the piano, black
and white keys marking the path you must climb step

by half-step with no compass but the blues, no company
but your distrust of the journey, of all that you hear, of arrival.

## Celestial Mechanics

I have always been the poor
student, failing
geometry and physics,

confusing quadratics
with differentials.
You could explain it, master

of calculus, the night sky
the screen of your overhead
projector as you distinguished

terrestrial from extra-
terrestrial, then sailed
ferocious Orion, south

by southwest,
a forty-five degree angle
off your back step.

Sir Isaac Newton implied, you said,
that it all came down to gravity
and motion; bodies

moving through space will attract
each other. But it is a law
of physics that they must keep

moving. In Newtonian mechanics the stars
are in their courses, grooved
and suspended in space, gravity

pulling bodies toward other bodies
as they themselves are pulled
toward something else.

This is known as balance, equilibrium,
grace. Space is everywhere,
endless and empty,

it both is and contains what we know
of the universe,
and we may safely deduce

that our world is as it should be
as this is how it is.
It is all so simple:

the stars are in their courses, moving
through their fates,
moved by the immutable laws

of gravity and motion that rule
the world,
and it is my fate to be here,

a moving body in motion,
in place, suspended,
balanced, and helpless.

# The Lovesong of Emmett Till

More than likely she was Irish
or Italian, a sweet child who knew him
only as a shy clown.
Colleen, Jenny or Marie, she
probably didn't even know
he had her picture,
that he had traded her cousin
for baseball cards or a pocketknife,
that her routine visage
sat smoldering in his wallet
beyond any price.
He carried his love
like a burden, and devotion
always has to tell.
Hell, he was just flirting
with that lady in the store,
he already had his white
woman back up in Chicago.
He wasn't greedy, just showing
off, showing the rustics
how it was done. He had an eye,
all right, and he was free
with it, he knew they loved it.
*Hey baby,* was all he said,
and he meant it as a compliment,
when he said it in Chicago
the white girls laughed.
So when they came to get
him, he thought it was
a joke, he proclaimed himself guilty
of love, he showed them
the picture and paid the price of
not innocence, but affection, affection
for a little black-haired, blue-eyed
girl who must by now be an older
woman in Chicago, a woman
who will never know

she was to die for, that he died
refusing to take back her name,
his right to claim he loved her.


## The Summer Was Too Long


The fever broke in October,
and I woke sweating in a compost
of leaves,
            the ashes of summer.

Asleep since spring,
                the scythe of winter
through my dreams.

What is summer but a dream,
implying more
            than it can mean?

Give me grey variations
of gray,
        shadows fanning through water, clouds,
space,
        I will trade hay for straw, daylight
for darkness.

Let me warm my hands on the blazing
trees,
        breathe the dark wind chasing long days
into silence,
                pass the long night in blankets
of snow.

# ELIZABETH ALEXANDER  *(1962–      )*

**E**lizabeth Alexander was born in New York City in 1962 and raised in Washington, DC. A graduate of Yale University, the Writing Program of Boston University, and the University of Pennsylvania, Alexander currently teaches at Smith College. Her first collection of verse, *The Venus Hottentot,* was published in 1990; her second volume, *Body of Life,* appeared in 1996. She has also authored numerous essays and book reviews.

Nostalgic yet empowering, Alexander's poetry most often engages with history in the form of the individual voice. Many of her best poems utilize the dramatic monologue to reveal the complexities and struggles of various African American personas. Autobiographical pieces merge with these historical works to create a palimpsest of relationships between African Americans both past and present.

## The Venus Hottentot

*(1825)*

### 1. Cuvier

Science, science, science!
Everything is beautiful

blown up beneath my glass.
Colors dazzle insect wings.

A drop of water swirls
like marble. Ordinary

crumbs become stalactites
set in perfect angles

of geometry I'd thought
impossible. Few will

ever see what I see
through this microscope.

Cranial measurements
crowd my notebook pages,

and I am moving closer,
close to how these numbers

signify aspects of
national character.

Her genitalia
will float inside a labeled

pickling jar in the Musée
de l'Homme on a shelf

above Broca's brain:
"The Venus Hottentot."

Elegant facts await me.
Small things in this world are mine.

2.

There is an unexpected sun today
in London, and the clouds that
most days sift into this cage
where I am working have dispersed.
I am a black cutout against
a captive blue sky, pivoting
nude so the paying audience
can view my naked buttocks.

I am called "Venus Hottentot."
I left Capetown with a promise

of revenue: half the profits
and my passage home: A boon!
Master's brother proposed the trip;
the magistrate granted me leave.
I would return to my family
a duchess, with watered-silk

dresses and money to grow food,
rouge and powders in glass pots,
silver scissors, a lorgnette,
voile and tulle instead of flax,
cerulean blue instead
of indigo. My brother would
devour sugar-studded non-
pareils, pale taffy, damask plums.

That was years ago. London's
circuses are florid and filthy,
swarming with cabbage-smelling
citizens who stare and query,
"Is it muscle? bone? or fat?"
My neighbor to the left is
The Sapient Pig, "The Only
Scholar of His Race." He plays

at cards, tells time and fortunes
by scraping his hooves. Behind
me is Prince Kar-mi, who arches
like a rubber tree and stares back
at the crowd from under the crook
of his knee. A professional
animal trainer shouts my cues.
There are singing mice here.

"The Ball of Duchess DuBarry":
In the engraving I lurch
toward the *belles dames,* mad-eyed, and
they swoon. Men in capes and pince-nez
shield them. Tassels dance at my hips.
In this newspaper lithograph

my buttocks are shown swollen
and luminous as a planet.

Monsieur Cuvier investigates
between my legs, poking, prodding,
sure of his hypothesis.
I half expect him to pull silk
scarves from inside me, paper poppies,
then a rabbit! He complains
at my scent and does not think
I comprehend, but I speak

English. I speak Dutch. I speak
a little French as well, and
languages Monsieur Cuvier
will never know have names.
Now I am bitter and now
I am sick. I eat brown bread,
drink rancid broth. I miss good sun,
miss Mother's *sadza*. My stomach

is frequently queasy from mutton
chops, the pale potatoes, blood sausage.
I was certain that this would be
better than farm life. I am
the family entrepreneur!
But there are hours in every day
to conjure my imaginary
daughters, in banana skirts

an ostrich-feather fans.
Since my own genitals are public
I have made other parts private.
In my silence I possess
mouth, larynx, brain, in a single
gesture. I rub my hair
with lanolin, and pose in profile
like a painted Nubian

archer, imagining gold leaf
woven through my hair, and diamonds.
Observe the wordless Odalisque.
I have not forgotten my Xhosa
clicks. My flexible tongue
and healthy mouth bewilder
this man with his rotting teeth.
If he were to let me rise up

from this table, I'd spirit
his knives and cut out his black heart,
seal it with science fluid inside
a bell jar, place it on a low
shelf in a white man's museum
so the whole world could see
it was shriveled and hard,
geometric, deformed, unnatural.

# Narrative: Ali

*A Poem in Twelve Rounds*

### Narrative

### I.

My head so big
they had to pry
me out.      I'm sorry
Bird (is what I call
my mother).      Cassius
Marcellus Clay,
Muhammad Ali,
you can say
my name in any
language, any
continent:      Ali.

2.

Two photographs
of Emmett Till,
born my year,
on my birthday.
One, he's smiling,
happy, and the other one
is after.       His mother
did the bold thing,
kept the casket open,
made the thousands look upon
his bulging eyes,
his twisted neck,
her lynched black boy.
I couldn't sleep
for thinking,
Emmett Till.

One day I went
down to the train tracks,
found some iron
shoe-shine rests
and planted them
between the ties
and waited
for a train to come,
and watched the train
derail, and ran,
and after that
I slept at night.

3.

I need to train
around people,
hear them talk,
talk back.       I need
to hear the traffic,
see people in

the barbershop,
people getting
shoeshines, talking,
hear them talk,
talk back.

4.

Bottom line:      Olympic gold
can't buy a black man
a Louisville hamburger
in nineteen-sixty.

Wasn't even real gold.
I watched the river
drag the ribbon down,
red, white, and blue.

5.

Laying on the bed,
praying for a wife,
in walk Sonji Roi.

Pretty little shape.
Do you like
chop suey?

Can I wash your hair
underneath
that wig?

Lay on the bed,
Girl.       Lie
with me.

Shake to the east,
to the north,
south, west—

but remember,
remember, I need
a Muslim wife.        So

Quit using lipstick.
Quit your boogaloo.
Cover up your knees.

like a Muslim
wife, religion,
religion, a Muslim

wife.        Eleven
months with Sonji,
first woman I loved.

6.

There's not
too many days
that pass that I
don't think
of how it started,
but I know
no Great White Hope
can beat
a true black champ.
Jerry Quarry
could have been
a movie star,
a millionaire,
a Senator,
a President—
he only had
to do one thing,
is whip me,
but he can't.

## 7. *Dressing Room Visitor*

He opened
up his shirt:
"KKK" cut
in his chest.
He dropped
his trousers:
latticed scars
where testicles
should be.      His face
bewildered, frozen,
in the Alabama woods
that night in 1966
when they left him
for dead, his testicles
in a Dixie Cup.
You a warning,
they told him,
to smart-mouth,
sassy-acting niggers,
meaning niggers
still alive,
meaning any nigger,
meaning niggers
like me.

## 8. *Training*

Unsweetened grapefruit juice
will melt my stomach down.
Don't drive if you can walk,
don't walk if you can run.
I add a mile each day
and run in eight-pound boots.

My knuckles sometimes burst
the glove.      I let dead skin
build up, and then I peel it,
let it scar, so I don't bleed

as much.       My bones
absorb the shock.

I train in three-minute
spurts, like rounds:       three
rounds big bag, three speed
bag, three jump rope, one
minute breaks,
no more, no less.

Am I too old?       Eat only
kosher meat.       Eat cabbage,
carrots, beets, and watch
the weight come down:
two-thirty, two-twenty,
two-ten, two-oh-nine.

9.

Will I go
like Kid Paret,
a fractured
skull, a ten-day
sleep, dreaming
alligators, pork-
chops, saxophones,
slow grinds, funk,
fishbowls, lightbulbs,
bats, typewriters,
tuning forks, funk,
clocks, red rubber
ball, what you see
in that lifetime
knockout minute
on the cusp?
You could be
let go,
you could be
snatched back.

## 10. *Rumble in the Jungle*

*Ali boma ye,*
*Ali boma ye,*
means kill him, Ali,
which is different
from a whupping
which is what I give,
but I lead them chanting
anyway, *Ali*
*boma ye,* because
here in Africa
black people fly
planes and run countries.

I'm still making up
for the foolishness
I said when I was
Clay from Louisville,
where I learned Africans
lived naked in straw
huts eating tiger meat,
grunting and grinning,
swinging from vines,
pounding their chests—

I pound my chest but of my own accord.

### 11.

I said to Joe Frazier,
first thing, get a good house
in case you get crippled
so you and your family
can sleep somewhere.     Always
keep one good Cadillac.
And watch how you dress
with that cowboy hat,
pink suits, white shoes—
that's how pimps dress,

or kids, and you a champ,
or wish you were, 'cause
I can whip you in the ring
or whip you in the street.
Now back to clothes,
wear dark clothes, suits,
black suits, like you the best
at what you do, like you
President of the World.
Dress like that.
Put them yellow pants away.
We dinosaurs gotta
look good, gotta sound
good, gotta be good,
the greatest, that's what
I told Joe Frazier,
and he said to me,
we both bad niggers.
We don't do no crawlin'.


### 12.

They called me "the fistic pariah."

They said I didn't love my country,
called me a race-hater, called me out
of my name, waited for me
to come out on a streetcar, shot at me,
hexed me, cursed me, wished me
all manner of ill-will,
told me I was finished.

*Here I am,*
like the song says,
*come and take me,*

"The People's Champ,"

myself,
Muhammad.

# REGINALD SHEPHERD (1963–   )

Reginald Shepherd's poetry is both passionate and intelligent, deftly mixing the poet's interest in myth with a respect for history and a wistful awe of love. Many strands of thought and allusion can occur simultaneously in a Shepherd poem, a careful layering that rewards repeated reading.

Born in New York City in 1963, Shepherd was raised in the Bronx and attended Bennington College. He received two M.F.A.'s—one from Brown University in 1991, another from the University of Iowa in 1993. A recipient of a "Discovery"/*The Nation* award and a National Endowment for the Arts creative writing fellowship, Shepherd is the author of *Some Are Drowning* (1994) and *Angel, Interrupted* (1996). His poetry has been published widely in literary journals, including *Poetry, Tri-Quarterly,* and *The Iowa Review,* as well as the 1995 and 1996 volumes of *The Best American Poetry.* Shepherd currently lives in Chicago and teaches at Northern Illinois University.


## Narcissus in Plato's Cave

The eye of the lake is on fire. Pluck it out:
a bloom of clotted blood that stains the palm
with wounded light. Sunset inflects surface tensions
with its bluster, then recedes

into the I-am-not-a-little-boy, rumors the skin becomes
of glass. This is my heart of running water
stilled, pooled sap from snapped stems and reeds
broken by a touch, now irretrievable. (Someone

who sank centuries ago is asking me to stir
a current, someone's asking for the underside
of my blurred face. This clearing in the myth of woods
was never mine.) My fascination multiplies

these flowers out of frost and cobwebs, filaments of morning
ice breath violates: their fragments
sink in concentric ripples. A skipped stone
bears no loss: drowned as I am

among the surfaces of things, my features
will never heal. These brackish waters
close over every sacrifice. Socrates once
told me, *Know thyself.* (Or twice, I can't recall.) I wanted that

myself, but here I am with dew
and drenched red petals, a cloud in bloom.


## Tantalus in May

When I look down, I see the season's blinding flowers,
the usual mesmerizing and repellent artifacts:
a frat boy who turns too sharply from my stare,
a cardinal capturing vision in a lilac bush

on my walk home. I'm left to long
even for simple dangers. From the waist up
it's still winter, I left world behind
a long time ago; waist down it's catching

up, a woodpecker out my window is mining grubs
from some nameless tree squirrels scramble over.
When I turn back it's gone, I hadn't realized
this had gone so far. (Everywhere I look

it's suddenly spring. No one asked
if I would like to open drastically. Look up.
It's gone.) Everywhere fruits dangle
I can't taste, their branches insurmountable,

my tongue burnt by frost. White boys, white flowers,
and foul-mouthed jays, days made of sky-blue boredoms
and everything seen much too clearly:
the utterance itself is adoration, kissing

stolid air. I hate every lovely thing about them.


## Slaves


These are the years of the empty hands. And what
were those just past, swift with the flash of alloyed hulls
but carrying no cargo? Outside our lives, my mythical
America, dingy rollers fringed with soot deposit
cracked syringes and used condoms on beaches tinted gray
by previous waves, but when an hour waits just for a moment,
everything begins again. All of it is yours, the longed-for
mundane: men falling from a cloud-filled sky like flakes of snow
onto the ocean, your mother immersed in ordinary misery
and burning breakfast, still alive in the small tenement
kitchen. You understand I use the second person
only as a marker: beyond these sheltered bays are monsters,
and tarnished treasures of lost galleons
it's death to bring to light. The ships put out
and they sink; before the final mast descends, the shadow
of a single sailor is burned across the sun, then wrapped
in strands of cirrus, his European skin a gift
to the black and unknown ocean floor. Of the slaves
thrown overboard to save the ship, no words
remain. What memorials the public beach becomes
in late October, scattered with Puerto Rican families
on muddied sand still lighter than a black man's
pound of flesh: it abrades my skin. I can't touch
that perfected picture of myself, no white wave
will wash either hand clean. There is a wind
riding in on the tainted waves, and what it cannot
make whole it destroys. You would say that all along

I chose wrong, antonyms of my own face
lined up like buoys, but there is another shore
on the far side of that wind. Everything is there,
outside my unhealed history, outside my fears. I
can see it now, and every third or fourth wave is clear.

# SELECTED BIBLIOGRAPHIES

### ELIZABETH ALEXANDER

**Poems:** *The Venus Hottentot* (1990), *Body of Life* (1996).

### BENJAMIN BANNEKER

**Other:** *The Pennsylvania, Delaware, Maryland, and Virginia Almanac and Ephemeris* (1791–1802).

### AMIRI BARAKA (LEROI JONES)

**Poems:** *Preface to a Twenty Volume Suicide Note* (1961), *The Dead Lecturer* (1964), *Black Magic: Sabotage, Target Study, Black Art; Collected Poetry, 1961–1967* (1969), *It's Nation Time* (1970), *Spirit Reach* (1972), *Transbluesency: The Selected Poems of Amiri Baraka/LeRoi Jones (1961–1995)* (1995), *Funk Lore: New Poems (1984–1995)* (1996).

**Other:** *Dutchman* and *The Slave* [plays] (1964), *Blues People; Negro Music in White America* (1963), *The System of Dante's Hell* [novel] (1965), *Home; Social Essays* (1966), *The Baptism* and *The Toilet* [plays] (1966), *Tales* (1967), *Black Music* [criticism] (1967), *Raise Race Rays Raze* [essays] (1971), *The Motion of History* [plays] (1978), *Daggers and Javelins: Essays, 1974–1979* (1984), *The Music: Reflections on Jazz and Blues* (with Amina Baraka, 1987), *The LeRoi Jones/Amiri Baraka Reader* (1991), *Wise, Why's, Y's* (1995), *Eulogies* (1996), *The Autobiography of LeRoi Jones* (1997).

### GWENDOLYN BENNETT

No volumes; journal submissions

### WILLIAM STANLEY BRAITHWAITE

**Poems:** *Lyrics of Life* (1904), *The House of Falling Leaves* (1908), *Selected Poems* (1948), *The William Stanley Braithwaite Reader* (edited by Philip Butcher, 1972).

### GWENDOLYN BROOKS

**Poems:** *A Street in Bronzeville* (1945), *Annie Allen* (1949), *The Bean Eaters* (1960), *Selected Poems* (1963), *We Real Cool* (1966),

*The Wall* (1967), *In the Mecca* (1968), *Family Pictures* (1970), *Riot* (1970), *Black Steel: Joe Frazier and Muhammad Ali* (1971), *Aloneness* (1971), *Aurora* (1972), *Beckonings* (1975), *Black Love* (1981), *To Disembark* (1981), *The Near-Johannesburg Boy and Other Poems* (1986), *Blacks* (1987), *Winnie* (1988), *Children Coming Home* (1992).

**Other:** *Maud Martha, A Novel* (1953), *Bronzeville Boys and Girls* (1956), *The World of Gwendolyn Brooks* (1971), *Report from Part One: An Autobiography* (1972), *The Tiger Who Wore White Gloves: or, What You Are You Are* (1974), *Primer for Blacks* (1981), *Report from Part Two* (1996).

## STERLING A. BROWN

**Poems:** *Southern Road* (1932), *The Last Ride of Wild Bill and Eleven Narrative Poems* (1975), *The Collected Poems of Sterling A. Brown* (1980).

**Other:** *Outline for the Study of the Poetry of American Negroes* (1931), *The Negro in American Fiction* (1937), *Negro Poetry and Drama* (1937), *A Son's Return: Selected Essays of Sterling A. Brown* (edited by Mark A. Sanders, 1996).

## LUCILLE CLIFTON

**Poems:** *Good Times* (1969), *Good News About the Earth* (1972), *An Ordinary Woman* (1974), *The Times They Used to Be* (1974), *Two-Headed Woman* (1980), *Here Is Another Bone to Pick with You* (1981), *Good Women: Poems and a Memoir, 1969–1980* (1987), *Next: New Poems* (1987), *Quilting: Poems 1987–1990* (1991), *The Book of Light* (1993), *The Terrible Stories* (1996).

**Other:** *Some of the Days of Everett Anderson* [children] (1970), *The Boy Who Didn't Believe in Spring* [children] (1973), *Generations: A Memoir* (1976), *Three Wishes* (1976), *Everett Anderson's Goodbye* [children] (1983).

## JOSEPH SEAMAN COTTER, SR.

**Poems:** *A Rhyming* (1895), *Links of Friendship* (1898), *A White Song and a Black One* (1909), *Collected Poems* (1938), *Sequel to the "Pied Piper of Hamelin," and Other Poems* (1939), *Negroes and Others at Work and Play* (1947).

**Other:** *Caleb, the Degenerate, a Play in Four Acts* (1903).

## COUNTEE CULLEN

**Poems:** *Color* (1925), *The Ballad of the Brown Girl* (1927), *Copper Sun* (1927), *The Black Christ and Other Poems* (1929), *One Way to Heaven* (1932), *The Medea and Some Poems* (1935), *On These I Stand: An Anthology of the Best Poems of Countee Cullen* (1947).

**Other:** *The Lost Zoo* [stories] (1940), *My Lives and How I Lost Them* [stories] (1942), *My Soul's High Song: The Collected Writings of Countee Cullen* (edited by Gerald Early, 1991).

## TOI DERRICOTTE

**Poems:** *Captivity* (1989), *Tender* (1997).

**Other:** *The Black Notebooks* (1997).

## RITA DOVE

**Poems:** *The Yellow House on the Corner* (1980), *Museum* (1983), *Thomas and Beulah* (1986), *Grace Notes* (1989), *Mother Love* (1995), *On the Bus with Rosa Parks* (1999).

**Other:** *Fifth Sunday* [stories] (1985), *Through the Ivory Gate* [novel] (1992), *The Darker Face of the Earth: A Play* (1996).

## PAUL LAURENCE DUNBAR

**Poems:** *Oak and Ivy* (1893), *Majors and Minors* (1895), *Lyrics of Lowly Life* (1896), *Lyrics of the Hearthside* (1899), *Poems of Cabin and Field* (1899), *Candle-Lightin' Time* (1901), *In Old Plantation Days* (1903), *Lyrics of Love and Laughter* (1903), *When Malindy Sings* (1903), *Li'l Gal* (1904), *Chris'mus' Is A'Comin', and Other Poems* (1905), *Howdy, Honey, Howdy* (1905), *Lyrics of Sunshine and Shadow* (1905), *Joggin' Erlong* (1906), *I Greet the Dawn* (1978), *The Collected Poetry of Paul Laurence Dunbar* (edited by Joanne Braxton, 1993).

**Other:** *Folks from Dixie* (1892), *The Uncalled* (1898), *The Love of Landry* (1900), *The Fanatics* (1901), *The Sport of the Gods* (1902), *The Heart of Happy Hollow* (1904), *The Best Stories of Paul Laurence Dunbar* (edited by Benjamin Brawley, 1938).

## CORNELIUS EADY

**Poems:** *Victims of the Latest Dance Craze* (1986), *The Gathering of My Name* (1991), *You Don't Miss Your Water* (1995).

## C. S. GISCOMBE

**Poems**: *Postcards* (1977), *At Large* (1989), *Giscombe Road, Second Section* (1994), *Here* (1994), *Two Selections from Giscombe Road* (1995), *Giscombe Road* (1998).

## JUPITOR HAMMON

**Poems**: *America's First Negro Poet: The Complete Works of Jupitor Hammon of Long Island* (edited by Stanely Austin Ranson, Jr., 1983).

## FRANCES E. W. HARPER

**Poems**: *Poems on Miscellaneous Subjects* (1854), *Moses: A Story of the Nile* (1869), *Poems* (1871), *Sketches of Southern Life* (1873), *Atlanta Offering* (1895), *Idylls of the Bible* (1901), *Complete Poems of Frances E. W. Harper* (1988), *A Brighter Coming Day: A Frances Ellen Watkins Harper Reader* (edited by Frances Smith Foster, 1990).

**Other**: *Iola Leroy; or, Shadows Uplifted* (1893), *Minnie's Sacrifice; Sowing and Reaping; Trial and Triumph: Three Rediscovered Novels* (edited by Frances Smith Foster, 1994).

## MICHAEL S. HARPER

**Poems**: *Dear John, Dear Coltrane* (1970), *History Is Your Own Heartbeat* (1971), *Song: I Want a Witness* (1972), *Debridement* (1973), *Nightmare Begins Responsibility* (1974), *Images of Kin: New and Selected Poems* (1977), *Healing Song for the Inner Ear* (1985), *Honorable Amendments* (1995).

## ROBERT HAYDEN

**Poems**: *Heart-Shape in the Dust* (1940), *A Ballad of Remembrance* (1962), *Selected Poems* (1966), *Words in the Mourning Time* (1970), *The Night-Blooming Cereus* (1972), *Angle of Ascent: New and Selected Poems* (1975), *American Journal* (1978, 1980), *Collected Poems* (1985).

**Other**: *Collected Prose* (1984).

## GEORGE MOSES HORTON

**Poems**: *The Hope of Liberty, Containing a Number of Poetical Pieces* (1829), *Poems by a Slave* (1837), *The Poetical Works* (1845),

*Naked Genius* (1865), *The Black Bard of North Carolina: George Moses Horton and His Poetry* (edited by Joan R. Sherman, 1997).

## LANGSTON HUGHES

**Poems:** *The Weary Blues* (1926), *Fine Clothes to the Jew* (1927), *Shakespeare in Harlem* (1942), *Montage of a Dream Deferred* (1951), *Selected Poems* (1959), *Ask Your Mama: Twelve Moods for Jazz* (1961).

**Other:** *Not Without Laughter* [memoir] (1930), *The Ways of White Folks* [stories] (1934), *The Big Sea: An Autobiography* (1940), *Simple Speaks His Mind* (1950), *I Wonder as I Wander: An Autobiographical Journey* (1956), *The Langston Hughes Reader* (1958), *Five Plays by Langston Hughes* (edited by Webster Smalley, 1963), *The Panther and the Lash* (1967).

## GEORGIA DOUGLAS JOHNSON

**Poems:** *The Heart of a Woman and Other Poems* (1918), *Bronze: A Book of Poems* (1922), *An Autumn Love Cycle* (1928), *Share My World: A Book of Poems* (1962), *The Selected Works of Georgia Douglass Johnson* (edited by Claudia Tate, 1997).

**Other:** *Plumes: A Play in One Act* (1927).

## JAMES WELDON JOHNSON

**Poems:** *Fifty Years and Other Poems* (1917), *God's Trombones: Seven Negro Sermons in Verse* (1927), *Saint Peter Relates an Incident of the Resurrection Day* (1930), *Saint Peter Relates an Incident: Selected Poems* (1935).

**Other:** *The Autobiography of an Ex-Colored Man* (1912, 1927), *Black Manhattan* (1930), *Along This Way: The Autobiography of James Weldon Johnson* (1933), *Negro Americans, What Now?* (1938), *The Selected Writing of James Weldon Johnson* (edited by Sondra Kathryn Wilson, 1995).

## GAYL JONES

**Poems:** *Song for Anninho* (1981), *The Hermit Women: Poems* (1983), *Xarque and Other Poems* (1985).

**Other:** *Corregidora* [fiction] (1975), *Eva's Man* [fiction] (1976), *Liberating Voices: Oral Traditions in African-American Literature* (1991), *The Healing* [fiction] (1998), *Mosquito* [fiction] (1999).

## BOB KAUFMAN

**Poems:** *Solitudes Crowded with Loneliness* (1965), *The Ancient Rain: Poems, 1956–1978* (1981), *Cranial Guitar: Selected Poems* (1996).

## ETHERIDGE KNIGHT

**Poems:** *Poems from Prison* (1968), *Belly Song and Other Poems* (1973), *Born of a Woman: New and Selected Poems* (1980), *The Essential Etheridge Knight* (1992).

**Other:** *Black Voices from Prison* [anthology] (1970).

## YUSEF KOMUNYAKAA

**Poems:** *Copacetic* (1984), *I Apologize for the Eyes in My Head* (1986), *Dien Cau Dau* (1988), *Magic City* (1992), *Neon Vernacular: New and Selected Poems* (1994), *Thieves of Paradise* (1998).

## AUDRE LORDE

**Poems:** *Cables to Rage* (1970), *From a Land Where Other People Live* (1973), *Between Our Selves* (1974), *Coal* (1976), *The Black Unicorn* (1978), *Chosen Poems, Old and New* (1982), *Our Dead Behind Us* (1986), *Undersong: Chosen Poems, Old and New* (1992), *The Marvelous Arithmetics of Distance: Poems 1987–1992* (1993), *The Collected Poems of Audre Lorde* (1997).

**Other:** *The Cancer Journals* (1980), *Zami: A New Spelling of My Name* (1982), *Sister Outsider: Essays and Speeches* (1984), *A Burst of Light: Essays* (1988).

## NATHANIEL MACKEY

**Poems:** *Septet for the End of Time* (1983), *Eroding Witness* (1985), *School of Udhra* (1993), *Song of the Andoumboulou, 18–20* (1994).

**Other:** *Bedouin Hornbook* [fiction] (1986), *Discrepant Engagement: Dissonance, Cross-Culturality, and Experimental Writing* (1993).

## HAKI MADHUBUTI (DON L. LEE)

**Poems:** *Directionscore: Selected and New Poems* (1971), *We Walk the Way of the New World* (1972), *Killing Memory, Seeking*

*Ancestors* (1987), *GroundWork: New and Selected Poems of Don L. Lee/Haki R. Madhubuti, from 1966–1996* (1996).

**Other:** *Dynamite Voices* (1971), *From Plan to Planet: Life Studies; the Need for Afrikan Minds and Institutions* (1973), *Enemies: The Clash of Races* (1978), *Claiming Earth: Race, Rage, Rape, Redemption; Blacks Seeking a Culture of Enlightened Empowerment* (1994).

## CLAUDE MCKAY

**Poems:** *Songs of Jamaica* (1912), *Constab Ballads* (1912), *Spring in New Hampshire and Other Poems* (1920), *Harlem Shadows* (1922), *Selected Poems of Claude McKay* (1953), *The Dialect Poetry of Claude McKay* (edited by Wayne F. Cooper, 1972), *The Passion of Claude McKay: Selected Poetry and Prose, 1912–1948* (edited by Wayne F. Cooper, 1973).

**Other:** *Home to Harlem* [novel] (1928), *Banjo: A Story Without a Plot* [novel] (1929), *Gingertown* [stories] (1932), *Banana Bottom* [novel] (1933), *A Long Way from Home* [autobiography] (1937), *Harlem: Negro Metropolis* [essays] (1940), *Trial by Lynching* [stories] (1977), *My Green Hills of Jamaica* [stories] (1979), *The Negroes in America* [essays] (1979).

## THYLIAS MOSS

**Poems:** *Hosiery Seams on a Bowlegged Woman* (1983), *Pyramid of Bone* (1988), *Rainbow Remnants in Rock Bottom Ghetto Sky* (1991), *Small Congregations: New and Selected Poems* (1993), *Last Chance for the Tarzan Holler* (1998).

## MARILYN NELSON

**Poems:** *For the Body* (1978), *Martha's Promises* (1985), *The Homeplace* (1985), *The Fields of Praise: New and Selected Poems* (1997).

## RAYMOND PATTERSON

**Poems:** *Twenty-six Ways of Looking at a Blackman and Other Poems* (1969), *The Elemental Blues* (1985).

## CARL PHILLIPS

**Poems:** *In the Blood* (1992), *Cortege* (1995), *From the Devotions* (1998).

## ISHMAEL REED

**Poems:** *Catechism of the Neo-American Hoodoo Church* (1970), *Conjure: Selected Poems, 1963–1970* (1972), *Chattanooga* (1974), *A Secretary to the Spirits* (1978), *Cab Calloway Stands In for the Moon* (1986), *New and Collected Poems* (1988).

**Other:** *The Free-Lance Pallbearers* [novel] (1967), *Mumbo Jumbo* [novel] (1972), *The Last Days of Louisiana Red* (1974), *Flight to Canada* [novel] (1976), *Shrovetide in Old New Orleans* [novel] (1978), *God Made Alaska for the Indians: Selected Essays* (1982), *The Terrible Twos* (1982), *Reckless Eyeballing* [novel] (1986), *Airing Dirty Laundry* (1993), *Japanese by Spring* (1993), *MultiAmerican: Essays on Cultural Wars and Cultural Peace* (1997).

## SONIA SANCHEZ

**Poems:** *Homecoming* (1969), *We a BaddDDD People* (1970), *A Blues Book for Blue Black Magical Women* (1971), *Love Poems* (1973), *I've Been a Woman: New and Selected Poems* (1978), *Homegirls and Hand Grenades* (1981), *Generations: Selected Poetry, 1969–1985* (1986), *Under a Soprano Sky* (1987), *Does Your House Have Lions?* (1997), *Like the Singing Coming off the Drums: Love Poems* (1998), *Shake Loose My Skin: New and Selected Poems* (1999).

**Other:** *Sister Son/ji* [play] (1969).

## REGINALD SHEPHERD

**Poems:** *Some Are Drowning* (1994), *Angel, Interrupted* (1996).

## ANNE SPENCER

No volumes; journal submissions.

## MELVIN B. TOLSON

**Poems:** *Libretto for the Republic of Liberia* (1953), *Harlem Gallery: Book I, The Curator* (1966), *A Gallery of Harlem Portraits* (1979).

**Other:** *Rendezvous with America* (1944), *Caviar and Cabbage: Selected Columns by Melvin B. Tolson from the Washington Tribune* (edited by Robert M. Farnsworth, 1982).

## JEAN TOOMER

**Poems:** *Cane* (1923), *The Collected Poems of Jean Toomer* (edited by Robert B. Jones and Margery Toomer Latimer, 1988).

**Other:** *Essentials: Definitions and Aphorisms* (1931), *The Wayward and the Seeking* (edited by Darwin T. Turner, 1980), *A Jean Toomer Reader: Selected Unpublished Writings* (1993).

## GEORGE BOYER VASHON

**Poems:** "Vincent Ogé" in *Autographs for Freedom* (edited by Julia Griffiths, 1856).

## DEREK WALCOTT

**Poems:** *In a Green Night: Poems, 1948–1960* (1962), *Selected Poems* (1964), *The Castaway and Other Poems* (1965), *The Gulf and Other Poems* (1970), *Another Life* (1973), *Sea Grapes* (1976), *The Star-Apple Kingdom* (1979), *The Fortunate Traveller* (1981), *Midsummer* (1984), *Collected Poems* (1986), *The Arkansas Testament* (1987), *Omeros* (1990), *The Bounty* (1997).

**Other:** *Dream on Monkey Mountain, and Other Plays* (1970), *The Joker of Seville* and *O Babylon!: Two Plays* (1978), *Remembrance* and *Pantomine: Two Plays* (1980), *Three Plays* (1986), *The Poet in the Theatre* [essays] (1990), *The Antilles: Fragments of Epic Memory* [Nobel lecture] (1992), *The Odyssey: A Stage Version* (1993), *What the Twilight Says* (1998).

## MARGARET WALKER

**Poems:** *For My People* (1942), *Prophets for a New Day* (1970), *October Journey* (1973), *This Is My Century: New and Collected Poems* (1988).

**Other:** *Jubilee* [novel] (1966), *For Farish Street Green* (1988), *Richard Wright, Daemonic Genius: A Portrait of the Man, a Critical Look at His Work* (1988), *How I Wrote "Jubilee" and Other Essays on Life and Literature* (1990), *On Being Black Female and Free: Essays by Margaret Walker, 1932–1992* (1997).

## ANTHONY WALTON

**Poems:** *Cricket Weather* (1995).

**Other:** *Mississippi: An American Journey* (1996).

## PHILLIS WHEATLEY

**Poems:** *Poems on Various Subjects, Religious and Moral by Phillis Wheatley* (1793).

**Other:** *Letters of Phillis Wheatley, the Negro-Slave Poet of Boston* (1964).

## JAMES MONROE WHITFIELD

**Poems:** *America and Other Poems* (1853).

## SHERLEY ANNE WILLIAMS

**Poems:** *The Peacock Poems* (1975), *Some One Sweet Angel Chile* (1982).

**Other:** *Give Birth to Brightness* [criticism] (1972), *Dessa Rose* [novel] (1986), *Working Cotton* [fiction] (1992).

## JAY WRIGHT

**Poems:** *Death as History* (1967), *The Homecoming Singer* (1971), *Soothsayers and Omens* (1976), *Dimensions of History* (1976), *The Double Invention of Komo* (1980), *Explications/Interpretations* (1984), *Selected Poems* (1987), *Elaine's Book* (1988), *Boleros* (1991).

## AL YOUNG

**Poems:** *Dancing* (1969), *The Song Turning Back into Itself* (1971), *Geography of the Near Past* (1976), *The Blues Don't Change: New and Selected Poems* (1982), *Heaven: Collected Poems, 1958–1988* (1989).

**Other:** *Snakes* (1970), *Who Is Angelina?* (1975), *Sitting Pretty* (1976), *Ask Me Now* [novel] (1984), *Bodies and Soul: Musical Memoirs* (1981), *Kinds of Blue: Musical Memoirs* (1984), *Things Ain't What They Used to Be: Musical Memoirs* (1987), *Seduction by Light* [novel] (1988), *Mingus/Mingus* [memoirs] (1989), *Drowning in the Sea of Love: Musical Memoirs* (1995).

# PERMISSIONS ACKNOWLEDGMENTS

Grateful acknowledgment is made to the following for permission to reprint previously published material:

**Elizabeth Alexander**, "The Venus Hottentot" from *The Venus Hottentot* by Elizabeth Alexander (University Press of Virginia, 1990) and "Narrative: Ali" by Elizabeth Alexander (Tia Chucha Press, 1996). Reprinted by permission of the author.

**Amiri Baraka**, "Preface to a Twenty Volume Suicide Note," "Each Morning," "Three Modes of History and Culture," and "Clay" from *Selected Poetry* by Imamu Amiri Baraka, copyright © 1961, 1979 by Amiri Baraka; "Black Art" and "Black Bourgeoisie" from *Black Magic* by Amiri Baraka, copyright © 1969 by Amiri Baraka; and "Short Speech to My Friends" from *The Dead Lecturer* by Amiri Baraka, copyright © 1964 by Amiri Baraka. Reprinted by permission of Sterling Lord Literistic, Inc.

**Gwendolyn Brooks**, "The Bean-Eaters," "Sadie and Maud," "A Song in the Front Yord," "De Witt Williams on His Way to the Lincoln Cemetary," "We Real Cool," "The Mother," "To Be in Love," "Beverly Hills, Chicago," "An Old Black Woman, Homeless and Indistinct," "The Blackstone Rangers," "Mentors," "Negro Hero" from *Blacks* by Gwendolyn Brooks (Chicago: Third World Press), copyright © 1991 by Gwendolyn Brooks. Reprinted by permission of the author.

**Lucille Clifton**, "miss rosie," "the lost baby poem," "to ms. Ann," "light on my mother's tongue," "why some people be mad at me sometimes," "to my friend, jerina," "white lady," "4/30/92 for rodney king," and "slaveship" by Lucille Clifton. Reprinted by permission of the author.

**Countee Cullen**, "A Brown Girl Dead," "Yet Do I Marvel," "For My Grandmother," "For John Keats, Apostle of Beauty," "For Paul Laurence Dunbar," "For a Lady I Know," "Heritage," "Incident," and "Saturday's Child" from *Color* by Countee Cullen, copyright © 1925 by Harper & Brothers, copyright renewed 1952 by Ida M.

Cullen; "From the Dark Tower" and "Uncle Jim" from *Copper Sun* by Countee Cullen, copyright © 1927 by Harper & Brothers, copyright renewed 1954 by Ida M. Cullen; "Death to the Poor" and "Scottsboro, Too, Is Worth Its Song" from *The Medea and Some Poems* by Countee Cullen, copyright © 1935 by Harper & Brothers, copyright renewed 1962 by Ida M. Cullen; "A Negro Mother's Lullaby" from *On These I Stand* by Countee Cullen, copyright © 1947 by Harper & Brothers, copyright renewed 1975 by Ida M. Cullen. Reprinted by permission of the Estate of Ida M. Cullen. Special thanks to the Armistad Research Center, Tulane University.

**Toi Derricotte**, "Before Making Love," "On the Turning Up of Unidentified Black Female Corpses," and "Invisible Dreams" by Toi Derricotte. Copyright © 1989, 1997 by Toi Derricotte. Reprinted by permission of the University of Pittsburgh Press.

**Rita Dove**, "Teach Us to Number Our Days," "Banneker," "Parsley," "The Event," "Weathering Out," "The Great Palaces of Versailles," "Canary" from *Selected Poems* by Rita Dove (New York: Pantheon Books/Vintage Books, 1993), copyright © 1980, 1983, 1986 by Rita Dove. Reprinted by permission of the author.

**Cornelius Eady**, "Crows in a Strong Wind," "Leadbelly," "Muddy Waters and the Chicago Blues," "Radio," and "Travelin' Shoes," by Cornelius Eady. Reprinted by permission of the author.

**C. S. Giscombe**, "Dayton, O., the 50's & 60's" by C. S. Giscombe. Reprinted by permission of the author.

**Michael S. Harper**, "Dear John, Dear Coltrane," "For Bud," "We Assume," "Here Where Coltrane Is," "Last Affair: Bessie's Blues Song," "Br'er Sterling and the Rocker," "Nightmare Begins Responsibility," "In Hayden's College," "Angola (Louisiana)," "Psalm," "Release," "The Ghost of Soul-Making," and "My Father's Face" by Michael S. Harper, copyright © 2000 by Michael S. Harper. Reprinted by permission of the author and the University of Illinois Press.

**Robert Hayden**, "Ice Storm," copyright © 1982 by Irma Hayden, "Those Winter Sundays," "Frederick Douglass," "Homage to the Empress of the Blues," copyright © 1966 by Robert Hayden, "A Plague of Starlings," copyright © 1970 by Robert Hayden, "Paul

Laurence Dunbar," "A Letter from Phillis Wheatley," "The Islands," copyright © 1978 by Robert Hayden, "October," copyright © 1979 by Robert Hayden, from *Collected Poems of Robert Hayden,* edited by Frederick Glaysher. Reprinted by permission of Liveright Publishing Corporation.

**Langston Hughes**, "Cross," "Christ in Alabama," "Dream Variations," "Frosting," "Harlem Night Song," "Harlem Sweeties," "House in the World," "Madam and the Rent Man," "Mother to Son," "Passing Love," "Personal," "Suicide's Note," "The Negro Speaks of Rivers," "Theme for English B," and "Tower" from *Collected Poems* by Langston Hughes, copyright © 1994 by the Estate of Langston Hughes. Reprinted by permission of Alfred A. Knopf, a division of Random House.

**Gayl Jones**, "Deep Song" by Gayl Jones. Reprinted by permission of the author.

**Bob Kaufman**, "Jail Poems" and "Grandfather Was Queer Too" from *Solitudes Crowded with Loneliness* by Bob Kaufman, copyright © 1965 by Bob Kaufman. Reprinted by permission of New Directions Publishing Corp.

**Etheridge Knight**, "The Idea of Ancestry," "Haiku"—the sequence 1–9, "For Freckled-Faced Gerald," and "Dark Prophecy: I Sing of Shine" from *The Essential Etheridge Knight* by Etheridge Knight, copyright © 1986. Reprinted by permission of the University of Pittsburgh Press.

**Yusef Komunyakaa**, "Untitled Blues," "Elegy for Thelonius," "Between Days," "Facing It," "February in Sydney," "Euphony," and "My Father's Love Letters" by Yusef Komunyakka. Reprinted by permission of the author.

**Audre Lorde**, "Separation" and "Revolution Is One Form of Social Change," copyright © 1974 by Audre Lorde, "But What Can You Teach My Daughter," copyright © 1978 by Audre Lorde, from *Collected Poems* by Audre Lorde. Reprinted by permission of W. W. Norton & Company, Inc.

**Nathaniel Mackey**, "Winged Abyss" and "Black Snake Visitation" from *Eroding Witness* by Nathaniel Mackey, copyright © 1985 by Nathaniel Mackey. Reprinted by permission of the author.

Haki Madhubuti, "We Walk the Way of the New World" and "the self-hatred of don l. lee" from *Groundwork: New and Selected Poems from 1966–1996* by Haki Madhubuti, copyright © 1996 by Haki Madhubuti. Reprinted by permission of Third World Press, Inc., Chicago, IL.

Thylias Moss, "Lessons from a Mirror," "The Undertaker's Daughter Feels Neglect," "A Reconsideration of the Blackbird," and "Landscape with Saxophonist" from *Pyramid of Bone* by Thylias Moss, copyright © 1989 by Thylias Moss. Reprinted by permission of the University Press of Virginia.

Marilyn Nelson, "My Grandfather Walks in the Woods," "Emily Dickinson's Defunct," and "Tuskegee Airfield" from *The Fields of Praise* by Marilyn Nelson, copyright © 1997 by Marilyn Nelson. Reprinted by permission of the author and Louisiana State University Press.

Raymond Patterson, "Twenty-Six Ways of Looking at a Blackman" from *Twenty-Six Ways of Looking at a Blackman and Other Poems,* copyright © 1969 by Raymond R. Patterson. Reprinted by permission of the author.

Carl Phillips, "Cortege" and "Aubade for Eve Under the Arbor" from *Cortege* by Carl Phillips, copyright © 1995 by Carl Phillips. Reprinted by permission of Graywolf Press, Saint Paul, MN.

Ishmael Reed, "Dualism," "05," "Paul Laurence Dunbar in the Tenderloin," "I Am a Cowboy in the Boat of Ra," and "The Reactionary Poet" by Ishmael Reed. Reprinted by permission of the author.

Sonia Sanchez, "Reflections after the June 12th March for Disarmament" by Sonia Sanchez. Reprinted by permission of the author.

Reginald Shepherd, "Slaves," "Narcissus in Plato's Cave," and "Tantalus in May" from *Angel, Interrupted* by Reginald Shepherd, copyright © 1996. Reprinted by permission of the University of Pittsburgh Press.

Jean Toomer, "Cotton Song," "Evening Song," "Georgia Dusk," "Harvest Song," "November Cotton Flower," and "Reapers" from

## SELECTED POEMS OF LANGSTON HUGHES
### by Langston Hughes

Langston Hughes's poems celebrate the experience of invisible men and women: of slaves who "rushed the boots of Washington"; of musicians on Lenox Avenue; of the poor and the lovesick; of losers in "the raffle of night." They convey that experience in a voice that blends the spoken with the sung, that turns poetic lines into the phrases of jazz and blues, and that rips through the curtain separating high from popular culture. They span the range from the lyric to the polemic, ringing out "wonder and pain and terror—and the marrow of the bone of life."

The poems in this collection were chosen by Hughes himself shortly before his death in 1967 and represent work from his entire career, including "The Negro Speaks of Rivers," "The Weary Blues," "Still Here," "Song for a Dark Girl," "Montage of a Dream Deferred," and "Refugee in America." It gives us a poet of extraordinary range, directness, and stylistic virtuosity.

Poetry/0-679-72818-X

## SELECTED POEMS
### by Rita Dove

Here in one volume is a selection of the extraordinary poems of Rita Dove, who, as the nation's Poet Laureate from 1993 to 1995, brought poetry into the lives of millions of people. Along with a new introduction and poem, *Selected Poems* comprises Dove's collections *The Yellow House on the Corner*, which includes a group of poems devoted to the themes of slavery and freedom; *Museum*, intimate ruminations on home and the world; and finally, *Thomas and Beulah*, winner of the Pulitzer Prize in 1987, a verse cycle loosely based on her grandparents' lives. Precisely yet intensely felt, resonant with the voices of ordinary people, Rita Dove's *Selected Poems* is marked by lyric intensity and compassionate storytelling.

Poetry/0-679-75080-0

COLLECTED POEMS
by W. H. Auden

Between 1927 and his death in 1973, W. H. Auden endowed
poetry in the English language with a new face. Or, rather, with
several faces, since his work ranged from the political to the
religious, from the urbane to the pastoral, from the mandarin
to the invigoratingly plain-spoken. This collection presents all
his final approval. It includes the full contents of his previous
collected editions along with all the later volumes of his shorter
poems. Together, these works display the astonishing range of
Auden's voice and the breadth of his concerns, his deep knowl-
edge of the traditions he inherited, and his ability to recast those
traditions in modern times.

Poetry/0-679-73197-0

**VINTAGE BOOKS**

Available at your local bookstore, or call toll-free to order:

1-800-793-2665 (credit cards only)

## SIX AMERICAN POETS

### Edited by Joel Connaroe

Here are the most enduring works of six great American poets, collected in a single authoritative volume. From the overflowing pantheism of Walt Whitman to the exquisite precision of Emily Dickinson; from the democratic clarity of William Carlos Williams to the cerebral luxuriance of Wallace Stevens; and from Robert Frost's deceptively homespun dramatic monologues to Langston Hughes's exuberant jazz-age lyrics, this anthology presents the best work of six makers of the modern American poetic tradition.

Poetry/ 0-679-74525-4

## EIGHT AMERICAN POETS

### Edited by Joel Connaroe

In this generous anthology, Joel Connaroe has assembled the work of eight poets who have shaped American verse since 1940: Elizabeth Bishop, James Merrill, Sylvia Plath, Allen Ginsberg, Theodore Roethke, John Berryman, Anne Sexton, and Robert Lowell.

Poetry/0-679-77643-5

**VINTAGE BOOKS**
Available at your local bookstore, or call toll-free to order:
1-800-793-2665 (credit cards only)

## JAGUAR OF SWEET LAUGHTER:
## NEW AND SELECTED POEMS
### by Diane Ackerman

In *A Natural History of the Senses* Diane Ackerman revealed herself as a naturalist who writes with the sensuous immediately of a great poet. Now *Jaguar of Sweet Laughter* presents the work of a poet with the precise and wondering eye of a gifted naturalist.

Ackerman's Olympian vision records and transforms landscapes from Amazonia to Antarctica, while her imaginative empathy penetrates the otherness of hummingbirds, deer, and trilobites. But even as they draw readers into the wild heart of nature, Ackerman's poems are indelible reminders of what it is to be a human being—the "jaguar of sweet laughter" that, according to Mayan mythology, astonished the world because it was the first animal to speak.

Poetry/ 0-679-74304-9

## OPUS POSTHUMOUS
### by Wallace Stevens

When *Opus Posthumous* first appeared in 1957, it was an appropriate capstone to the career of one of the most important writers of the twentieth century. It included many poems missing from Stevens's *Collected Poems,* along with Stevens's characteristically inventive prose and pieces for the theater. Now Milton J. Bates, the author of the acclaimed *Wallace Stevens: A Mythology of Self*, has edited and revised *Opus Posthumous* to correct the previous edition's errors and to incorporate material that has come to light since its original publication. A third of the poems and essays in this edition are new to the volume. The resulting book is an invaluable literary document whose language and insights are fresh, startling, and eloquent.

Poetry/0-679-72534-2

## AS I WALKED OUT ONE EVENING: SONGS, BALLADS, LULLABIES, AND OTHER LIGHT VERSE
### by W. H. Auden

W. H. Auden once defined light verse as the kind that is written by poets who are democratically in tune with their audience and whose language is straightforward and close to general speech. Given that definition, the 123 poems in this collection all qualify; they are as accessible as popular songs yet have the wisdom and profundity of the greatest poetry.

*As I Walked Out One Evening* contains some of Auden's most memorable verse: "Now Through the Night's Caressing Grip," "Lullaby: Lay your Sleeping Head, My Love," "Under Which Lyre," and "Funeral Blues." Alongside them are less familiar poems, including seventeen that have never before appeared in book form. Here, among toasts, ballads, limericks, and even a foxtrot, are "Song: The Chimney Sweepers," a jaunty evocation of love, and the hilarious satire "Letter to Lord Byron." By turns lyrical, tender, sardonic, courtly, and risqué, *As I Walked Out One Evening* is Auden at his most irresistible and affecting.

Poetry/ 0-679-76170-5

### THE CINNAMON PEELER
### by Michael Ondaatje

If Michael Ondaatje's novels have the compression and imagistic power of poetry, his poems often read like narratives that have been pared down to their mysterious essence. The poems that have been brought together in this electrifying volume are stylish yet endlessly surprising explorations of friendship and passion, family history, and personal mythology.

Spanning twenty-seven years and representing the best poems from Ondaatje's hard-to-find earlier collections, *The Cinnamon Peeler* is a masterpiece of intelligence and ardor, informed by rueful wit, sensitivity to nature, and an exultant love of language.

Poetry/0-679-77913-2

### VINTAGE BOOKS
Available at your local bookstore, or call toll-free to order:
1-800-793-2665 (credit cards only)